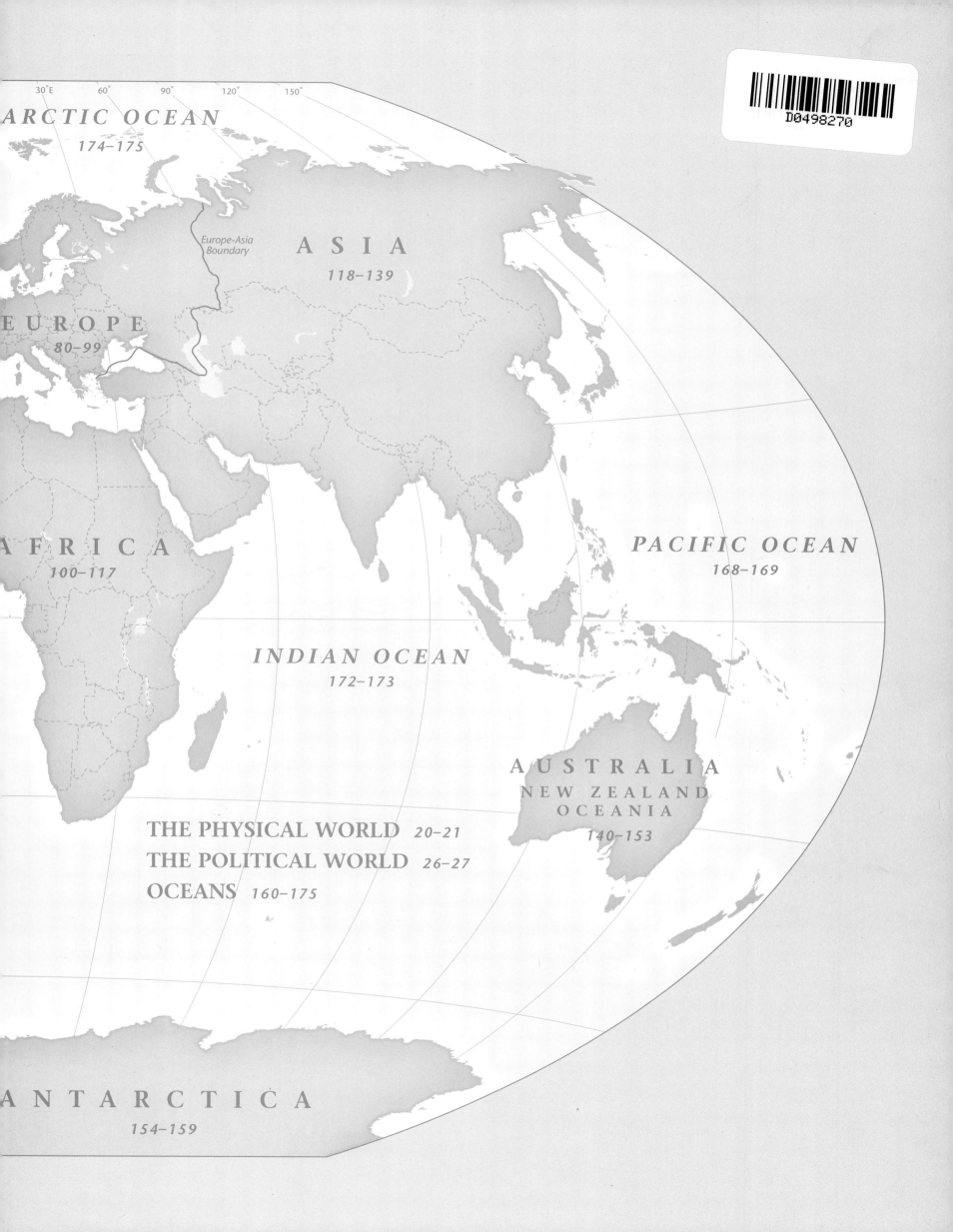

30°E 60° 90° 120° 150°

ARCTIC OCEAN

Europe-Asia Boundary

A S I A

EUROPE

A F R I C A

PACIFIC OCEAN

INDIAN OCEAN

A U S T R A L I A
NEW ZEALAND
OCEANIA

ANTARCTICA

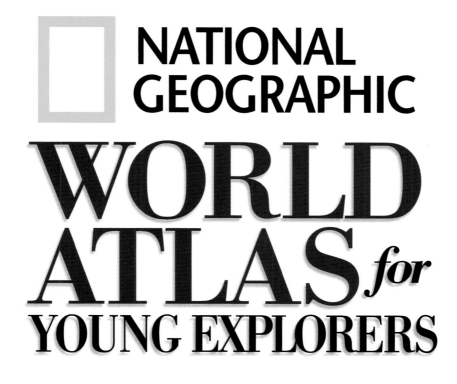

NATIONAL GEOGRAPHIC

WORLD ATLAS *for* YOUNG EXPLORERS

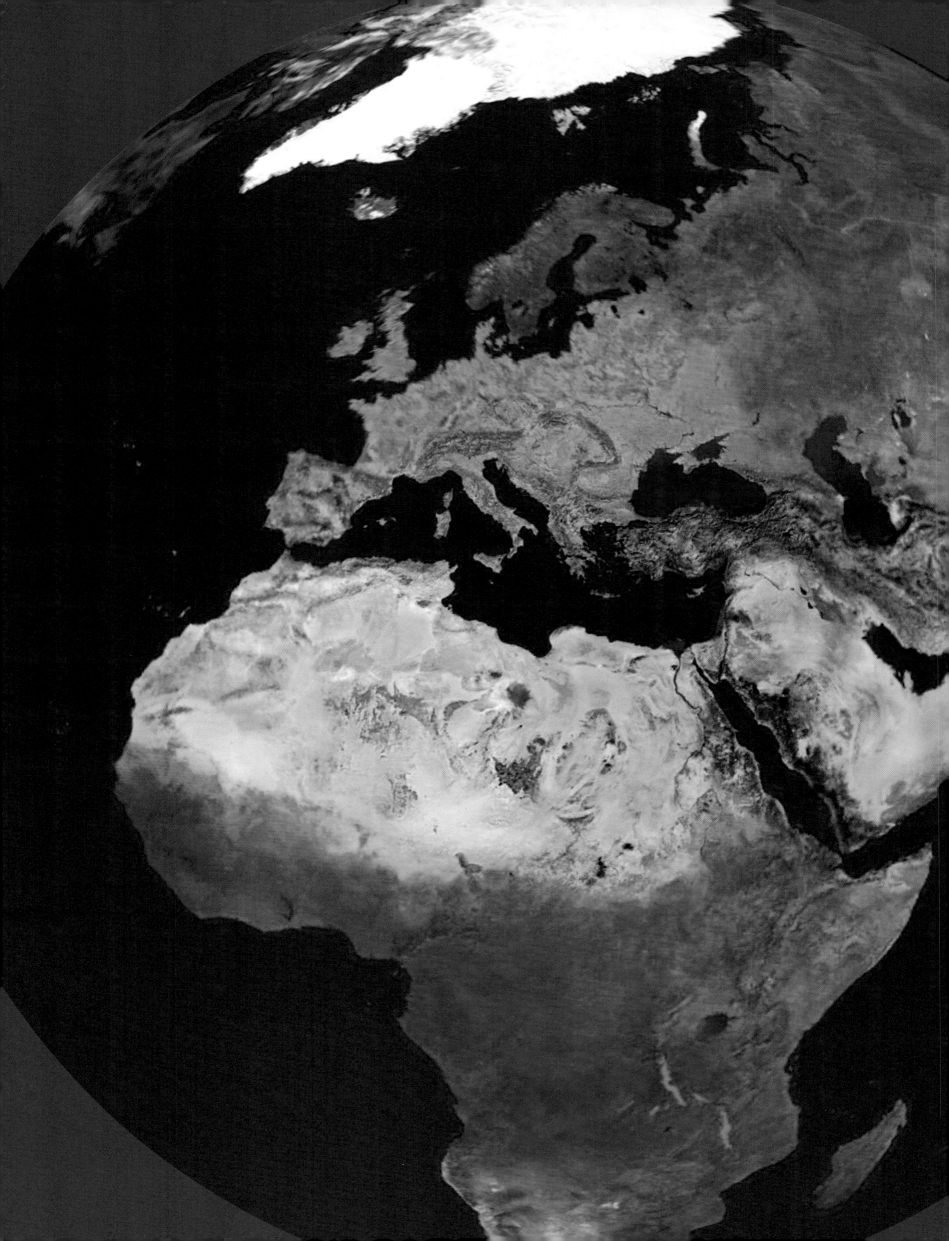

NATIONAL GEOGRAPHIC
WORLD ATLAS *for*
YOUNG EXPLORERS

NATIONAL GEOGRAPHIC

WASHINGTON, D.C.

SOUTH AMERICA:
THREE-TOED
SLOTH, PAGE 69

Contents

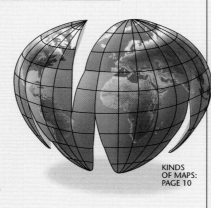

KINDS
OF MAPS:
PAGE 10

SOUTH AMERICA:
RIO DE JANEIRO,
PAGES 68–69

Conversion tables
and abbreviations
can be found on
the back endsheets.

ASIA: AFGHAN GIRL, PAGE 123

How to Use This Atlas

You can use this atlas for all kinds of exploration. To learn about maps, read the first section, Understanding Maps. Some basic facts about the Earth appear in the second part, Planet Earth. The world maps that follow will give you an overall picture of the planet. After that, the maps are arranged by continent. You can get an understanding of a continent's culture and people by reading the photographic essay. You can find cities, mountains, and rivers on the continent and regional maps. Or, you can just browse, and see where you end up!

Connections: Planet to Map

Each continent section in this atlas opens with a large photograph (like the one of Asia, above). This picture shows one part of a continent seen from space. In most cases, the photos were taken from the space shuttle. Can you make the connection? Look for these places on the maps.

▲ *Every continent photo is accompanied by a smaller photo. This one is the city of Dubai. The small photo shows a close-up of a place in the big picture.*

Projections

Every map in this atlas is drawn to a particular projection *(see also page 10)*. The projection determines how and how much land shapes are stretched. Our world political and physical maps use the Winkel Tripel projection (right), which gives a good overall picture of the continents' shapes. Many of our regional maps use an azimuthal equidistant projection, which shows accurate sizes on large-scale maps.

Flags and Stats

Each regional map has a box that shows the flag for each country or U.S. state featured. The box also lists each country's area, population, capital, and official or most common languages. Territories that belong to other countries are listed at the end of the box.

"You Are Here"

Locator globes help you see where an area is in relation to others. On regional maps, the area covered by the map is yellow on the globe and the continent it is part of is green. On continent maps, the whole continent is yellow. All the other land is brown.

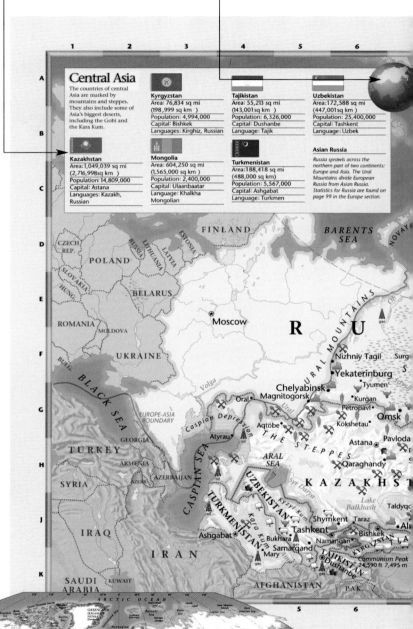

Index and Grid

Use the Index to find any place on these maps. It's arranged alphabetically. Look for the place-name you want. Next to it is a page number, a letter, and another number. Go to the page. Draw imaginary lines from the letter along the side of the map and the number along the top. Your place will be close to where the lines meet.

Uele (river), Democratic Republic of the Congo **115** D10
Ufa, Russia **89** D15, **98** B8
Uganda **108**, 112, **113**
Uinta Mountains, Utah **51** G9
Ujungpandang, Indonesia **139** J9
Ukiah, California **49** H10
Ukraine **89**, 95, **95**
Ulaanbaatar, Mongolia **129** H11

Corner Tabs

Every section in this atlas has its own color. Look for the color on the Contents pages and in the top right-hand corner of every page. Within that colored corner tab you'll see the name of the section and the title for each topic or map. These corner tabs give you a handy way to find the map you want.

North America
South America
Europe
Africa
Asia
Australia
Antarctica
Oceans

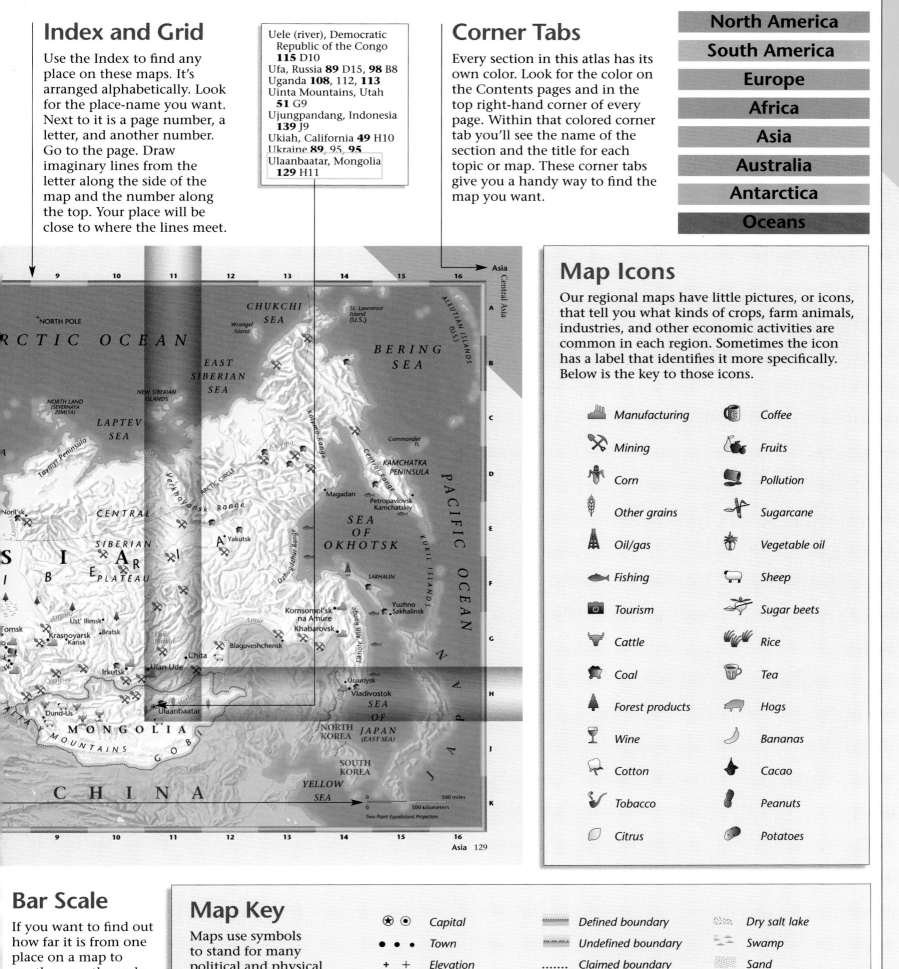

Map Icons

Our regional maps have little pictures, or icons, that tell you what kinds of crops, farm animals, industries, and other economic activities are common in each region. Sometimes the icon has a label that identifies it more specifically. Below is the key to those icons.

	Manufacturing		Coffee
	Mining		Fruits
	Corn		Pollution
	Other grains		Sugarcane
	Oil/gas		Vegetable oil
	Fishing		Sheep
	Tourism		Sugar beets
	Cattle		Rice
	Coal		Tea
	Forest products		Hogs
	Wine		Bananas
	Cotton		Cacao
	Tobacco		Peanuts
	Citrus		Potatoes

Bar Scale

If you want to find out how far it is from one place on a map to another, use the scale. A bar scale appears on every map. It shows how distance on paper corresponds to distance in the real world.

Map Key

Maps use symbols to stand for many political and physical features. At right is the key to the symbols used in this atlas. If you are wondering what you're looking at on a map, check here.

★ ◉	Capital		Defined boundary		Dry salt lake
● ● ●	Town		Undefined boundary		Swamp
+ +	Elevation	....	Claimed boundary		Sand
—⊩—	Waterfall		Offshore boundary		Lava
•	Depression		Rivers		Tundra
∴	Ruin		Canal		Below sea level
▼▼▼▼	Ice shelf		National Park		Glacier

From Local to World

About a hundred years ago, scientist Philip Henry Gosse taught his son Edmund about maps. He had Edmund stand on a stool in the middle of the living room and draw every curlicue of the Oriental rug's pattern onto a piece of paper. Then he had him add the furniture to his drawing, also as seen from the stool, and so on. Edmund learned these things about maps: A map is a drawing of a place as seen from above. It is flat. And it is smaller than the place it shows, shrinking all places and objects by the same amount.

Edmund grew up to be a writer with a passion for maps. Like many others who have grown up to be explorers, scientists, and dreamers of all kinds, he knew that maps could take him places in his imagination and, later, in reality. Maps not only describe places—the shape of a country or the location of mountains—they can reveal an astonishing variety of information, ranging from inches of rainfall by state to puppy ownership by county. Maps are still the same flexible tool Gosse introduced to his son. They are a way of organizing information in a universal language that you can fold up and stick in your pocket.

Downtown
Looking at maps is like looking at land from the sky. When you're close to the ground, you see a lot of detail but not much area—as in this view from above downtown Salt Lake City.

City
Zooming out from downtown lets you see the grid of surrounding streets.

State
Many miles up, you can see the whole state of Utah, but not much detail. The city and nearby lake look small.

Country
Higher yet, you notice that Utah is one piece of a larger country, the United States.

World
From space, you can see that a country is just part of a continent, the largest kind of landmass on the round Earth.

Make It Flat

To make a map—let's say, of your neighborhood—you need to know what to leave out. Maps show places from above, not from the ground. Objects in a map look flat. Your map will show only unchanging things, such as houses and streets. It won't show the dog that's walking by today.

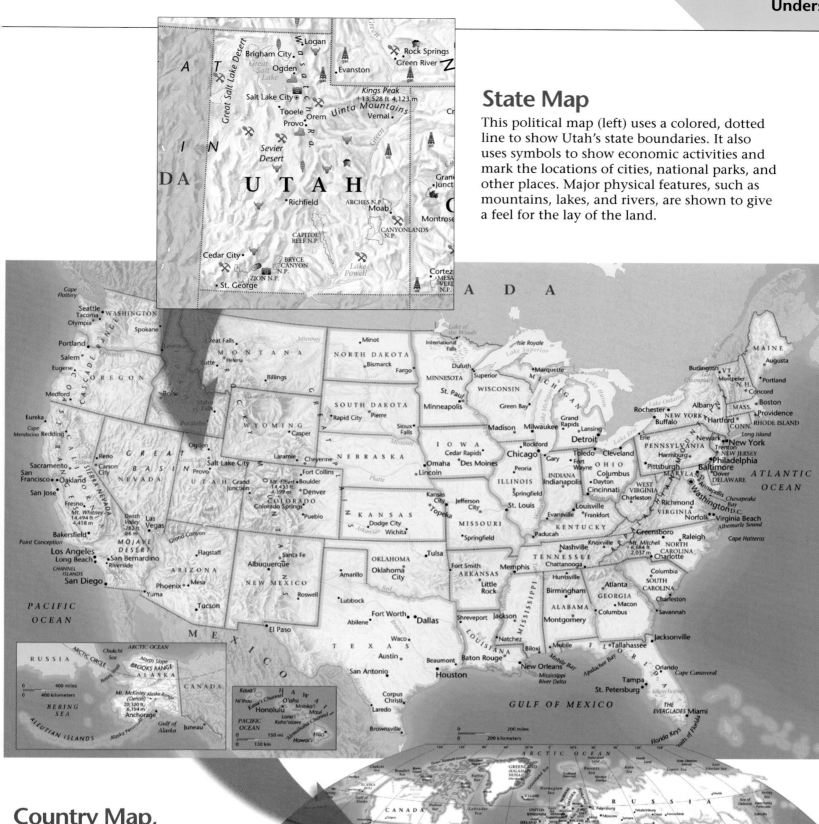

State Map

This political map (left) uses a colored, dotted line to show Utah's state boundaries. It also uses symbols to show economic activities and mark the locations of cities, national parks, and other places. Major physical features, such as mountains, lakes, and rivers, are shown to give a feel for the lay of the land.

Country Map, World Map

Like a state map, a country map (such as the one for the United States, above), shows major physical features as well as place-names, borders, and other information. Some maps, such as the one above, also have insets: boxes that contain their own maps, showing areas that can't be seen on the main map because they are too small or too far away. A world map, such as the one at right, shows even more area but less detail. It is called a small-scale map.

Kinds of Maps

Maps are amazingly useful tools. We use them to preserve information, to display data, and to reveal relationships between seemingly unrelated things. For instance, in the 19th century, Dr. John Snow made a map of London that plotted where deaths caused by cholera occurred compared to the locations of public water pumps. His map showed that victims lived only near certain pumps. Snow's map helped to prove that cholera is a disease carried by water.

One thing maps can't do is gather information. Humans have to do that themselves through exploration and by collecting data. Cartographers use computers to sort the data then use it to make an incredible variety of maps.

Projections

Because the Earth is round, its surface is best shown on a globe. But a globe can't show you the whole world at one time. So, cartographers project the round Earth onto a flat surface. Unfortunately, when Earth's surface is peeled off and flattened (below), big gaps appear. To fill in the gaps, mapmakers usually stretch parts of Earth's surface, choosing to show either the correct shapes of features or their correct sizes; it is impossible to show both. The map shape that results is called a projection. There are more than a hundred kinds of projections.

Physical Map

A physical map focuses on showing landforms and water features rather than cities. This physical map of northwestern Africa identifies rivers, lakes, mountains, and deserts. As on many physical maps, color identifies both elevation—the height of the land—and vegetation regions.

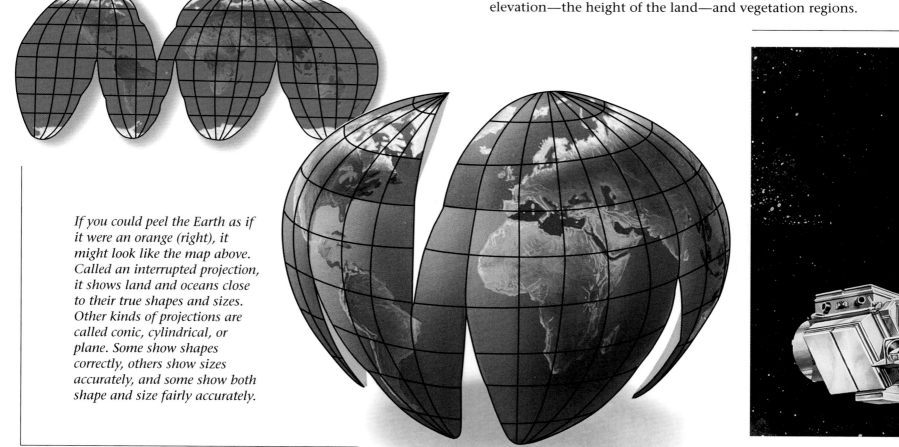

If you could peel the Earth as if it were an orange (right), it might look like the map above. Called an interrupted projection, it shows land and oceans close to their true shapes and sizes. Other kinds of projections are called conic, cylindrical, or plane. Some show shapes correctly, others show sizes accurately, and some show both shape and size fairly accurately.

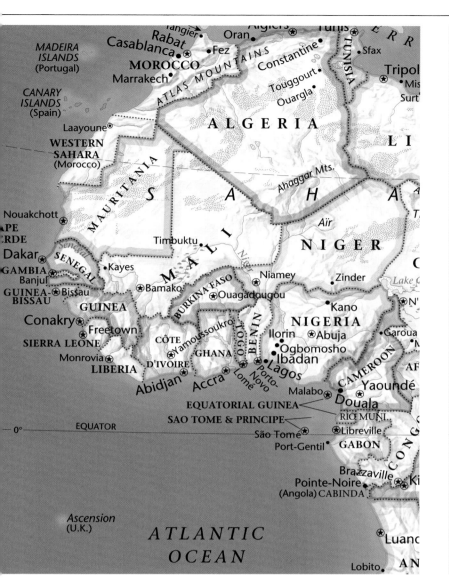

Political Map

A political map shows the names and boundaries of countries and identifies only major physical features. This political map shows countries in northwestern Africa. Dots mark cities. The larger the dot and the city name, the more populous the city. Stars in circles identify capital cities.

Thematic Map

Thematic maps display patterns, usually emphasizing one subject, or theme. This thematic map shows northwestern Africa's climates, with each climate zone marked by a color. Dark green means the area is tropical and wet. Yellow shows semiarid, meaning fairly dry. Orange is arid, or desert.

How Maps Are Made

The main reason we create maps—to organize our knowledge of the world—hasn't changed in 4,000 years of mapping. But the tools have. Today, most cartographers use computers with a program called Geographic Information Systems (GIS). Each kind of information on a map is kept as a separate "layer" in the map's digital files. This allows cartographers to make maps—and change them—more quickly and easily.

Eyes in Space

Monster mappers in the sky, satellites (left) collect data on what they "see" below. Landsat maps are the product of satellites surveying the Earth from 22,300 miles (35,887 kilometers) up. Equipment records sunlight reflecting from Earth's surface, converting it to numbers. Transmitters beam the numbers to Earth.

▲ *Mouse and monitor have replaced pen and paper for modern mapmakers. Here, due to political changes in Europe, a cartographer alters a country's name: Yugoslavia becomes Serbia and Montenegro.*

How to Read a Map

A map is more than just a diagram of a place from above. Encoded on an ordinary map is all sorts of information. Learn that code, and you can make any kind of map reveal its secrets.

Take latitude and longitude. These are imaginary measurement lines on a map or globe that form a grid like tic-tac-toe lines that come together at the North and South Poles. You won't find these lines on the ground because they don't exist in nature. They are simply an invention that helps pinpoint location—where a place is on Earth's surface.

Another way to pinpoint location is with a hand-held global positioning system (GPS). By timing radio waves from several orbiting satellites, it can zero in on your exact location. That's not all. It can also direct you to any other place on Earth.

Every map should have a scale, usually a bar scale. This little code tells you how to measure distances on the map. And many maps also offer a key. The key lists the symbols the cartographer has used on the map and explains what they stand for. Learn to read a key, translate scale, find a direction, and determine a location, and a map will keep no secrets from you.

Latitude and Longitude

Lines of latitude run around the globe horizontally, east and west (below left). Because latitude measures parts of a sphere, it is written in degrees, abbreviated as °. The Equator is 0° latitude. About 60 miles (111 kilometers) north is 1° N latitude. At the same distance south of the Equator is 1° S latitude, and so on, all the way up to 90° N and 90° S—the Poles.

Longitude runs vertically, north and south (below, right). Zero degrees longitude, the prime meridian, runs through Greenwich, England. There are 180 degrees east and west. Lines of latitude, or parallels, never meet. Lines of longitude, or meridians, meet at the Poles. The exact location of a place is where its lines of latitude and longitude meet.

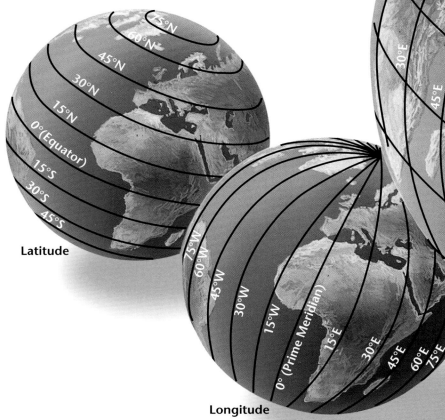

Latitude

Longitude

Zeroing In

Spot has run away. Fortunately, you had him outfitted with a radio-tracking collar, and the satellite positioning service tells you he's at 30° S, 60° W. Two clues are obvious: "S" means Spot is south of the Equator. "W" means he is west of the prime meridian. On a map, find 30° latitude running across the Southern Hemisphere. Trace it with your finger until you reach longitude 60° W. Hmm. Spot must be visiting cousin Ricardo in Argentina.

◀ *Lines of latitude and longitude form an imaginary grid that helps us locate places on a map. Here, the lines for 30° S, 60° W meet in Argentina near the Paraná River (see arrow, left).*

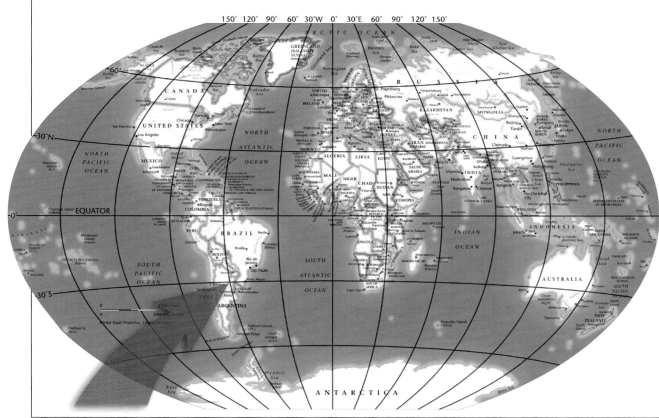

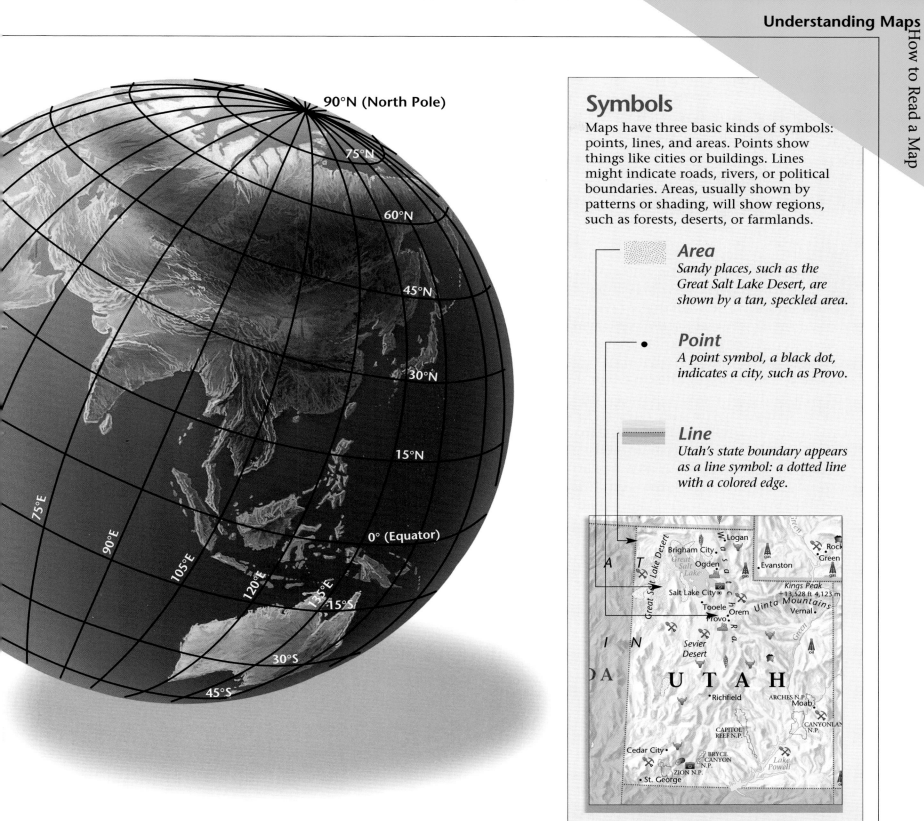

90°N (North Pole)

75°N
60°N
45°N
30°N
15°N
0° (Equator)
15°S
30°S
45°S

75°E
90°E
105°E
120°E
135°E

Symbols

Maps have three basic kinds of symbols: points, lines, and areas. Points show things like cities or buildings. Lines might indicate roads, rivers, or political boundaries. Areas, usually shown by patterns or shading, will show regions, such as forests, deserts, or farmlands.

Area

Sandy places, such as the Great Salt Lake Desert, are shown by a tan, speckled area.

Point

A point symbol, a black dot, indicates a city, such as Provo.

Line

Utah's state boundary appears as a line symbol: a dotted line with a colored edge.

Scale and Direction

A distance scale is a line or a bar that compares distance on the map to distance in the real world. Scales are often accompanied by the name of the map projection. Many maps also have an arrow that points north on the map; some use a compass rose to show all four directions. Maps in this atlas are oriented north; they do not use either device.

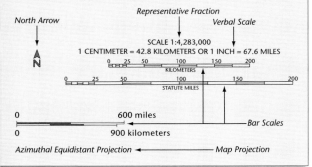

North Arrow

Representative Fraction

Verbal Scale

SCALE 1:4,283,000
1 CENTIMETER = 42.8 KILOMETERS OR 1 INCH = 67.6 MILES

KILOMETERS
STATUTE MILES

Bar Scales

0   600 miles
0   900 kilometers

Azimuthal Equidistant Projection ◄——   ——► Map Projection

Quick Look

▶ Looking for Luanda, but don't know where it is? Maps often use a grid around their edges that can help you. Look up the place-name in the index for the atlas or map. Our index tells you that Luanda, Angola, is on page 116, B2. Find the letter down the side of the map, then find the number along the top. Draw straight lines down and across the map with your fingers. You will find Luanda in the area where the lines meet.

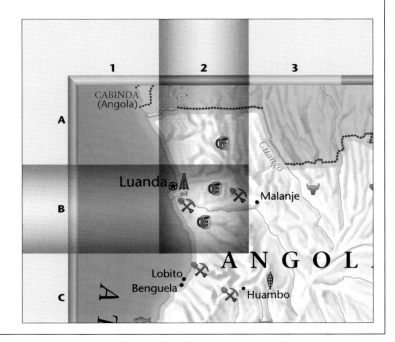

The Earth in Space

Earth, alone, seems vast and varied, with its continents, oceans, and polar caps. But Earth is part of a much larger system, and it is the workings of this system that dictate the rhythms of our days, seasons, and years.

Ours is one of nine planets that revolve around a star we call the sun, in a kind of cosmic family we call a solar system. Life on Earth depends on the sun for light, warmth, energy, and food. Our year is defined by the sun. The sun's gravity locks Earth onto an invisible, oval track around it that takes roughly 365 days to complete.

The sun also defines our day. As Earth revolves around the sun, it also rotates on its axis—an invisible line through the Poles—like a spinning top. Thus every place on the planet whirls to face the sun, turns past, and returns every 24 hours. When Africa faces the sun, it is day there. As it turns away, night falls.

Earth's Family

Earth is the third of nine planets orbiting the sun. It is dwarfed by the gas giants Jupiter, Saturn, Uranus, and Neptune. The planets, in turn, are tiny compared with the sun, which contains 99 percent of the matter in the solar system. The painting at right shows the planets' sizes compared with one another and to the sun. Distances are not to scale.

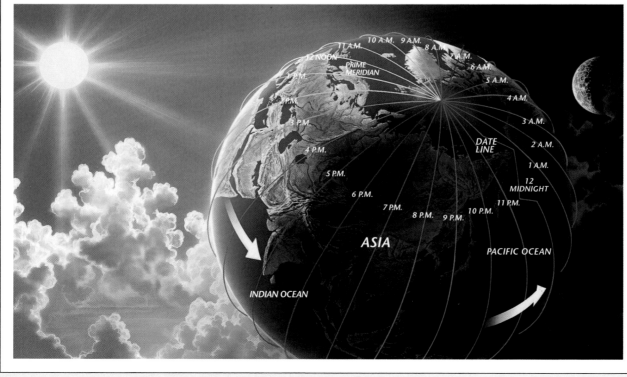

Time Zones

In olden times it was noon when the sun was overhead wherever you happened to be. Then, in the late 1800s, as transportation and communication technology advanced, countries recognized the need to establish a standard system of time. Earth's surface was divided into 24 standard time zones based on the fact that the planet rotates west to east 15 degrees every hour. Time is counted from the prime meridian (labeled "noon" on the art at left), which runs through Greenwich, England. For each 15 degrees you travel east of Greenwich, the time is one hour later. The opposite is true when you travel west.

Air Cover

Earth's atmosphere surrounds the planet with a life-giving blanket of nitrogen, oxygen, and other gases. Within it, all Earth's weather takes place, driven by the sun's energy, Earth's rotation, and ocean currents. Great rafts of air heated at the Equator rise and spin away north and south toward the Poles as polar air flows south, creating weather systems. Powerful currents of air called jet streams, 5 to 9 miles (8 to 15 kilometers) above the planet's surface, move this weather around the globe, unleashing storms and bringing in sunny days.

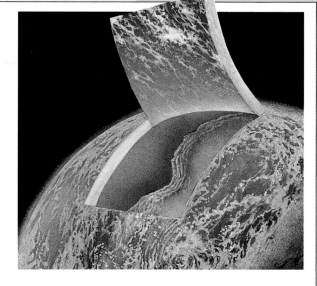

▲ *About 300 miles (480 kilometers) from top to bottom, Earth's atmosphere is thin compared to the planet it covers. All weather occurs in the lowest layer, about 10 miles (16 kilometers) thick.*

▲ *Storm clouds hang low over the Great Plains of the United States. Hot and cold air masses often collide violently over the flat lands of the Plains, producing anything from a thundershower to a deadly tornado.*

The Seasons

We have seasons because Earth is tilted on its axis. This means that as the Earth orbits the sun, the sun's vertical rays (direct sunlight) fall on different parts of the planet. When the Northern Hemisphere (the area north of the Equator) tilts toward the sun, it's summer there. Six months later when that hemisphere is tilted away from the sun, it has winter. Halfway between these two extremes spring and fall occur. Just the opposite happens in the Southern Hemisphere. Not all places have four distinct seasons.

Spring
Northern
Hemisphere
/ North Pole
South Pole /

Summer
Northern
Hemisphere
/ North Pole
South Pole /

Winter
Northern
Hemisphere
North Pole /
South Pole /

Fall
Northern
Hemisphere
North Pole /
Tropic of Cancer
Equator
Tropic of Capricorn
South Pole /

The Earth in Motion

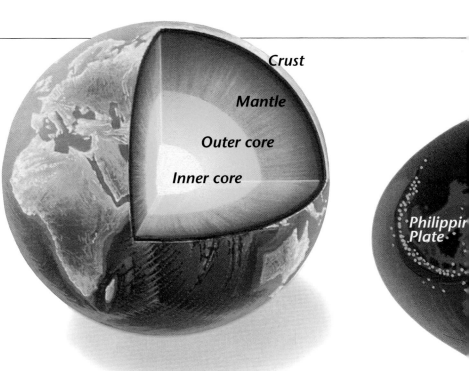

Crust

Mantle

Outer core

Inner core

Philippine Plate

I f ancient astronauts had photographed the planet as it was 500 million years ago, Earth as seen from space would not be anything we'd recognize. We wouldn't see North America as we know it today. We couldn't find Australia, Asia, or Africa. Most of the landmasses that make up our present-day continents were part of one large supercontinent called Pangaea. Over millions of years, this supercontinent has broken apart into continents, which in turn have drifted and recombined, all at a pace slower than a snail's.

What causes the continents to wander about? Earth's crust—the thin, rocky outer shell that makes up the land and ocean floors—forms a puzzle of rigid plates, floating on partially molten rock in the upper mantle. There, heat and currents shove the plates around, shaping Earth's surface.

Into the Core

If you could slice into the Earth (above), you would see that its outer layer, the crust, is thin—only 2 miles (3 kilometers) in some spots. Beneath it lie the rocky mantle, a liquid outer core, and a hot, solid inner core.

Giant Plates

Red lines on the map at right show the boundaries between Earth's largest plates. Yellow dots mark the locations of volcanoes. Always on the move, plates collide, grind past each other, or spread apart. The movement of these giant slabs of Earth's crust is called plate tectonics.

Continents on the Move

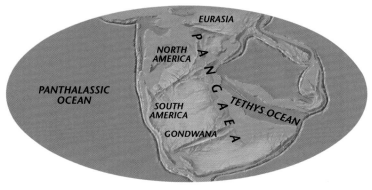

1 *Pangaea About 240 million years ago, Earth's continents had collided in a giant pile-up called Pangaea, stretching from Pole to Pole.*

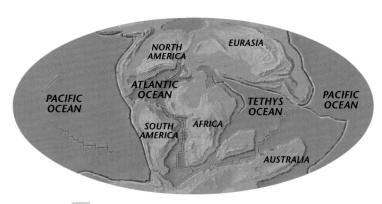

2 *Drifting Apart By 94 million years ago, Pangaea had been pulled apart into smaller continents. In the warm climate, dinosaurs evolved into Earth's most extensive animal group.*

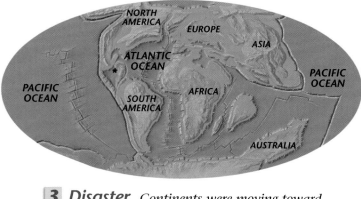

3 *Disaster Continents were moving toward their current positions by 65 million years ago. The impact of an asteroid (∗) in the Gulf of Mexico may have extinguished half of the world's species.*

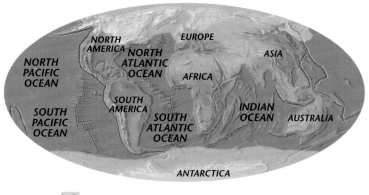

4 *Deep Freeze By 18,000 years ago, the continents had close to their modern shapes, but a great ice age had the far north and south locked under glaciers.*

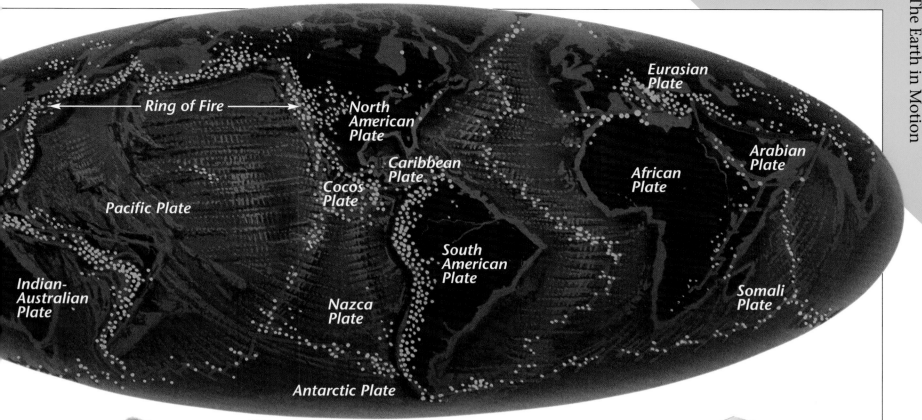

Ring of Fire

Eurasian Plate

North American Plate

Arabian Plate

Caribbean Plate

African Plate

Cocos Plate

Pacific Plate

South American Plate

Indian-Australian Plate

Somali Plate

Nazca Plate

Antarctic Plate

Earth Shapers

The planet's biggest features—its continents, oceans, and mountain ranges—are shaped by slowly moving plates. Where plates collide, they push up mountains. Where they spread apart, molten rock flows out. Where one plate dives beneath another, crust melts, fueling volcanoes. Eruptions and earthquakes often result.

◄ **Volcanoes** *Most volcanoes form where one plate dives beneath another, a process called subduction. The rocky plate melts as it moves downward. This molten rock, or magma, rises to the surface where it can erupt to form a volcano.*

▼ **Faulting** *Sometimes plates grind past each other, creating cracks called faults. One famous fault is the San Andreas, in California. Tension builds up along faults as plates stick. A sudden shift in the plates causes an earthquake.*

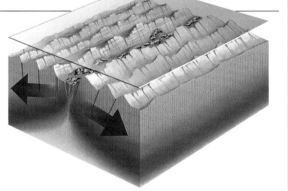

▲ **Spreading** *Where plates move apart, the crust cracks and molten rock rises up in the rift. Spreading occurs down the middle of the Atlantic Ocean's floor, pulling Europe away from North America.*

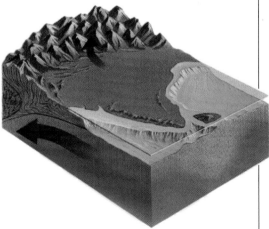

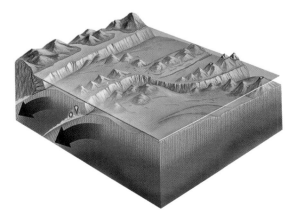

▲ **Accretion** *In accretion, pieces of crust join as two plates collide. This causes land to grow out as well as up, as seen along Alaska's coast.*

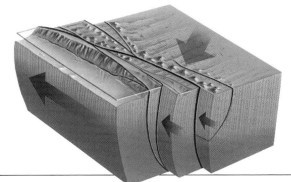

▲ **Collision** *When two pieces of continental crust collide, their edges may crumple up into mountains. Just such a collision built the Himalaya when the plate carrying India plowed into the Eurasian plate.*

The Land

Mesa. Butte. Lagoon. Archipelago. The names humans have given Earth's physical features make an intriguing language. They not only name the land but also distinguish between similar shapes. Take mesa and butte. Both are steep-sided hills found in deserts. A mesa has a flat table top—mesa means "table" in Spanish. A butte has the mesa's steep sides but is smaller and has an irregular top.

You can find the same kinds of shapes all over the world. That's because similar forces shaped them—either the internal forces of plate movement or the external forces of wind and water. Water, as a liquid or as ice, is a powerful earth mover. Rivers cut valleys and canyons. Glaciers scoop wide, U-shaped mountain valleys, pushing rocks ahead like icy bulldozers. The ace of earth-movers is the ocean, which with one mighty wave can strip away an entire beach—or deposit a new one.

These natural forces continually reshape the land. The Mississippi River adds 200 million tons of mud each year to its great delta in the Gulf of Mexico. A new Hawaiian island (already named Loihi) is rising from the Pacific Ocean floor. Niagara Falls, carving away at its rocky ledges, is moving upstream toward a meeting with Lake Erie 20,000 years from now. Icebergs the size of Connecticut are breaking away from the continent of Antarctica. Even Mount Everest, highest of mountains, is being worn down by wind and water. Someday it will be no more than a rounded nubbin. In the far future, there will still be mountains and valleys, but they will not be the same mountains and valleys we recognize as landmarks today.

Dormant volcano · Ocean · Island · Strait · Archipelago · Point · Sound · Cape · Peninsula · Bay · Isthmus · Cliff · Spit · Reef · Gu...

River *As a river flows downhill, the slope gradually flattens, causing the river to wind back and forth—as seen in England's Thames, above.*

Canyon *Canyons are deep, narrow, steep-sided valleys. Like Utah's Buckskin Gulch (above), most are carved out of rock by rivers and streams.*

Desert *Deserts can be hot or cold, sandy or rocky—but they are always dry. The one above, with its tall cactuses, is typical of the American Southwest.*

Oasis *Fed by fresh water from underground, oases, such as this one in Oman, are islands of life in the desert, supporting trees and even crops.*

Mountain range

Mountain peak

Iceberg

Glacier

Desert

Mesa

Basin

Oasis

Divide

Plateau

Waterfall

Escarpment

Valley

Lake

Canyon

Canal

Fork

Lagoon   Plain

Hills

Delta

River

Harbor

Breakwater

Tributary

A Name for Every Feature

Land has a vocabulary all its own, each name identifying a specific feature of the landscape. Sometimes the difference between one feature and another is only a matter of size or shape. A cape, for example, is a wide chunk of land extending out into the sea. It is not pointed, however, for then it would be a point. Nor does it have a narrow neck. A sizable cape or point with a narrow neck would be a peninsula. The narrow neck, of course, is an isthmus. Such specific identifiers have proved useful for centuries. Sailors, for example, use peninsulas, bays, and straits as landmarks to guide ships to safe harbor.

◄ *The landscape at left is an imaginary one that contains many of Earth's major land-forms and features. Definitions for these terms and others can be found in the Glossary on page 177.*

Mountain *Mountains are the highest landforms. Everest, in Asia's Himalaya, is highest of all at 29,035 feet (8,850 meters) above sea level.*

Glacier *Alaska's Mendenhall Glacier shows why glaciers are called rivers of ice. Glacial ice covers about one-tenth of Earth's surface.*

Valley *Valleys come in all shapes. Wide, U-shaped, steep-sided valleys like this one in the Peruvian Andes show geologists where glaciers once passed.*

Waterfall *When a river tumbles over a rocky ledge, it becomes a waterfall. Oregon's Multnomah Falls (above), drops 850 feet (259 meters).*

The Physical World

Look at a physical map of the world, such as the one at right, and you will see one key fact right away. We live on an ocean planet. Water covers more than two-thirds of the Earth's surface. Although we give four different names to the four biggest bodies of water—the Pacific, Atlantic, Indian, and Arctic Oceans—in fact they all form one interconnected ocean. We also define the largest landmasses as continents. Geographers usually recognize seven of them. In order of size they are Asia, Africa, North America, South America, Antarctica, Europe, and Australia.

On the Surface

The world physical map, right, shows natural features of the land such as river systems, mountain ranges, deserts, and plains. Certain landforms stand out. Long mountain belts run along the western coasts of North and South America and east-west across Europe and Asia. In the middle of most continents are large flat areas called plains or plateaus. Massive rivers, such as the Amazon, Congo, and Ganges, create green and fertile areas on the land.

NORTH PACIFIC OCEAN

SOUTH PACIFIC OCEAN

POLYNESIA

Hawaiian Islands
Kauai
Hawaii

Line Islands

EQUATOR

Phoenix Islands

Marquesas Islands

Samoa Is.

Cook Islands

Society Is.
Tahiti

Tuamotu Archipelago

Fiji Is.
Tonga Is.

Austral Islands

Easter Island

North Magnetic Pole
Queen Elizabeth Islands
Ellesmere Island
Melville Island
Victoria Island
Baffin Island
Baffin Bay

Chukchi Sea
Beaufort Sea
SIBERIA
Brooks Range
ALASKA
Mackenzie
Great Bear Lake
Great Slave Lake
Mt. McKinley (Denali) 20,320 feet 6,194 meters
Alaska Range
Yukon
Bering Sea
Kodiak I.
Alexander Archipelago
Queen Charlotte Islands
Vancouver Island
Coast Mountains

Canadian Shield
Hudson Bay
Nelson
Labrador Sea
Labrador
Island of Newfoundland
Nova Scotia

NORTH AMERICA
ROCKY MOUNTAINS
Great Plains
Missouri
Lake Winnipeg
Great Lakes
Cascade Range
Great Salt Lake
Central Lowland
Appalachian Mountains
Mississippi

Death Valley -282 feet -86 meters
Colorado

Baja California
Sierra Madre Occidental
Rio Grande
Sierra Madre Oriental

Gulf of Mexico
Bahama Islands
Cuba
Greater Antilles
Hispaniola
Jamaica
West Indies
Lesser Antilles
Trinidad

CENTRAL AMERICA
Caribbean Sea

NORTH ATLANTIC OCEAN

Llanos
Orinoco
Guiana Highlands
Negro

Galápagos Islands

Amazon
Amazon
Basin
Madeira
Tocantins

SOUTH AMERICA
Lake Titicaca
Mato Grosso Plateau
Brazilian Highlands
São Francisco

ANDES
Atacama Desert
Gran Chaco
Paraguay
Paraná

Cerro Aconcagua 22,834 feet 6,960 meters
Pampas

Isla Grande de Chiloé
Patagonia
Valdés Peninsula -131 feet -40 meters

Falkland Islands
Tierra del Fuego
Strait of Magellan
Scotia Sea

South Shetland Islands

Bellingshausen Sea
Ellsworth Land

Marie Byrd Land
Ross Sea
Ross Ice Shelf

ANTARCTIC PENINSULA
WEST
Ronne Ice Shelf
Vinson Massif 16,067 feet 4,897 meters

TRANSANTARCTIC M

30°N

0°

30°S

60°

60°

150° 120° 90°

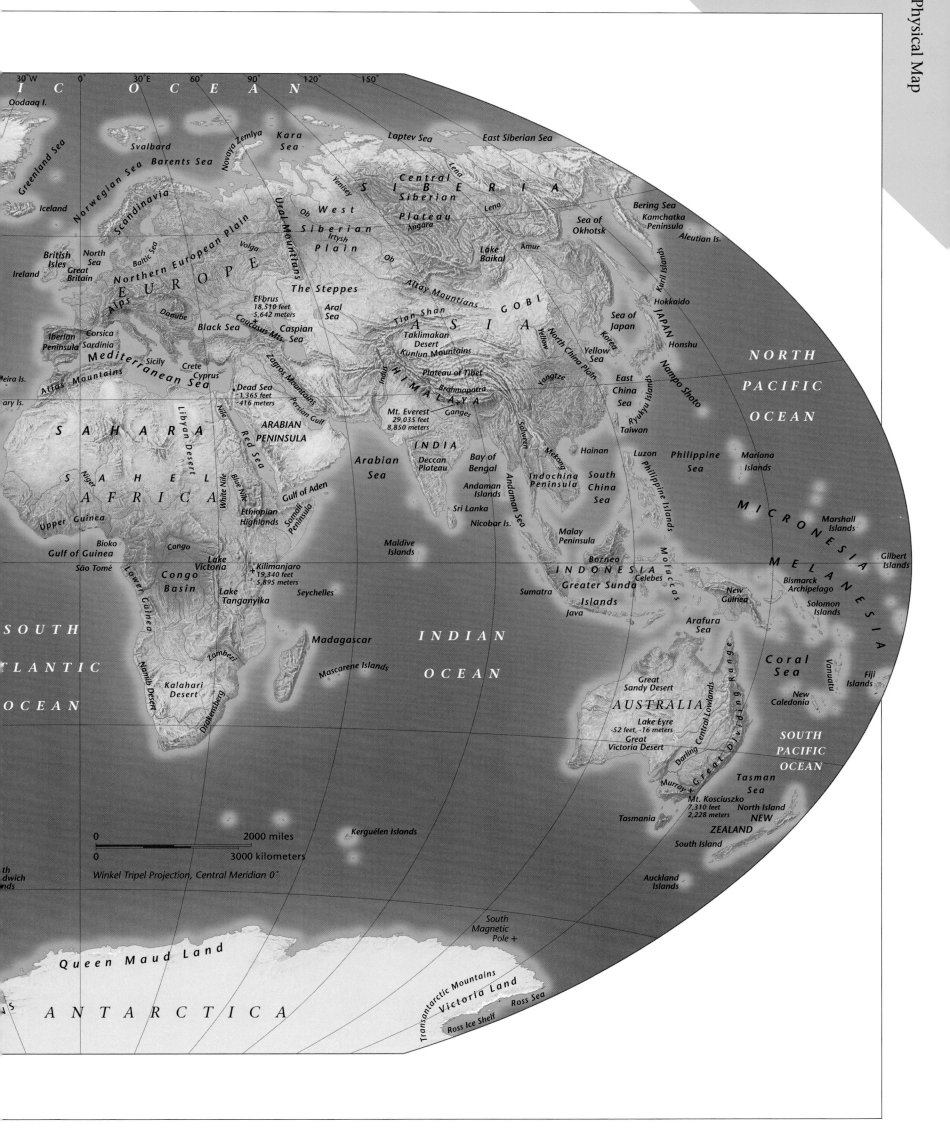

30°W 0° 30°E 60° 90° 120° 150°

A R C T I C   O C E A N

Oodaaq I.

Greenland Sea

Svalbard

Novaya Zemlya

Kara Sea

Laptev Sea

East Siberian Sea

Iceland

Norwegian Sea

Scandinavia

Barents Sea

C e n t r a l
S i b e r i a

Lena

Bering Sea

Kamchatka Peninsula

Aleutian Is.

British Isles

North Sea

Baltic Sea

Northern European Plain

Ural Mountains

Ob

West Siberian Plain

Yenisey

Central Siberian Plateau

Angara

Lena

Lake Baikal

Amur

Sea of Okhotsk

Karil Islands

Hokkaido

Ireland

Great Britain

EUROPE

Volga

The Steppes

Irtysh
Ob

Altay Mountians

A S I A

G O B I

Sea of Japan

JAPAN

NORTH

Alps

El'brus
18,510 feet
5,642 meters

Aral Sea

Tian Shan

Korea

Honshu

PACIFIC

Iberian Peninsula

Corsica
Sardinia

Danube

Black Sea

Caucasus Mts.

Caspian Sea

Taklimakan Desert

Kunlun Mountains

North China Plain

Yellow

Yellow Sea

OCEAN

Atlas Mountains

Sicily

Crete
Cyprus

Zagros Mountains

Plateau of Tibet

Yangtze

East China Sea

Nampo Shoto

eira Is.

Mediterranean Sea

H I M A L A Y A

Brahmaputra

Ryukyu Islands

Dead Sea
-1,365 feet
-416 meters

Taiwan

ary Is.

SAHARA

Libyan Desert

Nile

ARABIAN PENINSULA

Persian Gulf

Mt. Everest
29,035 feet
8,850 meters

Ganges

I N D I A

Salween

Hainan

Luzon

Philippine Sea

Mariana Islands

S A H E L

Red Sea

Arabian Sea

Deccan Plateau

Bay of Bengal

Mekong

South China Sea

M I C R O N E S I A

Niger

AFRICA

White Nile
Blue Nile

Gulf of Aden

Ethiopian Highlands

Somali Peninsula

Andaman Sea

Andaman Islands

Indochina Peninsula

Philippine Islands

Upper Guinea

Bioko

Congo

Sri Lanka

Nicobar Is.

Malay Peninsula

Marshall Islands

MELANESIA

Gulf of Guinea

São Tomé

Lake Victoria

Kilimanjaro
19,340 feet
5,895 meters

Maldive Islands

Borneo

I N D O N E S I A

Celebes

Moluccas

New Guinea

Bismarck Archipelago

Solomon Islands

Gilbert Islands

SOUTH

Congo Basin

Lower Guinea

Lake Tanganyika

Seychelles

Greater Sunda Islands

Java

Sumatra

ATLANTIC

Zambezi

Madagascar

Mascarene Islands

INDIAN

Arafura Sea

Coral Sea

Vanuatu

Fiji Islands

OCEAN

Namib Desert

Kalahari Desert

Drakensberg

OCEAN

Great Sandy Desert

AUSTRALIA

Central Lowlands

Great Dividing Range

New Caledonia

SOUTH PACIFIC OCEAN

Lake Eyre
-52 feet, -16 meters

Great Victoria Desert

Tasman Sea

th
dwich
nds

Kerguélen Islands

Murray

Mt. Kosciuszko
7,310 feet
2,228 meters

North Island

NEW ZEALAND

Darling

Tasmania

South Island

0   2000 miles
0   3000 kilometers

Winkel Tripel Projection, Central Meridian 0°

Auckland Islands

South Magnetic Pole +

as

Queen Maud Land

Transantarctic Mountains

Victoria Land

Ross Sea

A N T A R C T I C A

Ross Ice Shelf

Climate and Vegetation

Climate means all the weather that occurs in one place over a long time. Many factors work together to give a place its characteristic climate. These include latitude, elevation above sea level, distance from the ocean, prevailing winds, and location within a continent. In general, climate changes slowly over thousands of years. Some things can cause it to change more quickly, however. One agent of change is warming of the atmosphere caused by pollution. Most experts agree that people need to cut back on producing harmful gases such as carbon dioxide to help stop this global warming.

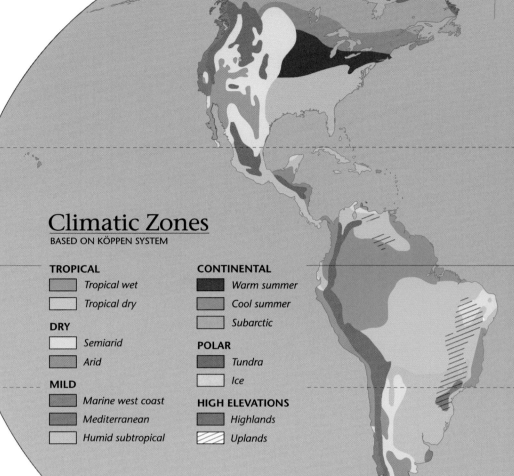

Climatic Zones
BASED ON KÖPPEN SYSTEM

TROPICAL
- Tropical wet
- Tropical dry

DRY
- Semiarid
- Arid

MILD
- Marine west coast
- Mediterranean
- Humid subtropical

CONTINENTAL
- Warm summer
- Cool summer
- Subarctic

POLAR
- Tundra
- Ice

HIGH ELEVATIONS
- Highlands
- Uplands

World Climate

The large map (right) shows the system for naming climates invented by Russian-born meteorologist Wladimir Köppen. It divides climates into six groups: tropical, dry, mild, continental, polar, and that of high elevations. The groups then split into types, such as tropical wet and tropical dry.

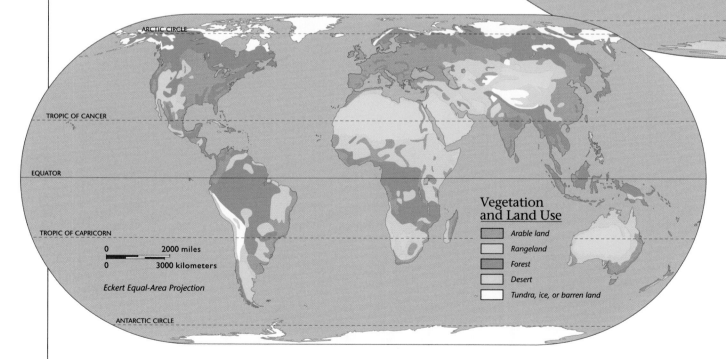

ARCTIC CIRCLE

TROPIC OF CANCER

EQUATOR

TROPIC OF CAPRICORN

0   2000 miles
0   3000 kilometers

Eckert Equal-Area Projection

ANTARCTIC CIRCLE

Vegetation and Land Use

- Arable land
- Rangeland
- Forest
- Desert
- Tundra, ice, or barren land

Vegetation and Land Use

Compare the two maps on these pages and you can see that vegetation—plant life in a place—is tied to climate. Five broad categories define vegetation and land use: arable (suitable for farming); rangeland (an open region where livestock can be kept); forest; desert; and tundra, ice, or barren land.

The Gulf Stream

▶ *Curling and swirling across the North Atlantic, the Gulf Stream current looks like a dark red river in this satellite image (near right). In a way, it is a river—a river of warm water that travels from the Gulf of Mexico up the east coast of the United States and across the ocean to Europe. Big currents like this one affect the world's climate. The northern branch of the Gulf Stream keeps northwestern Europe much warmer than it would be otherwise. Compare the region's climate with that of a similar latitude in North America.*

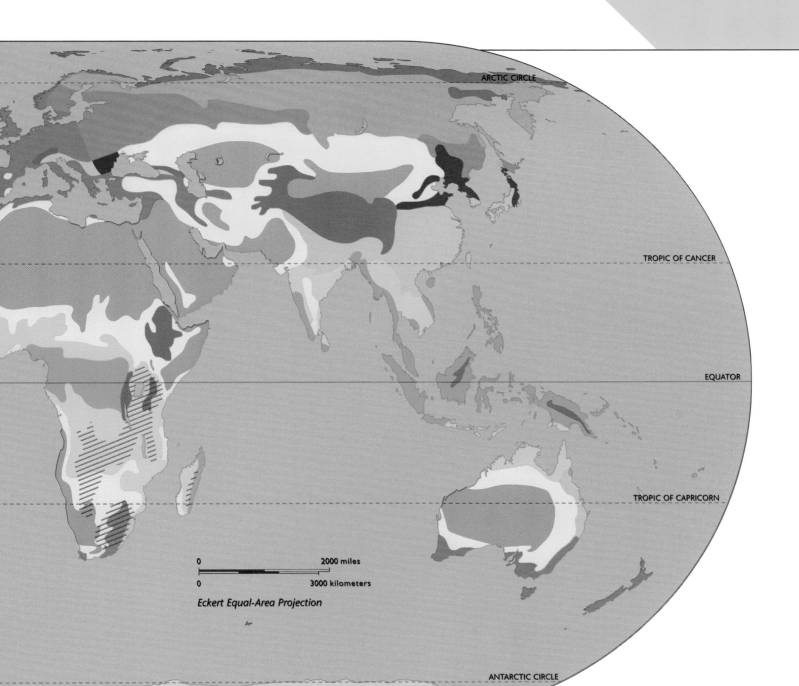

ARCTIC CIRCLE

TROPIC OF CANCER

EQUATOR

TROPIC OF CAPRICORN

ANTARCTIC CIRCLE

0   2000 miles

0   3000 kilometers

Eckert Equal-Area Projection

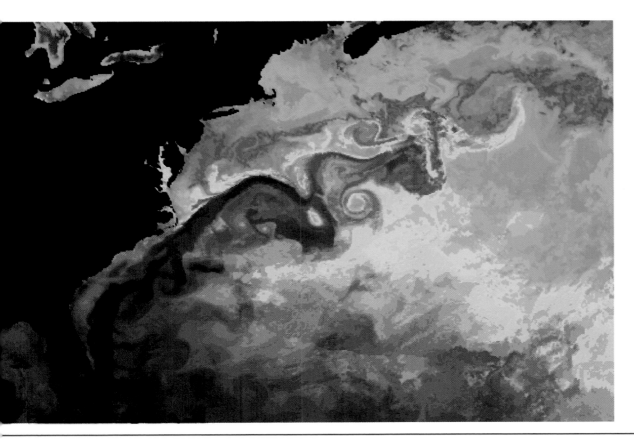

▲ *Thanks to the warming influence of the Gulf Stream, the climate in Cornwall, England, is mild enough to sustain this enormous gunnera plant (above). These plants are native to forests in humid tropical regions of South America.*

Environment
and Endangered Species

The environment is the sum of all the conditions surrounding a plant or animal. The map at right shows just a few ways in which human activities are changing—and threatening—the world's environments. In tropical and subtropical regions, ranchers, farmers, loggers, and miners have cleared nearly half of the world's original rain forests. About a fifth of the world's population lives in dry lands near deserts. Farming and other activities in these lands may damage them so much that they will become deserts.

Throughout the world, more than 1,800 species of animals and plants that once were thriving are now threatened with extinction. The map shows just a few of the most threatened animals around the world.

▼ Pollution from a nearby paper mill threatens wildlife in this wetland in the state of Georgia. Soil, air, and water pollution are global problems.

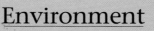

Environment

- Present rain forest
- Former rain forest
- Hyperarid lands
- Dry lands susceptible to desertification
- Most polluted cities

▼ Hunted for its highly decorative shell, the hawksbill turtle is endangered throughout its range in tropical and subtropical waters. Although the turtle is protected by international law, illegal hunting continues to threaten its existence.

◄ Africa's black rhinoceros, once numerous on the continent's savannas, is now endangered because of demand for its horn, which is ground up for use in Asian medicines.

▶ Loss of habitat due to human settlement has brought the giant panda's population down to a mere 1,000 to 2,000, all in western China.

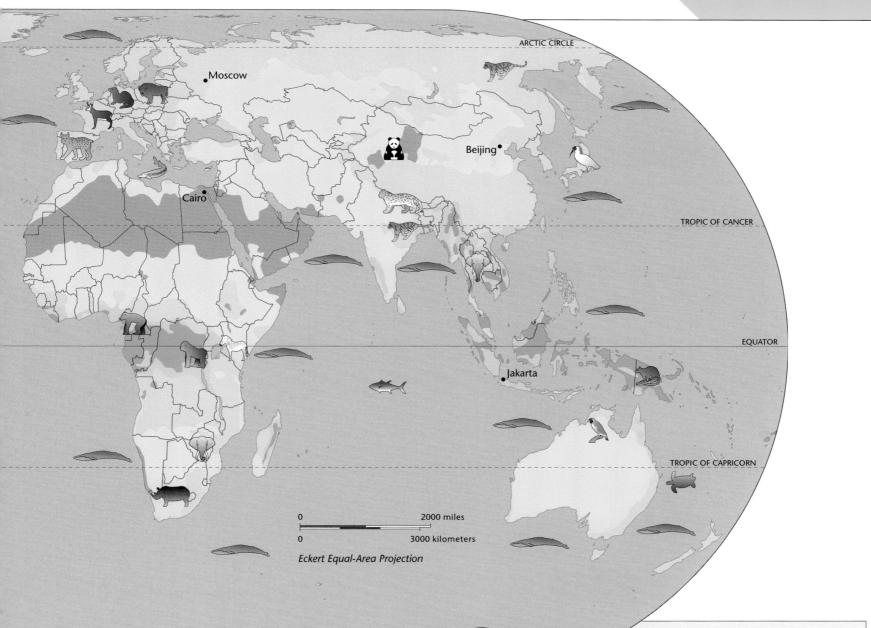

ARCTIC CIRCLE

Moscow

Cairo

Beijing

TROPIC OF CANCER

EQUATOR

Jakarta

TROPIC OF CAPRICORN

0   2000 miles

0   3000 kilometers

Eckert Equal-Area Projection

ANTARCTIC CIRCLE

▼ *Car exhaust adds to the smog in Bangkok, Thailand. Burning of fossil fuels is the main source of air pollution.*

▶ *A logger cuts through an African mahogany tree in a Congo rain forest. This logging is illegal, but the law is hard to enforce.*

▲ *When the 20th century began, about 100,000 tigers lived in Asia. Now humans have taken over so much of their land that the big cats are down to about 5,000 animals in the wild.*

Key to Endangered Species

Crested ibis	Gouldian finch
Goodfellow's tree kangaroo	Giant armadillo
Grevy's zebra	Spanish lynx
European bison	Chartreuse chamois
Mountain tapir	European mink
Snow leopard	American crocodile
Chimpanzee	Whooping crane
Mountain gorilla	California condor
African elephant	Beluga sturgeon
Asian elephant	Hawksbill turtle
Black-footed ferret	Tiger
Blue whale	Giant panda
Southern bluefin tuna	Black rhino

The Political World

When you look at a political map, like the one at right, you see things that aren't there. Countries and country boundaries are not natural features of the Earth. People create them. They agree that a certain area makes up a country. They decide that the government there is the highest authority over the land. Sometimes people change countries as well, creating new ones and merging old ones. Fifty years ago the political map of the world looked quite different from this one. In 50 more years, it will probably have changed again.

Countries and Capitals

This world political map shows countries of the world, ranging from such giants as Canada and Russia to the island nations of the Pacific. A star in a circle marks a country's capital city. Some countries control land outside their boundaries; Ecuador, for instance, owns the Galápagos Islands. Antarctica, a continent, is neither a country nor a possession, so it does not have a country boundary color.

150°   120°   90°

Chukchi Sea
Beaufort Sea
Banks Island
Queen Elizabeth Islands
Ellesmere Island
RUSSIA
Yukon
ALASKA (U.S.)
Anchorage
60°
Bering Sea
Gulf of Alaska
Aleutian Islands
Victoria Island
Great Bear Lake
Great Slave Lake
Mackenzie
Baffin Bay
Baffin Island
Nuuk
CANADA
Hudson Bay
Labrador Sea
Vancouver
Calgary
Seattle
Missouri
Toronto
Ottawa
Island of Newfoundland
San Francisco
UNITED STATES
Chicago
New York
Ohio
Washington
NORTH
30°N
Los Angeles
Atlanta
ATLANTIC
Houston
Rio Grande
Mississippi
Gulf of Mexico
OCEAN
NORTH PACIFIC OCEAN
Hawaiian Islands (U.S.)
MEXICO
Guadalajara
Havana
Nassau
BAHAMAS
DOMINICAN REP.
Santo Domingo
PUERTO RICO (U.S.)
Virgin Is. (U.S. & U.K.)
Mexico
CUBA
Belmopan
BELIZE
HAITI
ST. KITTS & NEVIS
ANTIGUA & BARBUDA
GUATEMALA
JAMAICA
Caribbean Sea
Guadeloupe (France)
Guatemala
HONDURAS
DOMINICA
San Salvador
Tegucigalpa
ST. LUCIA
Martinique (France)
NICARAGUA
GRENADA
BARBADOS
EL SALVADOR
Managua
ST. VINCENT & THE GRENADINES
COSTA RICA
Panama
TRINIDAD AND TOBAGO
San José
Caracas
PANAMA
VENEZUELA
Georgetown
Medellín
Bogotá
Paramaribo
Cayenne
SURINAME
FRENCH GUIANA (France)
COLOMBIA
GUYANA
EQUATOR
Christmas Island (Kiribati)
0°
Galápagos Islands (Ecuador)
Quito
ECUADOR
Manaus
Negro
Madeira
Amazon
PERU
BRAZIL
Recife
KIRIBATI
Marquesas Islands (France)
Lima
Ucayali
São Francisco
Salvador (Bahia)
AMERICAN SAMOA (U.S.)
La Paz
Brasília
SAMOA
Apia
BOLIVIA
Rio de Janeiro
FRENCH POLYNESIA (France)
Sucre
PARAGUAY
São Paulo
SOUTH PACIFIC OCEAN
Asunción
Porto Alegre
TONGA
Nuku'alofa
Córdoba
Paraná
URUGUAY
Santiago
Buenos Aires
Montevideo
30°S
CHILE
ARGENTINA
Chatham Is. (N.Z.)
Falkland Islands (U.K.)
Tierra del Fuego
South Georgia (U.K.)
Strait of Magellan
Drake Passage
60°
Antarctic Peninsula
Weddell Sea
Ross Sea
Bell Is.

0   2000 miles
0   3000 kilometers

Winkel Tripel Projection, Central Meridian 0°

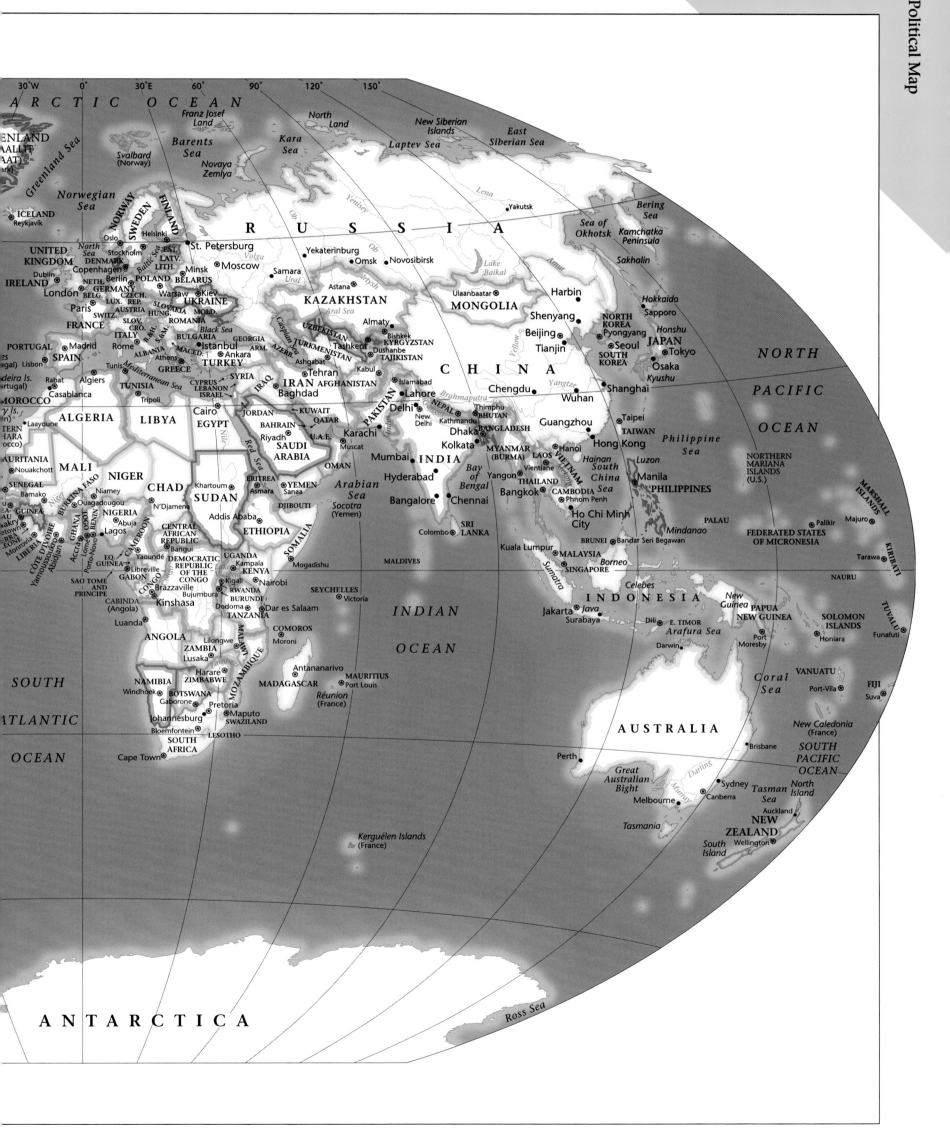

People

More than six billion people are living on Earth as the 21st century begins, with another 15,000 born every hour. Two countries—China and India—are home to one-third of the total population. In many nations of Asia, Africa, and South America, the population is growing quickly. Governments in these poorer countries are hard pressed to provide enough education, jobs, and food for their people. In wealthier countries, the birthrate is usually low. Although these countries add fewer people to the planet, their demands on Earth's natural resources add to the stresses on Earth's environment.

Where People Live

A map of population density shows where people live and how closely crowded they are. In recent years, people have been moving away from the countryside into cities. There are now more than 40 cities, such as Hong Kong (below), with more than 5 million people.

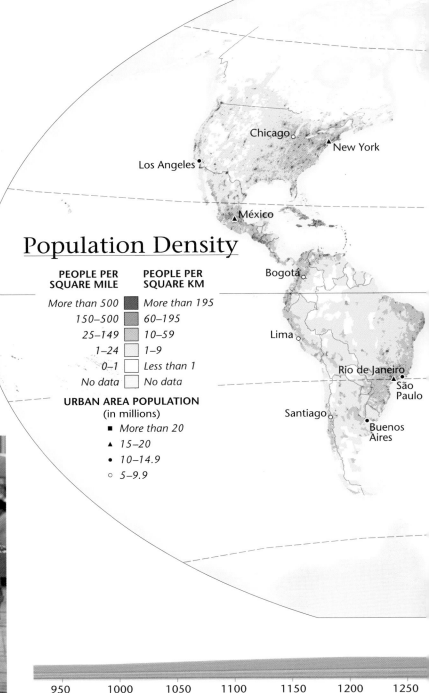

Population Density

PEOPLE PER SQUARE MILE	PEOPLE PER SQUARE KM
More than 500	More than 195
150–500	60–195
25–149	10–59
1–24	1–9
0–1	Less than 1
No data	No data

URBAN AREA POPULATION
(in millions)
- ■ More than 20
- ▲ 15–20
- ● 10–14.9
- ○ 5–9.9

Chicago, New York, Los Angeles, México, Bogotá, Lima, Rio de Janeiro, São Paulo, Santiago, Buenos Aires

950   1000   1050   1100   1150   1200   1250

Cultures on the Move

A culture is not confined to neat geographical boundaries. Instead, it is defined by the many things people have in common, such as their language, religion, food, clothing styles, customs, and music. When groups of people move from one part of the world to another, they often take their culture, or parts of it, with them. Languages take root as their speakers settle in new lands. Religions spread as their followers travel and win over new believers.

Common Languages

Two of the world's most commonly spoken languages, Mandarin Chinese and Hindi, reflect the huge numbers of native speakers in China and India. Other languages such as English, Spanish, and Portuguese spread around the world during European colonization.

Population (in millions)

Japanese	Russian	Portuguese	Arabic	Bengali	Spanish	English	Hindi	Chinese (Mandarin)
125	167	176	207	207	340	341	366	874

Note: Figures count only "first language" speakers. Arabic is treated as a single language.

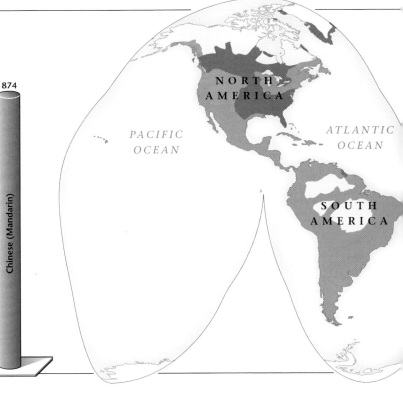

NORTH AMERICA

PACIFIC OCEAN

ATLANTIC OCEAN

SOUTH AMERICA

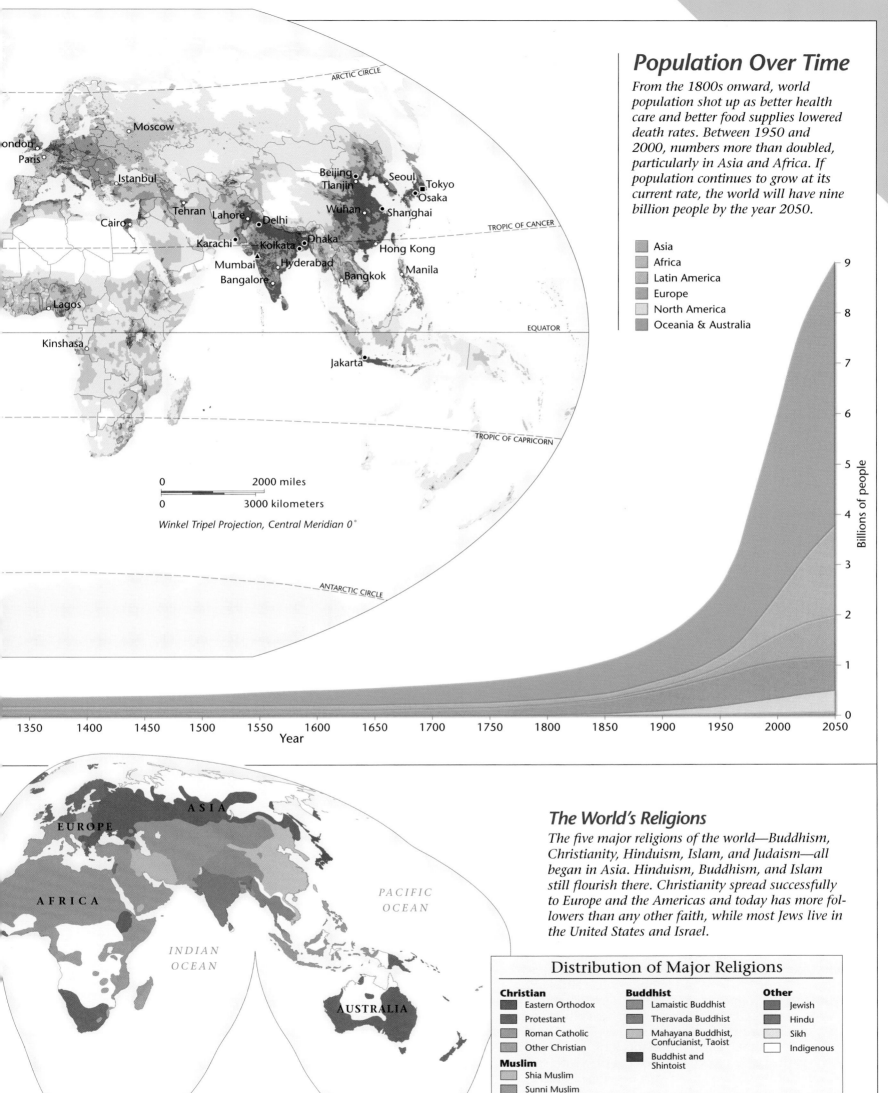

Moscow
London
Paris
Istanbul
Tehran
Cairo
Lahore
Karachi
Delhi
Kolkata
Dhaka
Mumbai
Hyderabad
Bangalore
Beijing
Tianjin
Wuhan
Seoul
Tokyo
Osaka
Shanghai
Hong Kong
Bangkok
Manila
Lagos
Kinshasa
Jakarta

ARCTIC CIRCLE
TROPIC OF CANCER
EQUATOR
TROPIC OF CAPRICORN
ANTARCTIC CIRCLE

0   2000 miles
0   3000 kilometers

Winkel Tripel Projection, Central Meridian 0°

Population Over Time

From the 1800s onward, world population shot up as better health care and better food supplies lowered death rates. Between 1950 and 2000, numbers more than doubled, particularly in Asia and Africa. If population continues to grow at its current rate, the world will have nine billion people by the year 2050.

- Asia
- Africa
- Latin America
- Europe
- North America
- Oceania & Australia

Billions of people

9
8
7
6
5
4
3
2
1
0

1350 1400 1450 1500 1550 1600 1650 1700 1750 1800 1850 1900 1950 2000 2050
Year

ASIA
EUROPE
AFRICA
PACIFIC OCEAN
INDIAN OCEAN
AUSTRALIA
ANTARCTICA

The World's Religions

The five major religions of the world—Buddhism, Christianity, Hinduism, Islam, and Judaism—all began in Asia. Hinduism, Buddhism, and Islam still flourish there. Christianity spread successfully to Europe and the Americas and today has more followers than any other faith, while most Jews live in the United States and Israel.

Distribution of Major Religions

Christian
- Eastern Orthodox
- Protestant
- Roman Catholic
- Other Christian

Muslim
- Shia Muslim
- Sunni Muslim

Buddhist
- Lamaistic Buddhist
- Theravada Buddhist
- Mahayana Buddhist, Confucianist, Taoist
- Buddhist and Shintoist

Other
- Jewish
- Hindu
- Sikh
- Indigenous

World Economies

From the tropical shores of Tuvalu to the chilly steppes of Russia, every country faces the same problem: how to use its resources to supply the goods and services its people want. (Goods are items such as food, clothing, or toys; services are work done for someone else, such as teaching or fighting fires.)

A country's economy is its system of producing these goods and services and getting them to the people who want them. The value of all those goods and services, added together, is called the gross domestic product (GDP). The countries with the highest standard of living are those with the highest GDP per person. Yet no country survives just on the goods and services it makes itself. Nations also trade with one another, selling the things that they can produce easily and buying the ones they can't. That's why kids in the U.S. have computer games made in Japan and Japanese kids have CDs made in the U.S.

Predominant Economy

- Agriculture
- Agriculture and forestry
- Fishing
- Forestry (lumber and pulpwood)
- Hunting, fishing and forestry
- Subsistence agriculture
- Little or no economic activity
- Manufacturing
- Nomadic herding
- Stock raising on ranges

Predominant World Economies

The map at right makes two things clear. One is that much of Earth's land is devoted to various primary economic activities, such as agriculture, fishing, forestry, and herding. The other is that almost all manufacturing can be found clustered around large cities in the Northern Hemisphere.

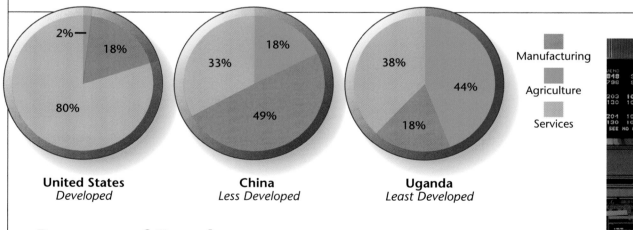

2%	18%	
80%		

United States
Developed

18%	
33%	
49%	

China
Less Developed

38%	
44%	
18%	

Uganda
Least Developed

- ■ Manufacturing
- ■ Agriculture
- ■ Services

Patterns of Development

Countries want their economies to develop so their people can have more food, better health care, and more opportunities for education and jobs—some of the measures of a high standard of living. Every economy is made up of three basic sectors: agriculture (which broadly defined includes farming, mining, fishing, and forestry), manufacturing (making and selling goods); and services (work that helps people). As countries develop, the portion of their GDP that comes from agriculture drops dramatically, while industry and services grow. The three graphs above show how these sectors look in a developed country (the U.S.), a less developed country with strong manufacturing China), and a least developed country (Uganda) that is working to improve its economy.

Services

These traders milling about on the floor of the Paris Stock Exchange (right) don't produce anything tangible, but their work—buying and selling contracts—is worth millions of dollars. Financial services like these account for about ten percent of all services in developed countries.

ARCTIC CIRCLE

TROPIC OF CANCER

EQUATOR

TROPIC OF CAPRICORN

ANTARCTIC CIRCLE

| 0 | 2000 miles |
| 0 | 3000 kilometers |

Winkel Tripel Projection, Central Meridian 0°

America's Big Spenders

Whether they're buying in-line skates, video games, or clothes, American teenagers pump a lot of money into the world economy. U.S. teens spend more than $150 billion each year. Much of their money ends up in China (for CD players, toys, or sports equipment), Japan (electronic games), and Mexico (music equipment).

Agriculture

Modern machinery, such as this combine harvesting wheat in Wisconsin, helps make farming very productive in the United States. Although fewer than 3 percent of U.S. workers are farmers, the country produces 15 percent of the world's grain, milk, and eggs, and 25 percent of its beef.

Manufacturing

Showering golden sparks, industrial robots put together cars in a factory in Durban, South Africa. Robotic machines allow companies to make more cars for less money; however, they also replace human workers, who then have to look for new jobs.

North Am

High mountains and winding rivers define the western regions of North America, a continent that has been the goal of immigrants since at least the last ice age, 25,000 years ago. Spanish settlers gave names to features in much of the southwestern United States and Mexico, including the Colorado River, shown flowing into the picture from the lower left. You can see the Gulf of California where the river ends at right. The Colorado provides water to farms and towns from Wyoming to Baja California, Mexico. Little of its torrent remains by the time it trickles into the gulf. Most of the land here is pale desert. Rivers and streams support trees and crops—the darker greenish brown in the photo.

Rafters enjoy a wild ride on the roaring Colorado River (below). The river cuts through six states, carving out the Grand Canyon on the way.

CONNECTION: *You can find the lower Colorado River on the maps on pages 52–53 and 60–61.*

erica

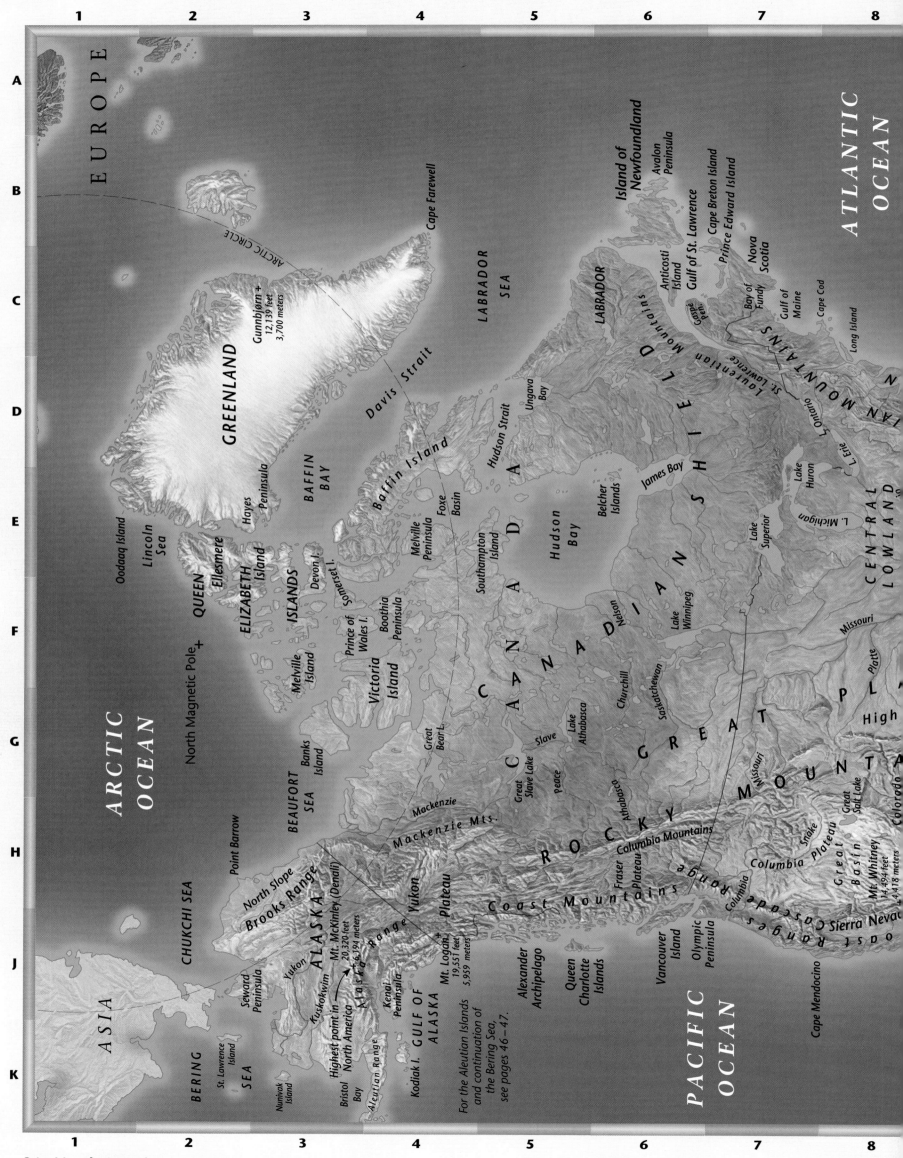

EUROPE

ATLANTIC OCEAN

ARCTIC OCEAN

GREENLAND

Gunnbjørn +
12,139 feet
3,700 meters

ARCTIC CIRCLE

Cape Farewell

LABRADOR SEA

Davis Strait

BAFFIN BAY

Baffin Island

Hudson Strait

Island of Newfoundland

Avalon Peninsula

Gulf of St. Lawrence

Cape Breton Island

Prince Edward Island

Nova Scotia

Bay of Fundy

Gulf of Maine

Cape Cod

Long Island

Gaspé Pen.

St. Lawrence

Anticosti Island

LABRADOR

Laurentian Mountains

Ungava Bay

Hudson Bay

Belcher Islands

James Bay

L. Ontario

L. Erie

CENTRAL LOWLAND

Lake Huron

Lake Superior

L. Michigan

APPALACHIAN MOUNTAINS

Oodaaq Island

Lincoln Sea

Ellesmere Island

Hayes Peninsula

QUEEN ELIZABETH ISLANDS

Devon I.

Somerset I.

Prince of Wales I.

Melville Peninsula

Foxe Basin

Southampton Island

CANADIAN SHIELD

Melville Island

Boothia Peninsula

North Magnetic Pole +

Victoria Island

Banks Island

BEAUFORT SEA

Great Bear L.

Mackenzie

Great Slave Lake

Slave

Lake Athabasca

Peace

Athabasca

Nelson

Churchill

Saskatchewan

Lake Winnipeg

Missouri

Missouri

Platte

ROCKY MOUNTAINS

GREAT PLAINS

High

ARCTIC OCEAN

CHUKCHI SEA

Point Barrow

North Slope

Brooks Range

ALASKA

Mt. McKinley (Denali) +
20,320 feet
6,194 meters

Highest point in North America

Kuskokwim

Yukon

Alaska Range

Kenai Peninsula

Seward Peninsula

Yukon

Mt. Logan +
19,551 feet
5,959 meters

Yukon

Plateau

Mackenzie Mts.

Coast Mountains

Fraser Plateau

Columbia Mountains

Columbia

Cascade Range

Columbia Plateau

Snake

Great Basin

Great Salt Lake

Mt. Whitney +
14,494 feet
4,418 meters

Sierra Nevada

Coast Ranges

Colorado

ASIA

BERING SEA

St. Lawrence Island

Nunivak Island

Bristol Bay

Aleutian Range

Kodiak I.

GULF OF ALASKA

For the Aleutian Islands
and continuation of
the Bering Sea,
see pages 46–47.

Alexander Archipelago

Queen Charlotte Islands

Vancouver Island

Olympic Peninsula

Cape Mendocino

PACIFIC OCEAN

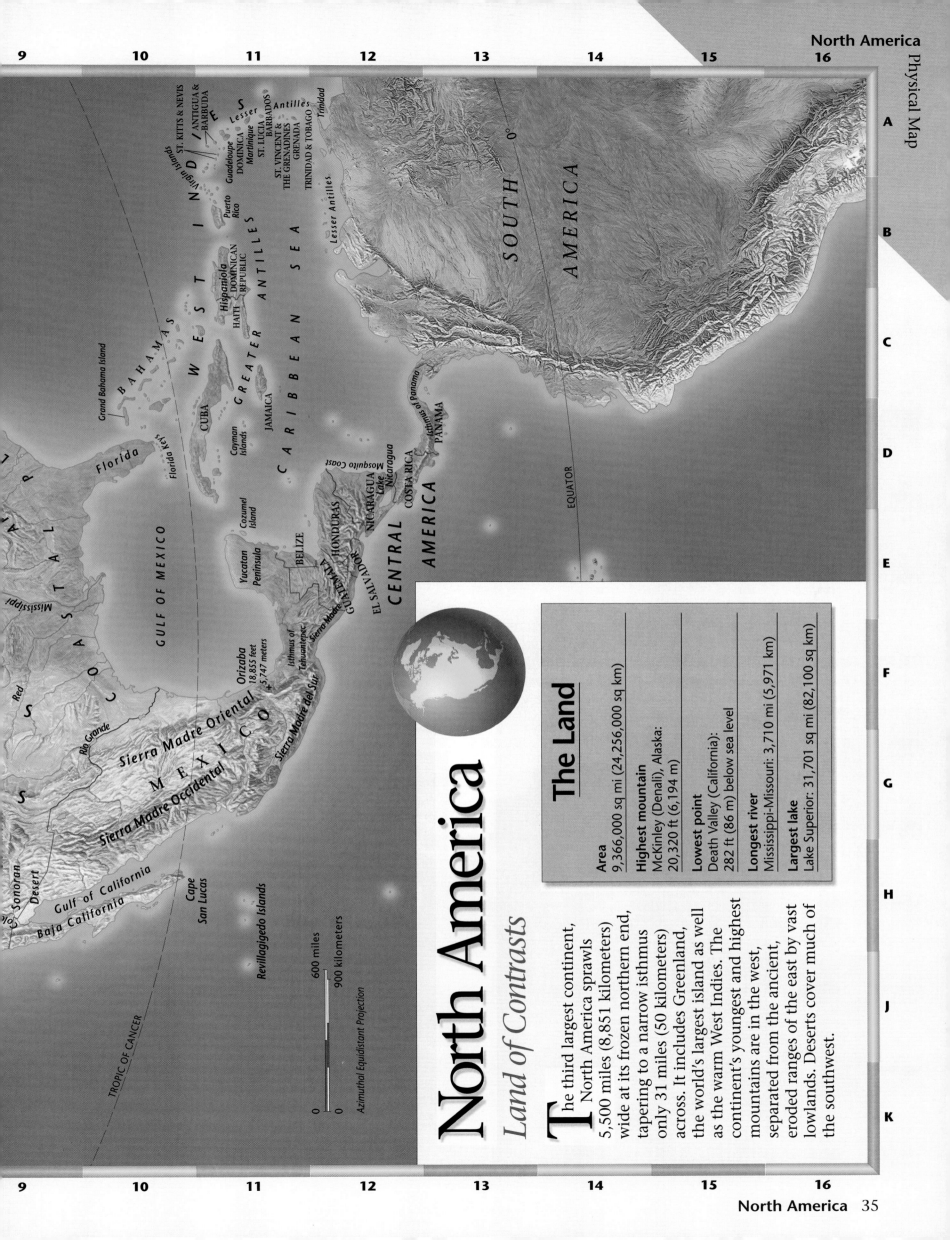

North America

Land of Contrasts

The third largest continent, North America sprawls 5,500 miles (8,851 kilometers) wide at its frozen northern end, tapering to a narrow isthmus only 31 miles (50 kilometers) across. It includes Greenland, the world's largest island as well as the warm West Indies. The continent's youngest and highest mountains are in the west, separated from the ancient, eroded ranges of the east by vast lowlands. Deserts cover much of the southwest.

The Land

Area
9,366,000 sq mi (24,256,000 sq km)

Highest mountain
McKinley (Denali), Alaska:
20,320 ft (6,194 m)

Lowest point
Death Valley (California):
282 ft (86 m) below sea level

Longest river
Mississippi-Missouri: 3,710 mi (5,971 km)

Largest lake
Lake Superior: 31,701 sq mi (82,100 sq km)

SOUTH AMERICA

EQUATOR

0°

WEST INDIES

BAHAMAS
Grand Bahama Island
CUBA
Florida
Florida Keys
GULF OF MEXICO
Cayman Islands
JAMAICA
Cozumel Island
GREATER ANTILLES
Hispaniola
HAITI
DOMINICAN REPUBLIC
Puerto Rico
Virgin Islands
ST. KITTS & NEVIS
ANTIGUA & BARBUDA
Lesser Antilles
Guadeloupe
DOMINICA
Martinique
ST. LUCIA
BARBADOS
ST. VINCENT & THE GRENADINES
GRENADA
TRINIDAD & TOBAGO
Trinidad
Lesser Antilles
LESSER ANTILLES
CARIBBEAN SEA

BELIZE
Yucatan Peninsula
GUATEMALA
HONDURAS
EL SALVADOR
NICARAGUA
Lake Nicaragua
Mosquito Coast
COSTA RICA
PANAMA
Isthmus of Panama
CENTRAL AMERICA

MEXICO
Sierra Madre Oriental
Sierra Madre Occidental
Sierra Madre del Sur
Sierra Madre
Isthmus of Tehuantepec
Orizaba
18,855 feet
5,747 meters
Rio Grande
Red
Mississippi
COASTAL PLAIN
Sonoran Desert
Gulf of California
Baja California
Cape San Lucas
Revillagigedo Islands

TROPIC OF CANCER

0   600 miles
0   900 kilometers
Azimuthal Equidistant Projection

North America

Continental Melting Pot

North America is a land of immigrants. The first people may have come to the continent 25,000 years ago from Asia. Their path was a wide land bridge between Siberia and the Alaskan Peninsula, long since covered by the rising sea. Vikings visited North America next, settling briefly in Newfoundland around 1000 A.D. In 1493 Italian explorer Christopher Columbus returned to Europe with word of new lands he'd seen. In Central America and the Caribbean, European countries such as Spain and England established plantation colonies. Europeans began to settle across North America, followed by people from South America and Asia. The flow of immigrants has never really stopped.

The immigrant's story is not always a happy one. From the 1500s to the 1800s Africans were brought to North America against their will as enslaved people. Native Americans, the first people here, were killed by European diseases and displaced by settlers moving onto their lands. Immigrants still are drawn to the United States and Canada because the countries offer personal freedom, stable governments, and opportunities for earning a good living.

▶ **AN ANCIENT STONE** *temple of the El Tajín civilization rises from the Mexican lowlands. Square openings represent the 365 days of the year.*

▲ **RAISING A RIPPLE** *in Alaska's Wonder Lake, a bull moose takes a watery stroll near the base of Mount McKinley. McKinley, the highest peak in North America, is also known as Denali, or "high one," in the language of the Athapascan people.*

◀ **THE BRIGHT** *lights of a big city illuminate Times Square in New York's famous theater district. With more than 20 million people in its metropolitan area, the city is the largest in the U.S.*

▶ **NATURALISTS** *credit the beaver with helping to shape much of North America. Felling trees and damming streams, beavers create ponds, which become swamps, then meadows.*

▶ **STEPPING LIGHTLY,** *a young girl dances along one of Antigua's many beaches. The islands of Antigua and Barbuda make up one Caribbean country.*

▼ **POLLUTION** *and overcrowding plague Los Angeles, the largest city on the Pacific coast. The city's strong Hispanic heritage is reinforced by many Mexican immigrants.*

▼ **GOLDEN TOADS,** *gleaming symbols of Costa Rica's rain forest, may be in trouble. Once numerous, the toads have mysteriously vanished from their usual habitat.*

▶ **ARIZONA'S PRIDE,** *the Grand Canyon at as much as 18 miles (29 kilometers) wide and 1 mile (1.6 kilometers) deep is the world's largest gorge. Its walls reveal the region's geologic history.*

▶ **AGAINST THE BACKDROP** *of the Twin Butte mountains, bales of hay rest on the fertile soil of Alberta, one of Canada's Prairie Provinces.*

▼ **THE BRIGHT BEAUTY** of autumn leaves brings tourists to Vermont every year. The forested slopes of the northern Appalachian Mountains cover much of New England.

▼ **A CANAL CUTS THROUGH** the Isthmus of Panama, the narrowest part of the continent. The canal is a shortcut between the Atlantic and Pacific Oceans.

▲ **THE CHÂTEAU FRONTENAC** hotel presides over Québec, Canada's oldest city. Two official languages—French and English—reflect Canada's colonial heritage.

▼ **A PUEBLO INDIAN ARTIST** in New Mexico's Nambe Pueblo shapes a stone. Native Americans throughout the continent struggle to retain their identity and culture.

A

B

ARCTIC CIRCLE

Cape Farewell

Greenland Sea

Wandel Sea

GREENLAND (KALAALLIT NUNAAT) (Denmark)

Nuuk (Godthåb)

Labrador Sea

Cartwright

Island of Newfoundland

Avalon Peninsula

St.-Pierre & Miquelon (Fr.)

Cape Breton Island

St. John's

ATLANTIC OCEAN

C

Oodaaq I. Peary Land

Lincoln Sea

QUEEN ELIZABETH ISLANDS

Ellesmere

SVERDRUP ISLANDS

Axel Heiberg I.

Knud Rasmussen Land

Qeqertarsuaq

Baffin Bay

Davis Strait

Iqaluit

Hudson Strait

NEWFOUNDLAND AND LABRADOR

LABRADOR

Scheffervile

Sept-Îles

QUEBEC

NOVA SCOTIA

Gulf of St. Lawrence

P.E.I.

N.B.

Halifax

Fredericton

Bangor

ME.

Concord, N.H.

Boston, MASS.

Providence, R.I.

Hartford, CONN.

N.J.

DEL.

Philadelphia, PA.

Washington

MD.

D

Wandel Sea

Lincoln Land

Devon I.

Borden Pen.

Prince Charles I.

Melville Peninsula

Southampton Island

N U N A V U T

Belcher Islands

James Bay

Chicoutimi

Quebec

Montréal

Ottawa

Toronto

Ontario L.

VT.

N.Y.

New York

Cleveland

OHIO

E

North Magnetic Pole

Prince Patrick I.

Mackenzie King I.

Borden Island

Melville Island

PARRY ISLANDS

Somerset I.

Brodeur Pen.

Boothia Peninsula

Prince of Wales I.

King William I.

Victoria Island

Banks Island

C A N A D A

Hudson Bay

Severn

ONTARIO

Rouyn-Noranda

Thunder Bay

Lake Superior

Lake Huron

MICH.

Detroit

Chicago

IND.

Indianapolis

ILL.

St. Lou.

F

ARCTIC OCEAN

Axel Heiberg I.

Point Barrow

Inuvik

NORTHWEST TERRITORIES

Yellowknife

Great Slave L.

MANITOBA

Lake Winnipeg

Churchill

Winnipeg

Fargo

N. DAK.

MINN.

Minneapolis

St. Paul

WIS.

Lake Michigan

IOWA

Des Moines

G

Beaufort Sea

Great Bear L.

Brooks Range

YUKON TERRITORY

Whitehorse

BRITISH COLUMBIA

Athabasca

SASK.

Saskatoon

Regina

ALBERTA

Edmonton

Calgary

Bismarck

S. DAK.

Sioux Falls

NEBR.

Omaha

Denver

COLO.

Cheyenne

WYO.

H

Mackenzie

Mackenzie Mts.

R O C K Y

Fraser

Spokane

WASH.

Seattle

Great Salt L.

UTAH

Salt Lake City

NEV.

MONT.

Butte

Billings

Boise

IDAHO

Cascade Range

J

Gulf of Alaska

Brooks Range

Fairbanks

Mt. McKinley (Denali) 20,320 ft 6,194 m

Anchorage

ALASKA (U.S.)

Yukon

Juneau

Glacier Bay

Alexander Archipelago

Queen Charlotte Islands

Vancouver Island

Vancouver

Victoria

Portland

OREG.

Eugene

Reno

Sacramento

San Francisco

CALIF.

Fresno

Sierra Nevada

-282 ft -86 m

Cape Mendocino

PACIFIC OCEAN

K

ASIA

Bering Str.

Seward Peninsula

Bering Sea

St. Lawrence Island

Nunivak Island

Bristol Bay

Aleutian Range

Kodiak I.

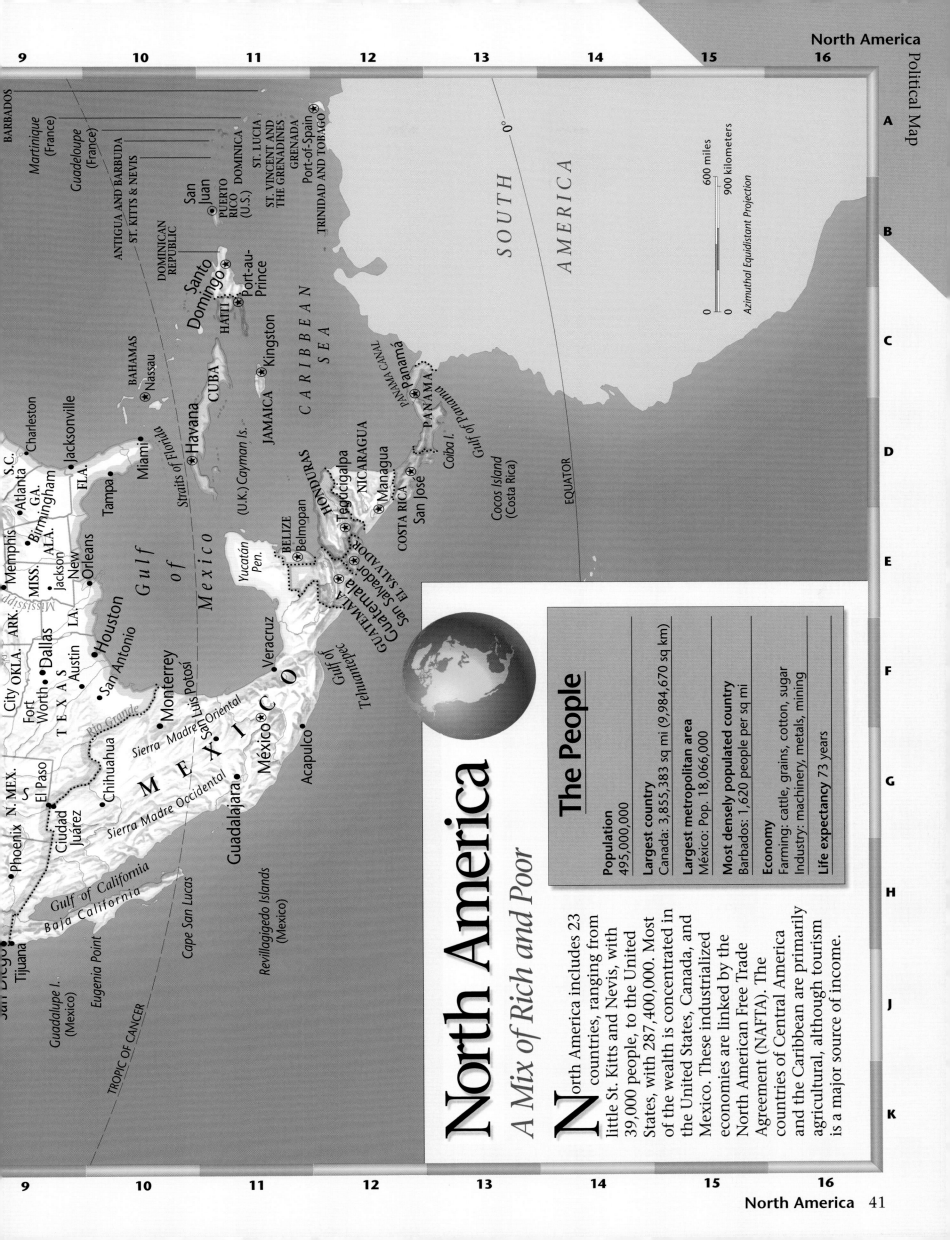

North America
A Mix of Rich and Poor

North America includes 23 countries, ranging from little St. Kitts and Nevis, with 39,000 people, to the United States, with 287,400,000. Most of the wealth is concentrated in the United States, Canada, and Mexico. These industrialized economies are linked by the North American Free Trade Agreement (NAFTA). The countries of Central America and the Caribbean are primarily agricultural, although tourism is a major source of income.

The People

Population
495,000,000

Largest country
Canada: 3,855,383 sq mi (9,984,670 sq km)

Largest metropolitan area
México: Pop. 18,066,000

Most densely populated country
Barbados: 1,620 people per sq mi

Economy
Farming: cattle, grains, cotton, sugar
Industry: machinery, metals, mining

Life expectancy 73 years

600 miles
900 kilometers
Azimuthal Equidistant Projection

Canada

Largest and least densely populated country in North America, Canada has fewer people than California. Most live within a hundred miles of the United States. Canada is one of the world's leading exporters of minerals, wheat, and timber products.

Canada
Area: 3,855,383 sq mi
(9,984,670 sq km)
Population: 31,414,000
Capital: Ottawa
Languages: English, French

Alberta
Area: 255,560 sq mi
(661,848 sq km)
Population: 3,113,600
Capital: Edmonton

British Columbia
Area: 364,791 sq mi
(944,735 sq km)
Population: 4,141,300
Capital: Victoria

Manitoba
Area: 250,134 sq mi
(647,797 sq km)
Population: 1,150,800
Capital: Winnipeg

New Brunswick
Area: 28,152 sq mi
(72,908 sq km)
Population: 756,700
Capital: Fredericton

Newfoundland and Labrador
Area: 156,465 sq mi
(405,212 sq km)
Population: 531,600
Capital: St. John's

Northwest Territories
Area: 519,772 sq mi
(1,346,106 sq km)
Population: 41,400
Capital: Yellowknife

Nova Scotia
Area: 21,347 sq mi
(55,284 sq km)
Population: 944,800
Capital: Halifax

Nunavut
Area: 808,244 sq mi
(2,093,190 sq km)
Population: 28,700
Capital: Iqaluit

Ontario
Area: 415,629 sq mi
(1,076,395 sq km)
Population: 12,068,300
Capital: Toronto

Prince Edward Island
Area: 2,185 sq mi
(5,660 sq km)
Population: 139,900
Capital: Charlottetown

Quebec
Area: 595,434 sq mi
(1,542,056 sq km)
Population: 7,455,200
Capital: Québec

Saskatchewan
Area: 251,385 sq mi
(651,036 sq km)
Population: 1,011,800
Capital: Regina

Yukon Territory
Area: 186,286 sq mi
(482,443 sq km)
Population: 29,900
Capital: Whitehorse

St.-Pierre and Miquelon
(France)

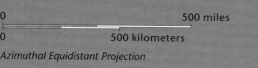

Azimuthal Equidistant Projection

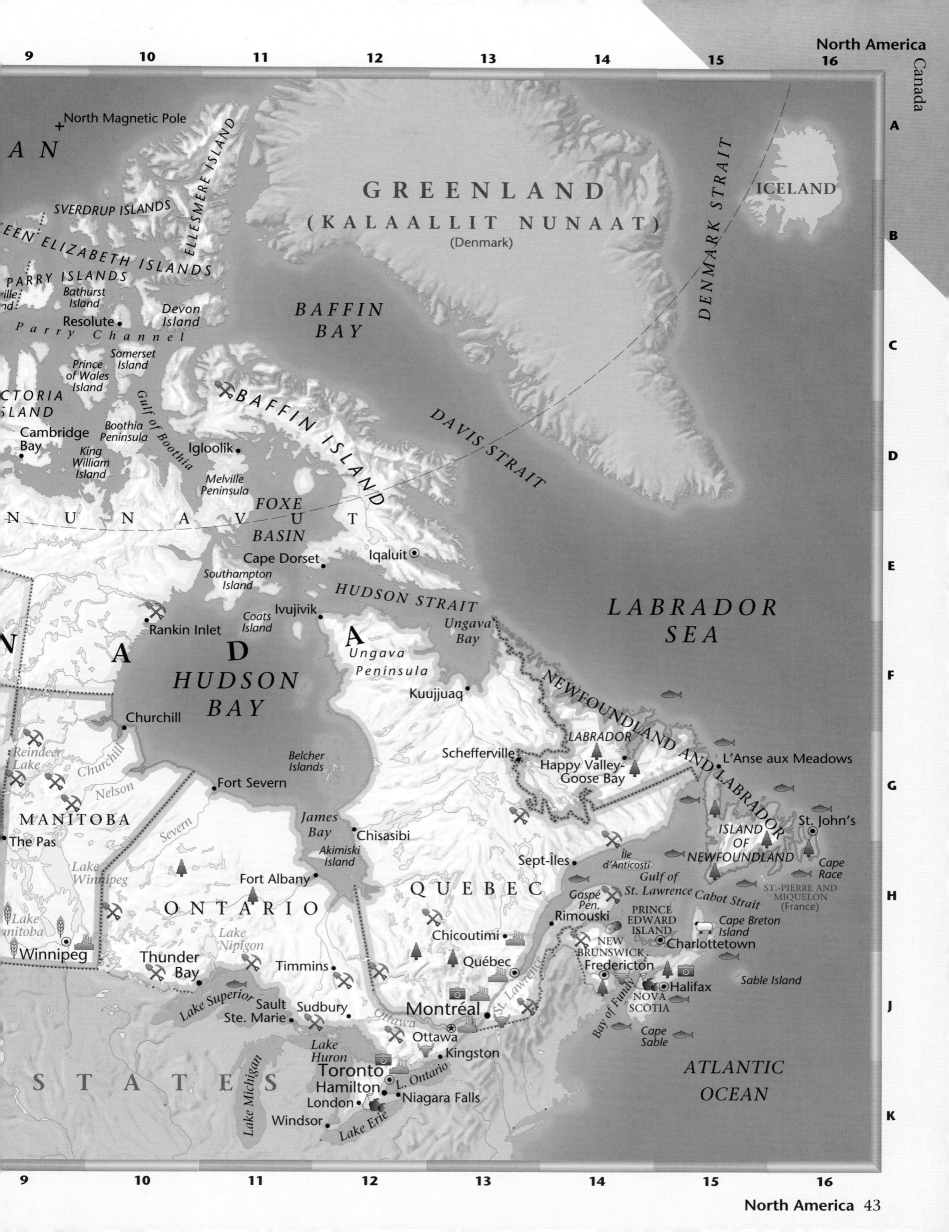

North Magnetic Pole

SVERDRUP ISLANDS

ELLESMERE ISLAND

EEN ELIZABETH ISLANDS

PARRY ISLANDS

Bathurst
Island

Devon
Island

Resolute

Parry Channel

Prince
of Wales
Island

Somerset
Island

CTORIA
ISLAND

Cambridge
Bay

Boothia
Peninsula

King
William
Island

Gulf of Boothia

Igloolik

BAFFIN ISLAND

Melville
Peninsula

FOXE
BASIN

Cape Dorset

Southampton
Island

Iqaluit

GREENLAND
(KALAALLIT NUNAAT)
(Denmark)

BAFFIN
BAY

DENMARK STRAIT

ICELAND

DAVIS STRAIT

HUDSON STRAIT

N U N A V U T

Rankin Inlet

Coats
Island

Ivujivik

Ungava
Bay

LABRADOR
SEA

C A N A D A

Ungava
Peninsula

HUDSON
BAY

Kuujjuaq

NEWFOUNDLAND AND LABRADOR

Churchill

Belcher
Islands

Scheffeville

Happy Valley-
Goose Bay

LABRADOR

L'Anse aux Meadows

Reindeer
Lake

Churchill

Nelson

Fort Severn

James
Bay

Chisasibi

Sept-Îles

ISLAND
OF
NEWFOUNDLAND

St. John's

MANITOBA

The Pas

Severn

Akimiski
Island

Fort Albany

QUEBEC

Île
d'Anticosti

Gulf of
St. Lawrence

Cape
Race

ST.-PIERRE AND
MIQUELON
(France)

Lake
Winnipeg

ONTARIO

Lake
manitoba

Lake
Nipigon

Chicoutimi

Gaspé
Pen.

Rimouski

PRINCE
EDWARD
ISLAND

Cabot Strait

Cape Breton
Island

Charlottetown

Winnipeg

Thunder
Bay

Timmins

Québec

NEW
BRUNSWICK

Fredericton

NOVA
SCOTIA

Halifax

Sable Island

Lake
Superior

Sault
Ste. Marie

Sudbury

Montréal

St. Lawrence

Bay of Fundy

Cape
Sable

ATLANTIC
OCEAN

Lake
Huron

Ottawa

Ottawa

Kingston

Lake Michigan

Toronto

Hamilton

London

L. Ontario

Niagara Falls

STATES

Windsor

Lake Erie

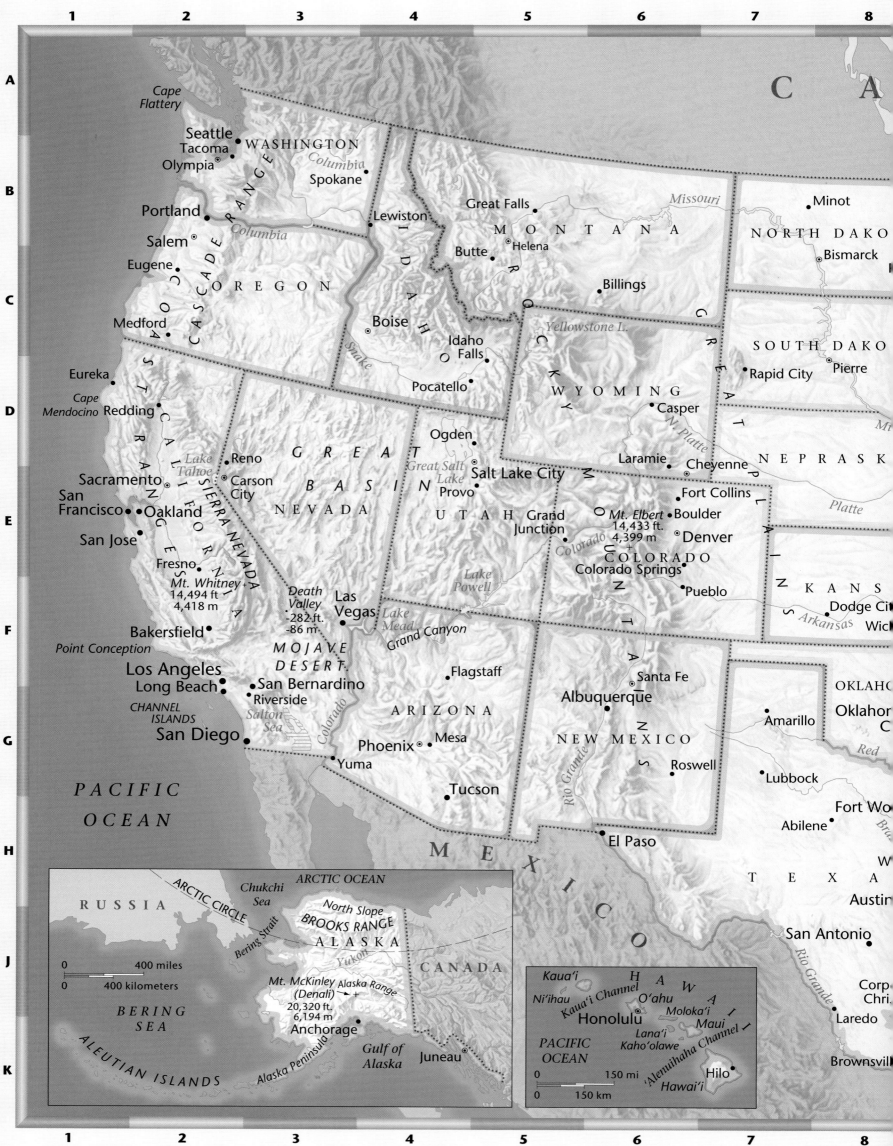

C A

WASHINGTON

Cape
Flattery

Seattle
Tacoma ◎
Olympia ◎

Portland •

Salem ◎

Eugene •

Medford •

Columbia

Spokane •

Columbia

O R E G O N

CASCADE RANGE

COAST RANGE

Great Falls •

M O N T A N A

Butte • ◎ Helena

Billings •

Missouri

Minot •

N O R T H   D A K O

• Bismarck

Lewiston •

I D A H O

Boise ◎

Idaho
Falls •

Pocatello •

Yellowstone L.

W Y O M I N G

Casper •

S O U T H   D A K O

Rapid City • ◎ Pierre

Eureka •

Cape
Mendocino Redding •

Lake
Tahoe Reno •
◎ Carson
City

Sacramento •
San
Francisco • • Oakland

San Jose •

Fresno •

Mt. Whitney +
14,494 ft
4,418 m

G R E A T

B A S I N

N E V A D A

Snake

*Great Salt
Lake* Salt Lake City •
Provo •

Ogden •

U T A H Grand
Junction •

Colorado

*Lake
Powell*

Laramie • ◎ Cheyenne

N E B R A S K

Mt. Elbert
14,433 ft.
4,399 m Boulder •
◎ Denver

C O L O R A D O

Colorado Springs •

Pueblo •

Fort Collins •

N. Platte

Platte

K A N S

SIERRA NEVADA

C A L I F O R N I A

Death
Valley
-282 ft.
-86 m

Las
Vegas •

*Lake
Mead*

Grand Canyon

Dodge Cit •
Arkansas Wich

Bakersfield •

Point Conception

Los Angeles •
Long Beach •

**CHANNEL
ISLANDS**

San Diego •

*M O J A V E
D E S E R T*

• San Bernardino
• Riverside

*Salton
Sea*

Yuma •

Flagstaff •

Colorado

A R I Z O N A

Phoenix ◎ • Mesa

Tucson •

Santa Fe •

Albuquerque •

N E W   M E X I C O

Roswell •

Rio Grande

Amarillo •

O K L A H O

Oklahom
C

Lubbock •

Fort Wo

Abilene •

PACIFIC

OCEAN

M E X I C O

El Paso •

T E X A

Austin

W

Rio Grande

San Antonio •

Corp
Chri

Laredo

Brownsvill

Red

Bria

Brazos

RUSSIA

ARCTIC CIRCLE

*Chukchi
Sea*

ARCTIC OCEAN

Bering Strait

North Slope
BROOKS RANGE
A L A S K A

Yukon

C A N A D A

0   400 miles
0   400 kilometers

B E R I N G

S E A

Mt. McKinley
(Denali) → +
20,320 ft.
6,194 m

Alaska Range

Anchorage •

A L E U T I A N   I S L A N D S

Alaska Peninsula

*Gulf of
Alaska*

Juneau •

Kaua'i **H** A W A **I**
Ni'ihau *Kaua'i Channel* O'ahu *Moloka'i* **I**
Honolulu ◎ *Lana'i* Maui
Kaho'olawe

**PACIFIC
OCEAN** *'Alenuihaha Channel*

Hilo •

Hawai'i

0   150 mi
0   150 km

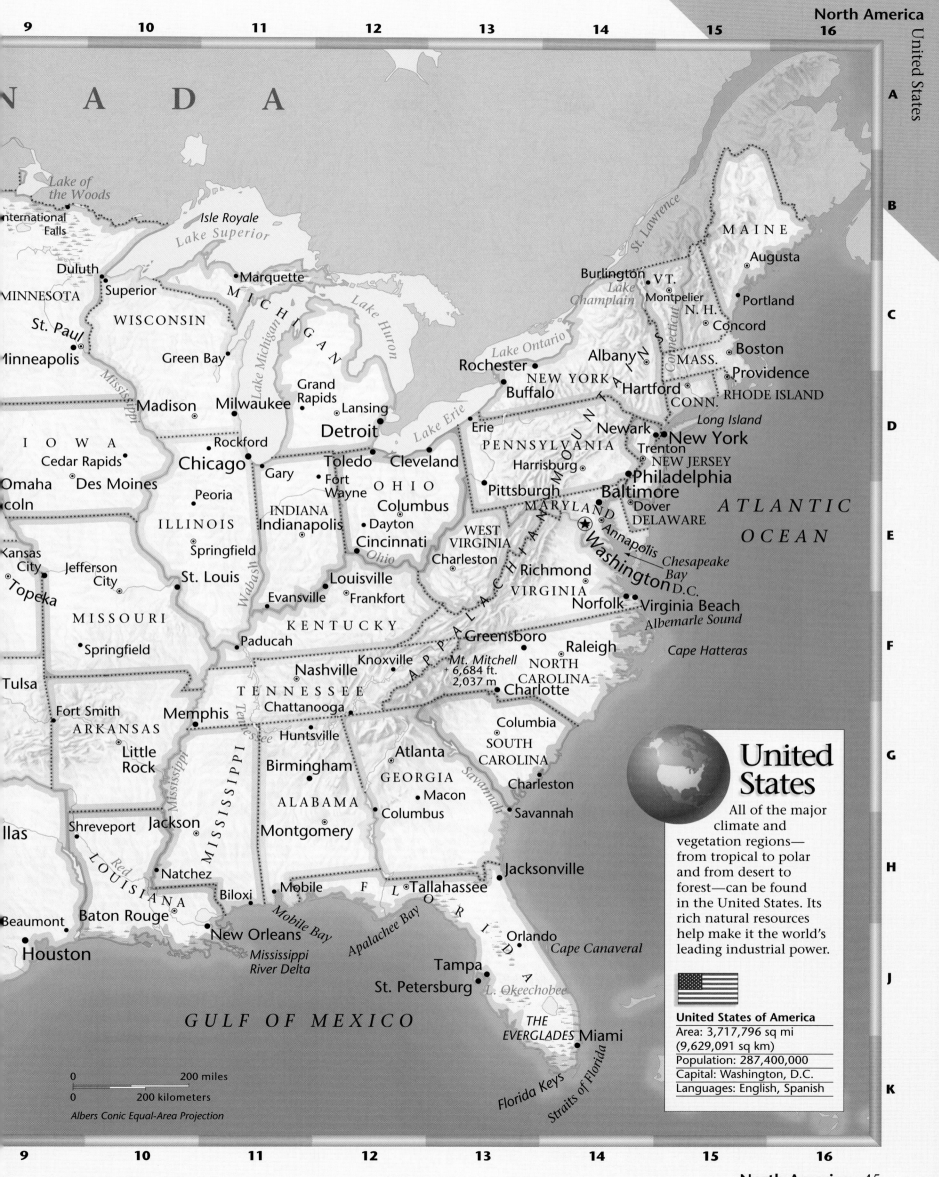

9 10 11 12 13 14 15 16

A

CANADA

Lake of the Woods

International Falls

Isle Royale

Lake Superior

MAINE

Burlington

• Augusta

B

Duluth

• Marquette

MICHIGAN

Lake Champlain

VT.

• Portland

Montpelier

N. H.

• Concord

MINNESOTA

Superior

WISCONSIN

• Green Bay

Lake Michigan

Lake Huron

Lake Ontario

Albany

Boston

C

St. Paul

Minneapolis

Madison

• Milwaukee

Grand Rapids

• Lansing

Rochester

Buffalo

Hartford

MASS.

Providence

CONN.

RHODE ISLAND

Long Island

D

IOWA

• Rockford

Chicago

Gary

Detroit

Toledo Cleveland

Erie

PENNSYLVANIA

Newark

New York

Cedar Rapids

Fort Wayne

OHIO

Harrisburg

Trenton

NEW JERSEY

Omaha

Des Moines

Peoria

INDIANA

Columbus

Pittsburgh

Philadelphia

Baltimore

ATLANTIC

E

coln

ILLINOIS

Indianapolis

Dayton

WEST VIRGINIA

MARYLAND

Dover

DELAWARE

OCEAN

Kansas City

Springfield

Cincinnati

Charleston

Washington

Annapolis

Jefferson City

St. Louis

Ohio

Richmond

D.C.

Chesapeake Bay

Topeka

Evansville

Frankfort

Louisville

VIRGINIA

Norfolk

Virginia Beach

F

MISSOURI

Wabash

KENTUCKY

APPALACHIAN

Greensboro

Albemarle Sound

Springfield

Paducah

Raleigh

Cape Hatteras

Tulsa

Knoxville

Mt. Mitchell
• 6,684 ft.
2,037 m

NORTH CAROLINA

Nashville

Fort Smith

ARKANSAS

Memphis

Chattanooga

MOUNTAINS

Charlotte

G

Little Rock

TENNESSEE

Huntsville

Atlanta

Columbia

SOUTH CAROLINA

Birmingham

GEORGIA

Charleston

Tennessee

Savannah

Macon

Savannah

llas

Shreveport

Jackson

ALABAMA

Columbus

H

Natchez

MISSISSIPPI

Montgomery

LOUISIANA

Red

Mobile

F L

Jacksonville

Beaumont

Baton Rouge

Biloxi

Mobile Bay

O

Tallahassee

R

Houston

New Orleans

Apalachee Bay

I

Orlando

Cape Canaveral

Mississippi River Delta

D

Tampa

A

J

St. Petersburg

L. Okeechobee

GULF OF MEXICO

THE EVERGLADES Miami

K

200 miles

200 kilometers

Florida Keys

Straits of Florida

Albers Conic Equal-Area Projection

United States

All of the major climate and vegetation regions—from tropical to polar and from desert to forest—can be found in the United States. Its rich natural resources help make it the world's leading industrial power.

United States of America

Area: 3,717,796 sq mi
(9,629,091 sq km)

Population: 287,400,000

Capital: Washington, D.C.

Languages: English, Spanish

9 10 11 12 13 14 15 16

Alaska and Hawaii

Alaska is almost a hundred times the size of Hawaii but has only half as many people. Its wealth lies in oil, natural gas, fisheries, and timber, while Hawaii earns most of its income from tourism. Both states have active volcanoes.

Alaska

Area:	615,230 sq mi (1,593,444 sq km)
Population:	635,000
Capital:	Juneau

Hawaii

Area:	6,459 sq mi (16,729 sq km)
Population:	1,224,000
Capital:	Honolulu

A R C T

CHUKCHI SEA

ARCTIC CIRCLE

RUSSIA

KO
VAL

Kotzebue Sound

Kotze

Bering Str.

SEWARD
PENINSU

Nome

Norton Sound

St. Lawrence
Island

St. Matthew Island

Bet

Nunivak
Island

B E R I N G

S E A

Pribilof
Islands

Bris

Ba

Attu
Island

Near Islands

A L E U T I A N   I S L A N D S

ALAS

Unimak I.

Unalaska

Rat Islands

FOX ISLANDS

ANDREANOF ISLANDS

P A C I F I C

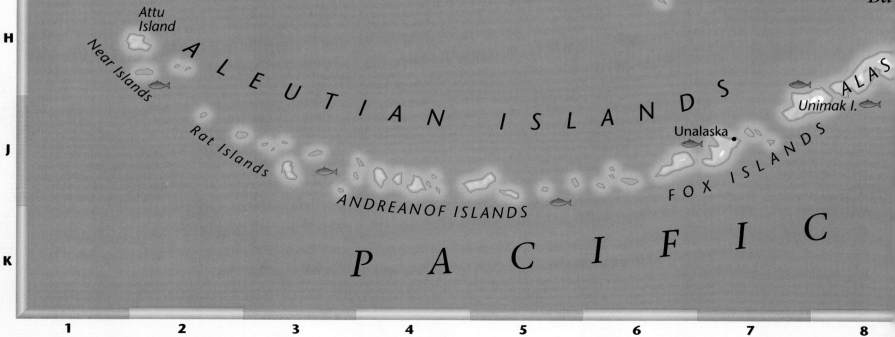

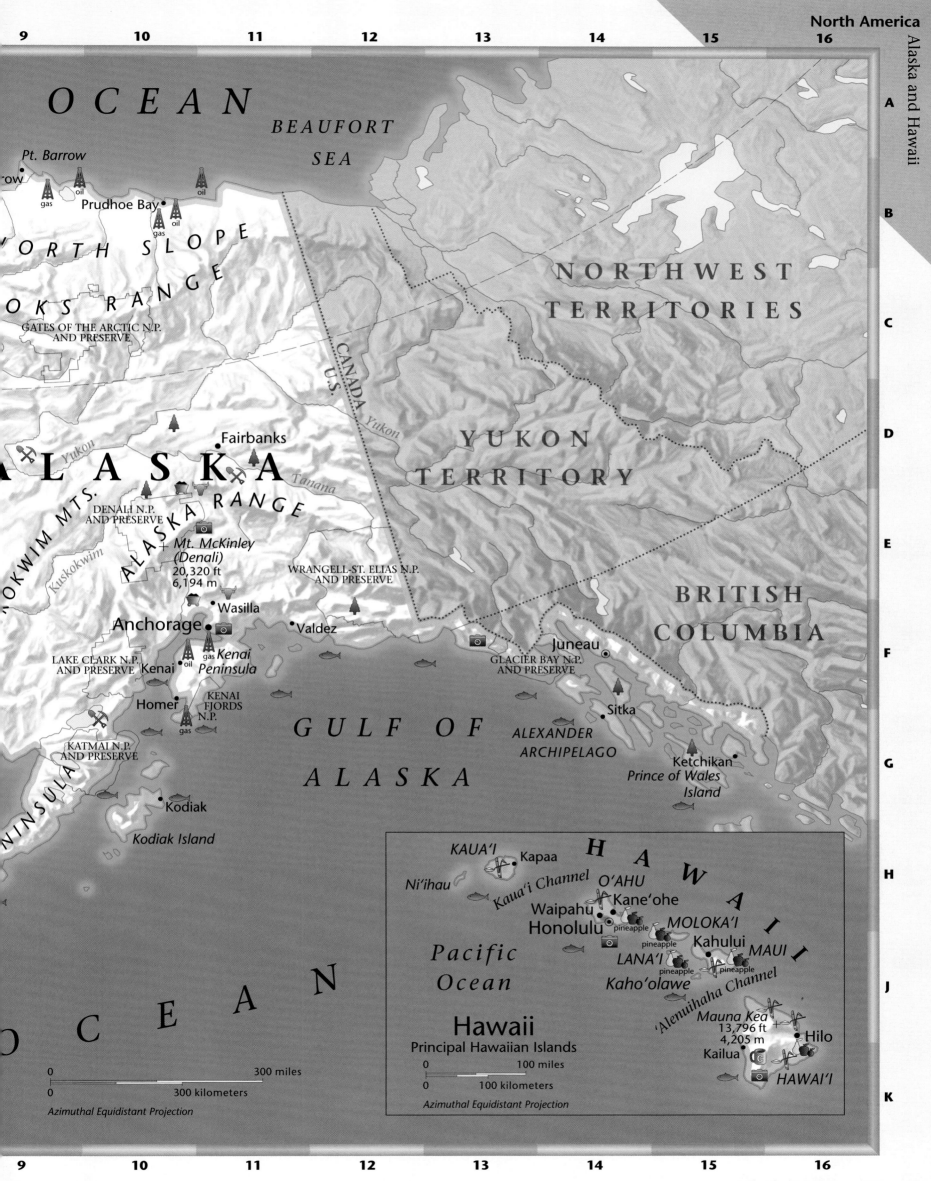

OCEAN

BEAUFORT SEA

Pt. Barrow

row

gas
oil
Prudhoe Bay
oil
oil
gas

ORTH SLOPE

OKS RANGE

GATES OF THE ARCTIC N.P.
AND PRESERVE

CANADA
U.S.

NORTHWEST
TERRITORIES

Yukon

YUKON
TERRITORY

Fairbanks

ALASKA

Yukon

Tanana

OKIM MTS.

DENALI N.P.
AND PRESERVE

ALASKA RANGE

Kuskokwim

Mt. McKinley
(Denali)
20,320 ft
6,194 m

WRANGELL-ST. ELIAS N.P.
AND PRESERVE

BRITISH
COLUMBIA

Wasilla

Anchorage

Valdez

Juneau

GLACIER BAY N.P.
AND PRESERVE

LAKE CLARK N.P.
AND PRESERVE
Kenai
gas
oil
Kenai
Peninsula

Homer
KENAI
FJORDS
N.P.
gas

Sitka

KATMAI N.P.
AND PRESERVE

GULF OF
ALASKA

ALEXANDER
ARCHIPELAGO

Ketchikan
Prince of Wales
Island

NINSULA

Kodiak

Kodiak Island

bo

OCEAN

KAUA'I
Kapaa

H
A
W
A
I
I

Ni'ihau
Kaua'i Channel

O'AHU

Waipahu
Kane'ohe

MOLOKA'I

Honolulu
pineapple

Kahului

Pacific
Ocean

LANA'I
pineapple
pineapple

MAUI

Kaho'olawe

'Alenuihaha Channel

Hawaii
Principal Hawaiian Islands

Mauna Kea
13,796 ft
4,205 m

Hilo

Kailua

HAWAI'I

0   100 miles
0   100 kilometers
Azimuthal Equidistant Projection

0   300 miles
0   300 kilometers
Azimuthal Equidistant Projection

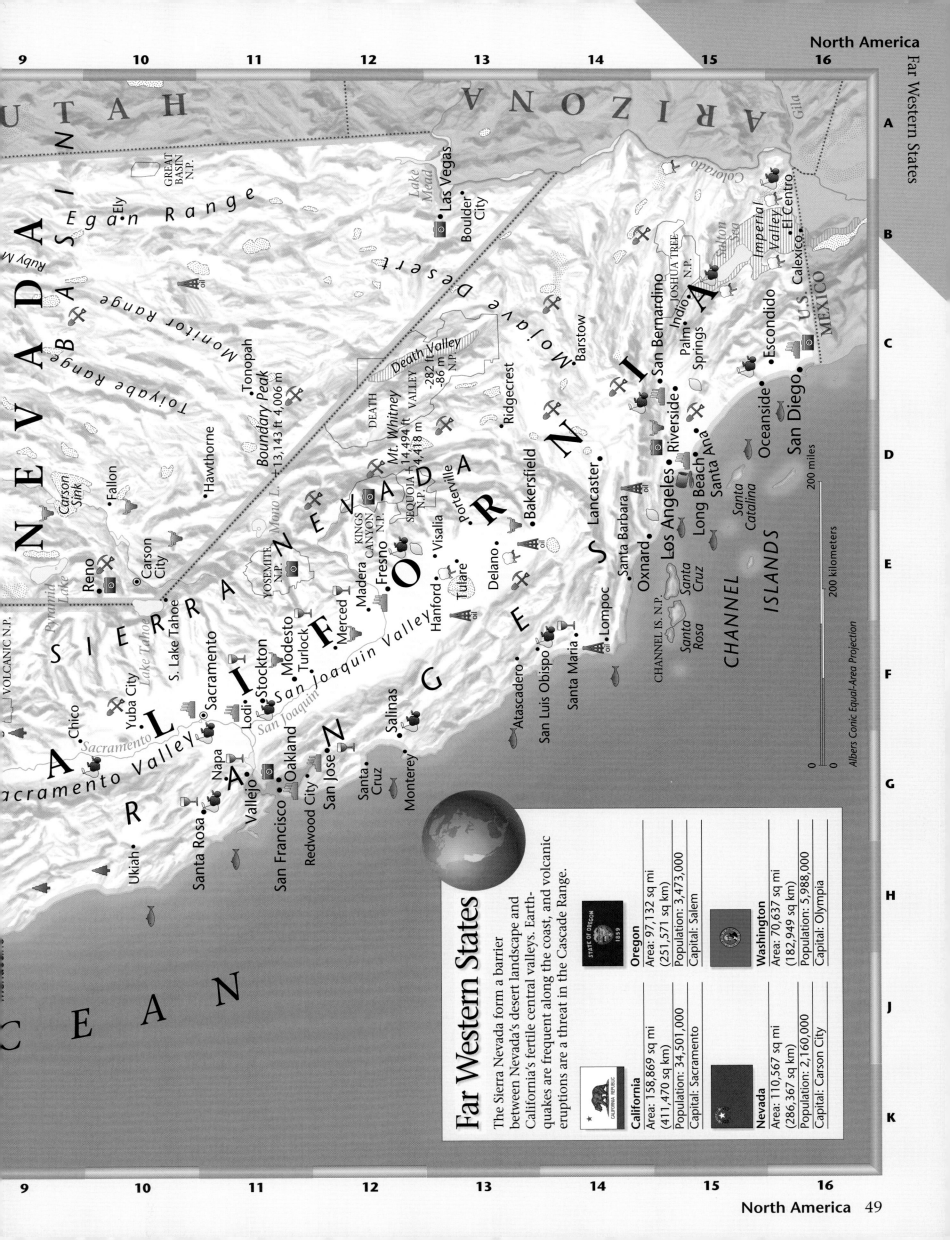

Far Western States

The Sierra Nevada form a barrier between Nevada's desert landscape and California's fertile central valleys. Earthquakes are frequent along the coast, and volcanic eruptions are a threat in the Cascade Range.

California
Area: 158,869 sq mi
(411,470 sq km)
Population: 34,501,000
Capital: Sacramento

Nevada
Area: 110,567 sq mi
(286,367 sq km)
Population: 2,160,000
Capital: Carson City

Oregon
Area: 97,132 sq mi
(251,571 sq km)
Population: 3,473,000
Capital: Salem

Washington
Area: 70,637 sq mi
(182,949 sq km)
Population: 5,988,000
Capital: Olympia

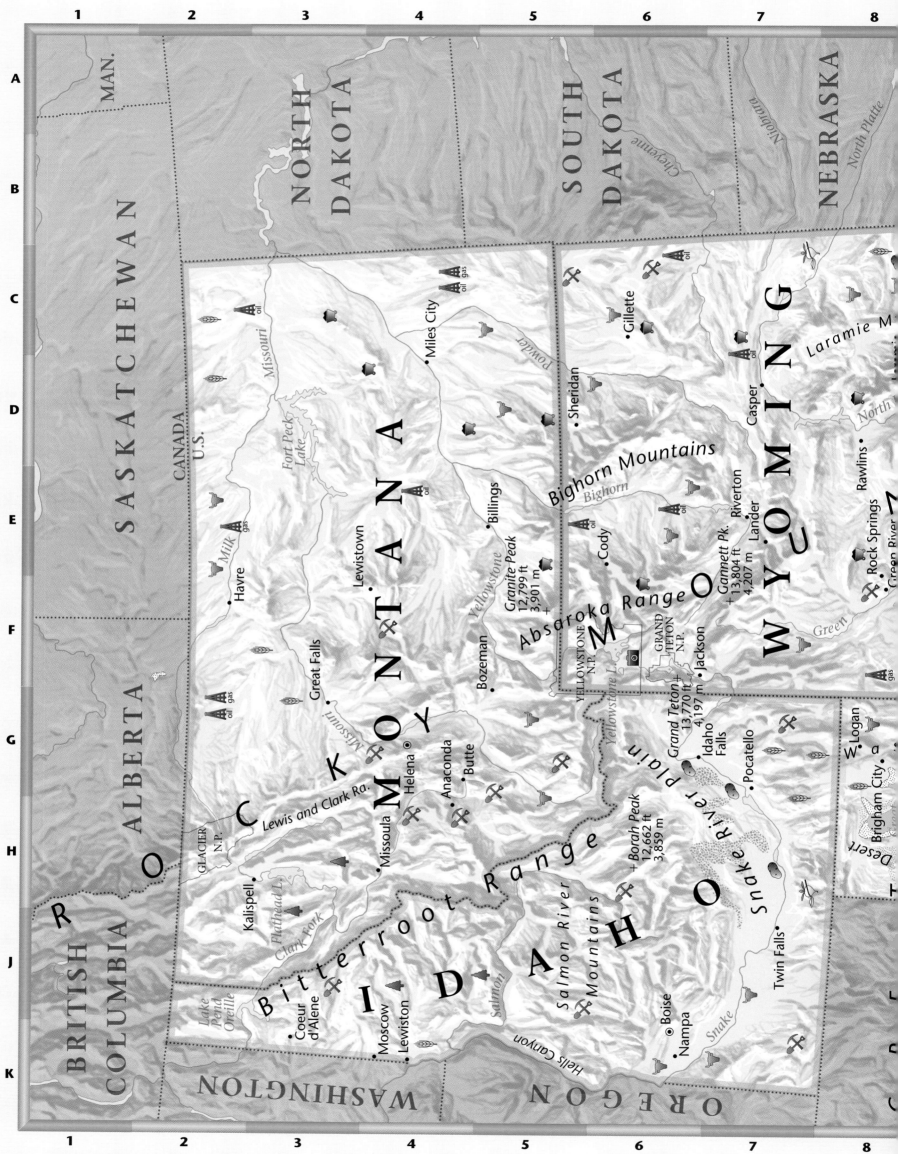

A

B

C

D

E

F

G

H

J

K

MAN.

SASKATCHEWAN

BRITISH COLUMBIA

ALBERTA

NORTH DAKOTA

SOUTH DAKOTA

NEBRASKA

Cheyenne

Niobrara

North Platte

CANADA
U.S.

Missouri

oil

oil gas

Miles City

Powder

Gillette

WYOMING

Laramie M

Milk
gas
Havre

Lewistown

Fort Peck Lake

oil

Billings

Yellowstone

Granite Peak
12,799 ft
3,901 m
+

Bighorn Mountains

Bighorn

Sheridan

oil

oil

•Cody

Casper

Riverton

+Gannett Pk.
13,804 ft
4,207 m
Lander

Rawlins

North

Rock Springs

Green River

Green

MONTANA

ROCKY

Missouri

Great Falls

Helena ◉

Anaconda
Butte

Lewis and Clark Ra.

Absaroka Range

M
O
U
N

YELLOWSTONE
N.P.

GRAND
TETON
N.P.

Yellowstone L.

Jackson

Grand Teton+
13,770 ft
4,197 m

Idaho
Falls

Pocatello

Snake River Plain

Logan

W   a

Brigham City

Desert

GLACIER
N.P.

Kalispell•

Flathead L.

Missoula•

Clark Fork

Bitterroot Range

Lake Pend Oreille

Coeur
d'Alene•

Moscow•
Lewiston•

Salmon

+Borah Peak
12,662 ft
3,859 m

IDAHO

Salmon River

Salmon River Mountains

Snake

•Boise
•Nampa

Twin Falls•

Snake

Hells Canyon

WASHINGTON

OREGON

KANSAS

OKLA.

T E X A S

Cimarron

Canadian

Pecos

Rio Grande

Lamar

Arkansas

Fort Morgan

Colorado Springs

Greeley

Longmont

Boulder

Denver oil

ROCKY MT. N.P.

Loveland

Pueblo

Trinidad

C O L O R A D O

Mt. Elbert
+14,433 ft 4,399 m

Canon City

Sangre de Cristo Mts.

Alamosa

San Juan Mountains

Aspen

Glenwood Springs

Springs

Craig

Colorado

Grand Junction

Montrose

Durango

gas

Cortez

MESA
VERDE
N.P.

oil

oil

N E W

M E X I C O

Vernal

Green

Uinta Mountains

CANYONLANDS
N.P.

Moab

ARCHES N.P.

*Lake
Powell*

Tooele

Orem

Provo

R a.

*Sevier
Desert*

Richfield

CAPITOL
REEF N.P.

BRYCE
CANYON
N.P.

Cedar City

ZION N.P.

St. George

U T A H

A R I Z O N A

Colorado

B A S I N

N E V A D A

Great

C A L I F O R N I A

Colorado

oil

Wyoming
Area: 97,818 sq mi
(253,349 sq km)
Population: 494,000
Capital: Cheyenne

Utah
Area: 84,904 sq mi
(219,902 sq km)
Population: 2,270,000
Capital: Salt Lake City

Montana
Area: 147,046 sq mi
(380,849 sq km)
Population: 904,000
Capital: Helena

Idaho
Area: 83,574 sq mi
(216,456 sq km)
Population: 1,321,000
Capital: Boise

Colorado
Area: 104,100 sq mi
(269,618 sq km)
Population: 4,418,000
Capital: Denver

200 miles

200 kilometers

0

0

Albers Conic Equal-Area Projection

Rocky Mountain States

Rising like a wall from the Great Plains, the Rockies dominate the landscape. Most people live on either side of the barrier in Denver or Salt Lake City.

9 10 11 12 13 14 15 16

A B C D E F G H J K

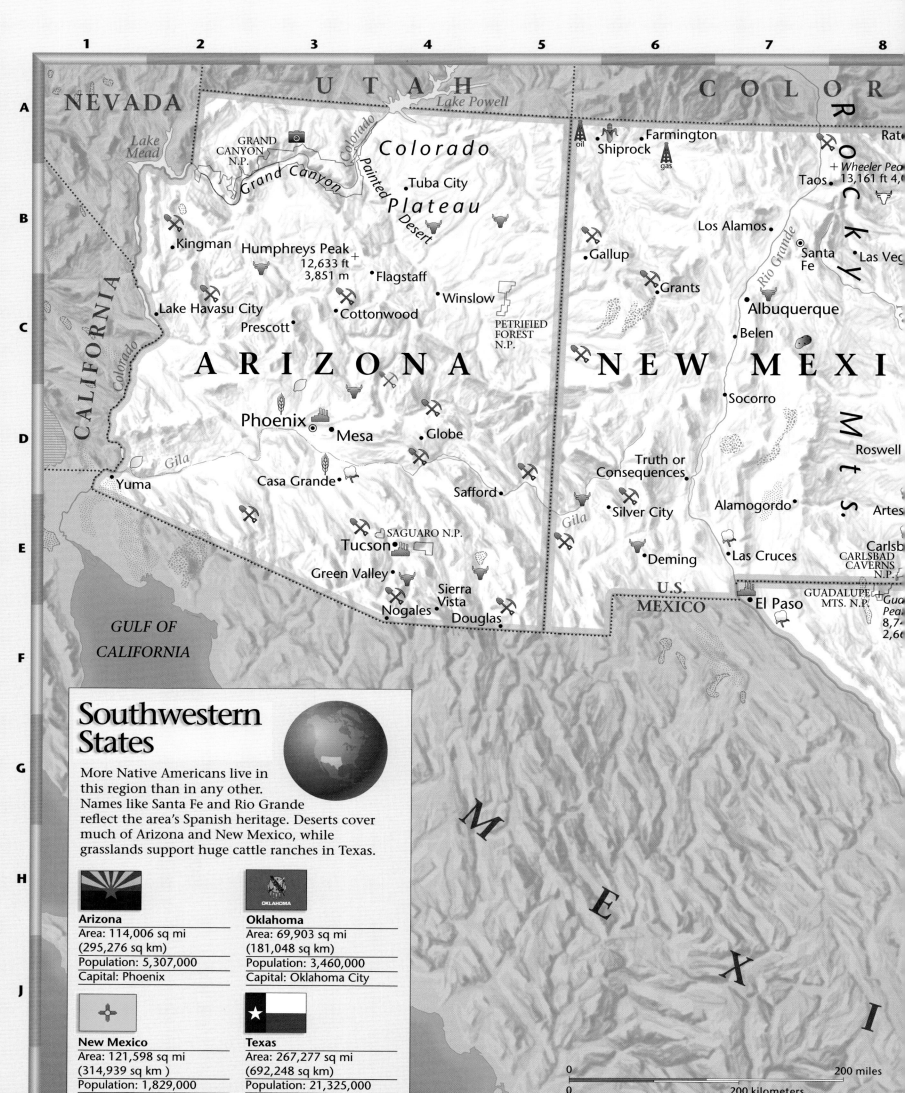

NEVADA

UTAH

COLOR

Lake Powell

Lake Mead

GRAND CANYON N.P.

Colorado

Colorado

Grand Canyon

Painted Desert

Plateau

Tuba City

oil

Shiprock

Farmington

gas

Rat

Wheeler Pea
13,161 ft 4,0

Taos

Los Alamos

Kingman

Humphreys Peak
12,633 ft
3,851 m

Gallup

Santa Fe

Las Veg

Flagstaff

Grants

Lake Havasu City

Cottonwood

Winslow

Albuquerque

CALIFORNIA

Prescott

PETRIFIED FOREST N.P.

Belen

ARIZONA

NEW MEXI

Colorado

Socorro

Phoenix

Mesa

Globe

Roswell

Gila

Truth or Consequences

Yuma

Casa Grande

Safford

Alamogordo

Artes

Gila

Silver City

Carlsb
CARLSBAD CAVERNS N.P.

SAGUARO N.P.

Tucson

Deming

Las Cruces

Green Valley

U.S.
MEXICO

GUADALUPE MTS. N.P.

Sierra Vista

El Paso

Gua
Pea
8,7
2,6

Nogales

Douglas

GULF OF CALIFORNIA

M

E

X

I

Southwestern States

More Native Americans live in this region than in any other. Names like Santa Fe and Rio Grande reflect the area's Spanish heritage. Deserts cover much of Arizona and New Mexico, while grasslands support huge cattle ranches in Texas.

Arizona
Area: 114,006 sq mi
(295,276 sq km)
Population: 5,307,000
Capital: Phoenix

Oklahoma
Area: 69,903 sq mi
(181,048 sq km)
Population: 3,460,000
Capital: Oklahoma City

New Mexico
Area: 121,598 sq mi
(314,939 sq km)
Population: 1,829,000
Capital: Santa Fe

Texas
Area: 267,277 sq mi
(692,248 sq km)
Population: 21,325,000
Capital: Austin

OKLAHOMA

0   200 miles
0   200 kilometers

Albers Conic Equal-Area Projection

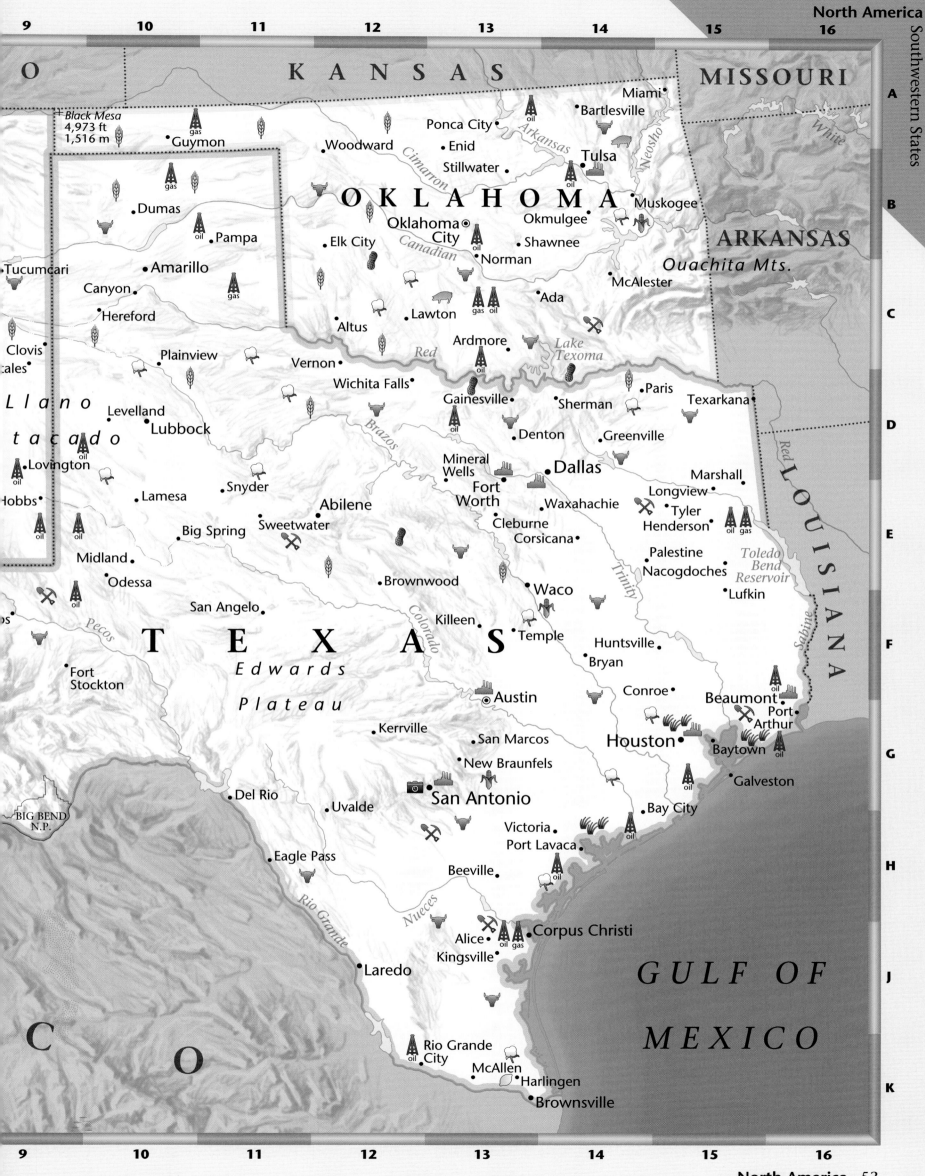

KANSAS

MISSOURI

OKLAHOMA

ARKANSAS

Ouachita Mts.

LOUISIANA

Black Mesa
4,973 ft
1,516 m
Guymon
Dumas
Pampa
Tucumcari
Canyon
Hereford
Amarillo
Clovis
ales
Llano
Levelland
Lubbock
tacado
Lovington
Hobbs
Lamesa
Snyder
Midland
Odessa
San Angelo
Fort
Stockton
BIG BEND
N.P.
Del Rio
Eagle Pass
Laredo
Pecos
Plainview
Vernon
Wichita Falls
Gainesville
Abilene
Big Spring
Sweetwater
Brownwood
Killeen
Kerrville
Rio Grande
Nueces
Alice
Kingsville
Rio Grande
City
McAllen
Harlingen
Brownsville
Woodward
Elk City
Altus
Lawton
Red
Ardmore
Canadian
Denton
Mineral
Wells
Fort
Worth
Cleburne
Corsicana
Colorado
Waco
Temple
Austin
San Marcos
New Braunfels
San Antonio
Uvalde
Victoria
Port Lavaca
Beeville
Brazos
Miami
Bartlesville
Ponca City
Enid
Stillwater
Tulsa
Oklahoma
City
Norman
Okmulgee
Shawnee
Muskogee
McAlester
Ada
Sherman
Paris
Texarkana
Greenville
Dallas
Marshall
Longview
Tyler
Henderson
Waxahachie
Palestine
Nacogdoches
Lufkin
Huntsville
Bryan
Conroe
Beaumont
Port
Arthur
Houston
Baytown
Galveston
Bay City
Corpus Christi

Arkansas
Cimarron
Neosho
White
Lake
Texoma
Trinity
Sabine
Toledo
Bend
Reservoir

TEXAS

Edwards

Plateau

GULF OF

MEXICO

CO

O

gas
gas
oil
oil
oil
oil
gas oil
oil
oil
oil
oil
oil
gas
oil
oil gas
oil
oil
oil
oil
oil
oil
oil
oil gas

SASKATCHEWAN

MANITOBA

CANADA
U.S.

Lake of the Woods

A

MONTANA

Williston
oil

Minot

Devils Lake

Lake Sakakawea

THEODORE ROOSEVELT N.P.

B

Thief River Falls

Upper Red Lake
Lower Red Lake

International Falls

VOYAGEURS N.P.

Rainy Lake

ISLE ROYA

Eagle Mt.+ 2,301 ft 701 m

Virginia

Hibbing

N O R T H
D A K O T A

Grand Forks

Bemidji

Dickinson

Bismarck

Jamestown

Fargo Moorhead

Duluth

Superior
Ironwood

Lak

C

Missouri

+White Butte
3,506 ft
1,069 m

oil

MINNESOTA

Fergus Falls

Brainerd

Mille Lacs Lake

St. Croix

Timms Hill
1,952 ft
595 m

Lake Oahe

Aberdeen

Willmar

St. Cloud

Mississippi

D

Spearfish

Cheyenne

Watertown

Minnesota

St. Paul

Menomonie

Eau Claire

Wisconsin Rapids

Black Hills

S O U T H
D A K O T A

Rapid City

Pierre

Huron

Minneapolis

Red Wing

Marshall

Faribault

Winona

WISCON

Harney Peak+
7,242 ft
2,207 m

Mankato

Rochester

La Crosse

WIND CAVE N.P. BADLANDS N.P.

Mitchell

James

Fairmont

Ste
Po

E

WYO.

Niobrara

Sioux Falls

Yankton

Spencer

Des Moines

Mason City

Watert

Madison

Janesvi
Bel

N E B R A S K A

Vermillion

Fort Dodge

Iowa

Cedar Falls

Dubuque

Alliance

Scottsbluff

North Platte

Sioux City

I O W A

Waterloo

Rockford

DeK

F

COLORADO

South Platte

North Platte

Columbus

Fremont

Missouri

Ames

Cedar Rapids

Iowa City

Clinton

Davenport

Moline

Grand Island

Omaha

Des Moines

Rock Island

Galesburg

Peoria

Pekin

Platte

Kearney

York

Council Bluffs

Indianola

G

McCook

Hastings

Lincoln

Ottumwa

Burlington

Republican

Beatrice

Maryville

Keokuk

Bloomington

Kirksville

Quincy

ILLINO

St. Joseph

H

K A N S A S

Mt. Sunflower
+4,039 ft
1,231 m

Smoky Hill

Hays

Atchison

Leavenworth

Kansas

Kansas City

Hannibal

Jacksonville

Springfield

Salina

Topeka

Kansas City

Marshall

Manhattan

Lawrence

Columbia

St. Charles

Alton

I

Great Bend

McPherson

Emporia

Neosho

Missouri

Jefferson City

St. Louis

Garden City

Hutchinson

oil

M I S S O U R I

Belle

Dodge City

gas

Wichita

Fort Scott

Nevada

Rolla

J

Arkansas

Liberal

Winfield

Pittsburg

Parsons

Springfield

Ozark Plateau

+Taum Sauk Mt.
1,772 ft
540 m

Carbon

Cape Girardeau

Ca

Coffeyville

Joplin

Poplar Bluff

Sikeston

Cimarron

Kennett

K

Canadian

O K L A H O M A

ARKANSAS

TEXAS

9 10 11 12 13 14 15 16

O N T A R I O

0   200 miles
0   200 kilometers

Albers Conic Equal-Area Projection

Midwestern States

Vast fields of wheat and corn make this region the nation's breadbasket. Most U.S. hogs and dairy cows are raised here as well. Chicago is the area's most populous city.

Illinois
Area: 57,918 sq mi
(150,007 sq km)
Population: 12,482,000
Capital: Springfield

Missouri
Area: 69,709 sq mi
(180,546 sq km)
Population: 5,630,000
Capital: Jefferson City

Indiana
Area: 36,420 sq mi
(94,328 sq km)
Population: 6,115,000
Capital: Indianapolis

Nebraska
Area: 77,358 sq mi
(200,358 sq km)
Population: 1,713,000
Capital: Lincoln

Iowa
Area: 56,276 sq mi
(145,754 sq km)
Population: 2,923,000
Capital: Des Moines

North Dakota
Area: 70,704 sq mi
(183,123 sq km)
Population: 634,000
Capital: Bismarck

Kansas
Area: 82,282 sq mi
(213,130 sq km)
Population: 2,695,000
Capital: Topeka

Ohio
Area: 44,828 sq mi
(116,103 sq km)
Population: 11,374,000
Capital: Columbus

Michigan
Area: 96,705 sq mi
(250,465 sq km)
Population: 9,991,000
Capital: Lansing

South Dakota
Area: 77,121 sq mi
(199,744 sq km)
Population: 757,000
Capital: Pierre

Minnesota
Area: 86,943 sq mi
(225,182 sq km)
Population: 4,972,000
Capital: St. Paul

Wisconsin
Area: 65,499 sq mi
(169,643 sq km)
Population: 5,402,000
Capital: Madison

Superior

Royale

Keweenaw Peninsula

Mt. Arvon
1,979 ft
603 m

Marquette
Sault Ste. Marie
Escanaba
Marinette
Green Bay
Door Pen.
MICHIGAN
Alpena
Traverse City
Lake Huron
Saginaw Bay
gas
Lake Winnebago
Sheboygan
Fond du Lac
Mt. Pleasant
Bay City
Saginaw
Muskegon
Grand Rapids
Flint
Port Huron
Milwaukee
Grand
Lansing
Lake St. Clair
Battle Creek
Detroit
Kalamazoo
Ann Arbor
Lake Erie
Waukegan
Jackson
Ashtabula
Chicago
Toledo
Lorain
Cleveland
Aurora
Gary
Elkhart
Sandusky
Akron
South Bend
CUYAHOGA VALLEY N.P.
PENNSYLVANIA
Kankakee
Fort Wayne
Mansfield
Canton
Lima
Marion
Steubenville
Kokomo
Marion
OHIO
Champaign
Lafayette
Muncie
Columbus
Danville
INDIANA
Springfield
Zanesville
Lancaster
Indianapolis
Dayton
Athens
Mattoon
Terre Haute
Hamilton
Chillicothe
Ohio
Effingham
Columbus
Cincinnati
WEST VIRGINIA
Bloomington
Madison
Portsmouth
Vincennes
Scioto
Kanawha
Wabash
Evansville

KENTUCKY
VIRGINIA

Ohio
Tennessee
Cumberland

TENNESSEE
NORTH CAROLINA

A B C D E F G H J K

Southeastern States

This is the land of cotton—at least in the South. Baltimore and New Orleans are among the region's busiest ports.

Alabama
Area: 52,237 sq mi
(135,293 sq km)
Population: 4,464,000
Capital: Montgomery

Arkansas
Area: 53,182 sq mi
(137,742 sq km)
Population: 2,692,000
Capital: Little Rock

Delaware
Area: 2,396 sq mi
(6,206 sq km)
Population: 796,000
Capital: Dover

District of Columbia (D.C.)*
(Washington, D.C.)
Area: 68 sq mi
(177 sq km)
Population: 572,000
Nation's capital
*Washington, D.C., is a federal district, not a state.

Florida
Area: 59,928 sq mi
(155,214 sq km)
Population: 16,397,000
Capital: Tallahassee

Georgia
Area: 58,997 sq mi
(152,750 sq km)
Population: 8,384,000
Capital: Atlanta

Kentucky
Area: 40,411 sq mi
(104,665 sq km)
Population: 4,066,000
Capital: Frankfort

Louisiana
Area: 49,651 sq mi
(128,595 sq km)
Population: 4,465,000
Capital: Baton Rouge

Maryland
Area: 12,297 sq mi
31,849 sq km)
Population: 5,375,000
Capital: Annapolis

Mississippi
Area: 48,286 sq mi
(125,060 sq km)
Population: 2,858,000
Capital: Jackson

North Carolina
Area: 52,672 sq mi
(136,421 sq km)
Population: 8,186,000
Capital: Raleigh

South Carolina
Area: 31,189 sq mi
(80,779 sq km)
Population: 4,063,000
Capital: Columbia

Tennessee
Area: 42,146 sq mi
(109,158 sq km)
Population: 5,740,000
Capital: Nashville

Virginia
Area: 42,326 sq mi
(109,625 sq km)
Population: 7,188,000
Capital: Richmond

West Virginia
Area: 24,231 sq mi
(62,753 sq km)
Population: 1,802,000
Capital: Charleston

0 ⎯ 200 miles
0 ⎯ 200 kilometers
Albers Conic Equal-Area Projection

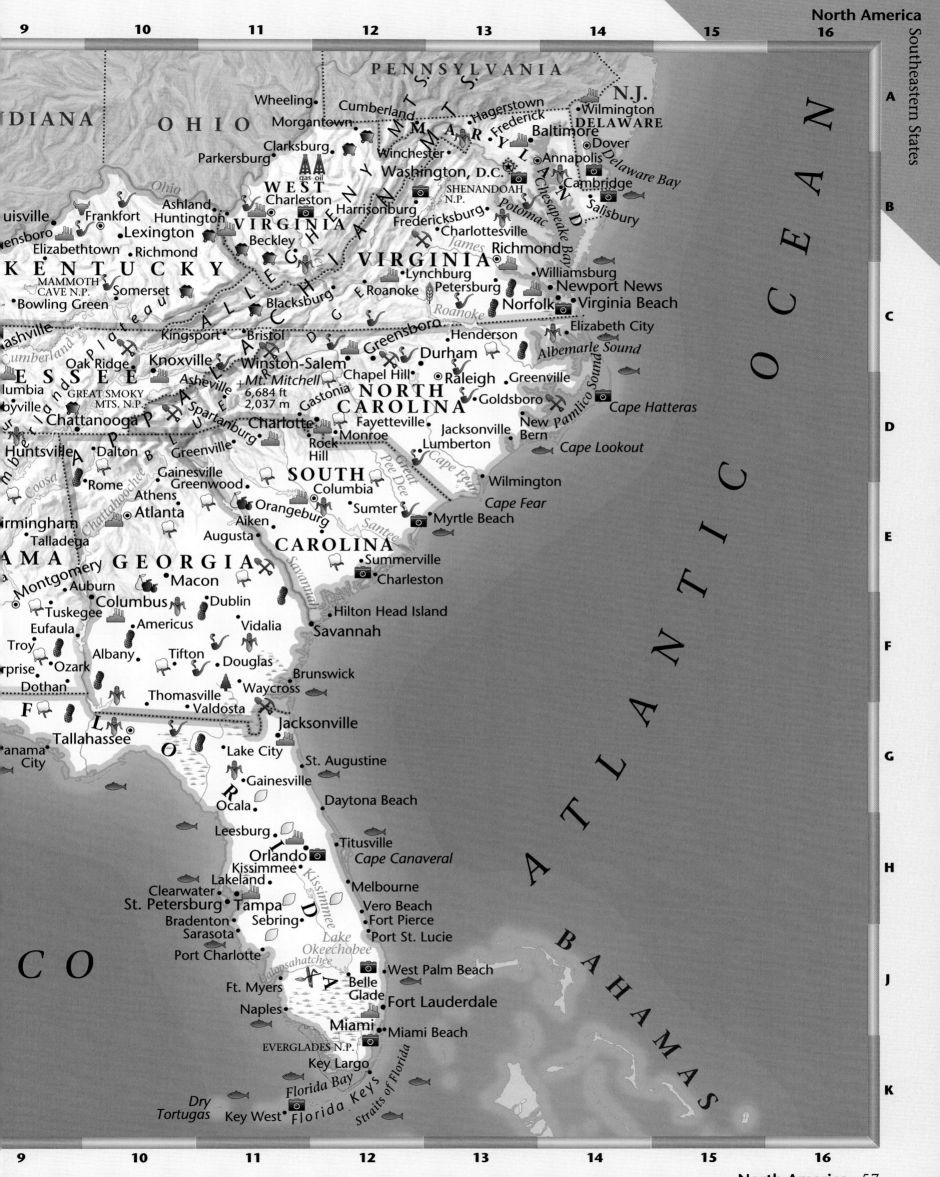

9   10   11   12   13   14   15   16

A

B

C

D

E

F

G

H

J

K

PENNSYLVANIA

INDIANA

OHIO

Wheeling • Cumberland • Hagerstown
Morgantown • Frederick • Baltimore
Clarksburg N.J. Wilmington
Parkersburg DELAWARE
Winchester Dover
gas oil Washington, D.C. Annapolis
WEST Charleston Harrisonburg Cambridge
Ashland SHENANDOAH Salisbury
Huntington N.P. Chesapeake Bay
Louisville VIRGINIA Potomac Delaware Bay
Frankfort
Lexington Fredericksburg
Elizabethtown Richmond Charlottesville
Beckley VIRGINIA Richmond
KENTUCKY James Williamsburg
MAMMOTH Lynchburg Newport News
CAVE N.P. Somerset Roanoke Petersburg Norfolk Virginia Beach
Bowling Green Blacksburg Roanoke
Nashville Kingsport Bristol Greensboro Henderson Elizabeth City
Oak Ridge Albemarle Sound
Columbia Knoxville Winston-Salem Durham
byville Mt. Mitchell Chapel Hill Raleigh Greenville
Chattanooga GREAT SMOKY Asheville 6,684 ft NORTH Goldsboro Pamlico Sound Cape Hatteras
Huntsville MTS. N.P. 2,037 m Gastonia CAROLINA
Dalton Spartanburg Charlotte Fayetteville New Cape Lookout
Rome Greenville Rock Monroe Jacksonville Bern
Gainesville Hill Lumberton
Coosa Greenwood SOUTH Columbia Great Cape Fear
Athens CAROLINA Pee Dee Wilmington
Birmingham Atlanta Aiken Sumter Santee Cape Fear
Talladega Orangeburg Myrtle Beach
Augusta Summerville
Montgomery GEORGIA Macon Charleston
ALABAMA Auburn
Columbus Dublin Savannah Hilton Head Island
Tuskegee Americus Vidalia Savannah
Eufaula Tifton
Troy Albany Douglas Brunswick
Enterprise Ozark Thomasville Waycross
Dothan Valdosta Jacksonville
FLORIDA
Tallahassee
Panama City Lake City St. Augustine
Gainesville
Ocala Daytona Beach
Leesburg
Titusville
Orlando Cape Canaveral
Kissimmee
Clearwater Lakeland Melbourne
St. Petersburg Tampa Vero Beach
Bradenton Sebring Fort Pierce
Sarasota Port St. Lucie
Lake
Okeechobee
Port Charlotte Caloosahatchee West Palm Beach
Ft. Myers Belle Fort Lauderdale
Naples Glade
Miami
Miami Beach
EVERGLADES N.P.
Key Largo
Florida Bay
Dry Florida Keys
Tortugas Key West Straits of Florida

ATLANTIC OCEAN

BAHAMAS

MEXICO

9   10   11   12   13   14   15   16

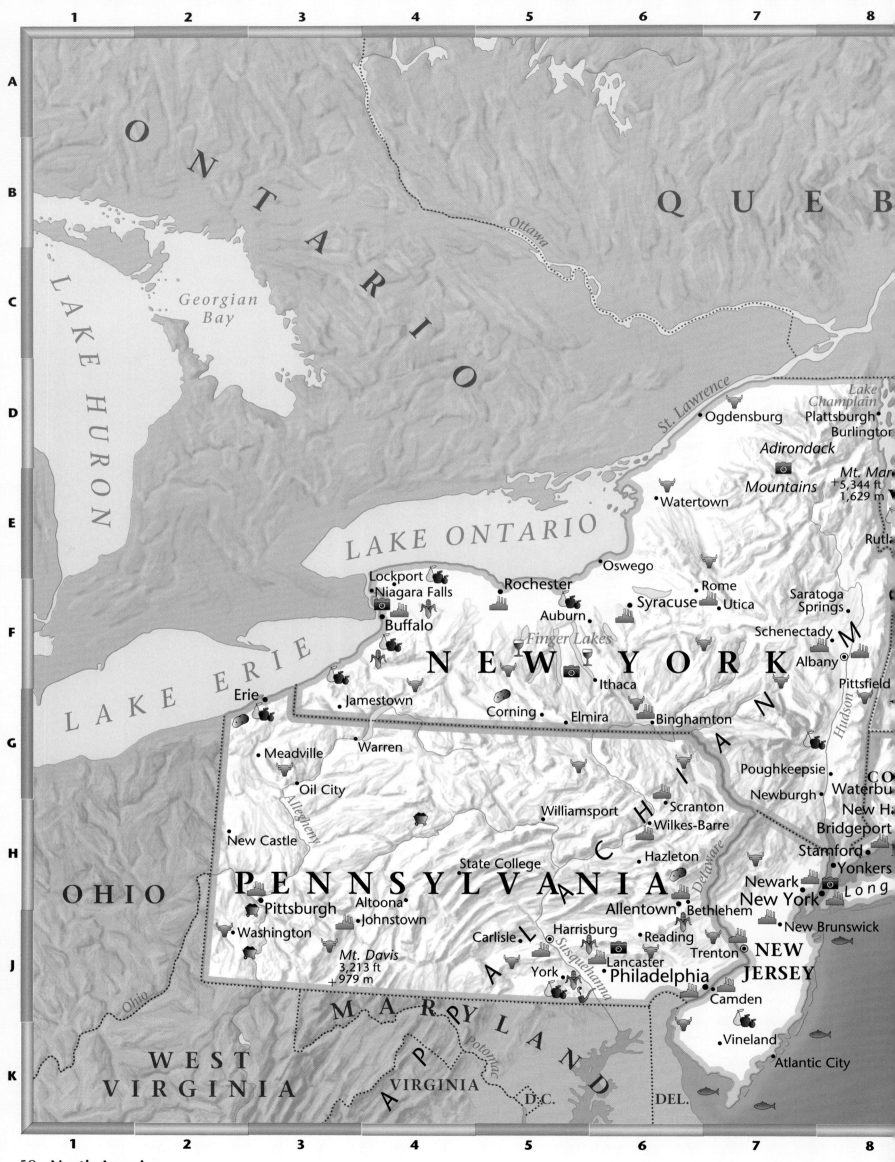

ONTARIO

QUEBE

Georgian
Bay

LAKE HURON

Ottawa

St. Lawrence

Lake
Champlain

• Ogdensburg   Plattsburgh •
                              Burlington •

Adirondack

□ +5,344 ft
Mountains 1,629 m   *Mt. Mar*

• Watertown

LAKE ONTARIO

Rutla

Oswego •

Lockport   Rome •   Saratoga
Niagara Falls • Rochester Syracuse • Utica   Springs

Buffalo   Auburn •   Schenectady •

Finger Lakes   Albany ◉

N E W   Y O R K   Pittsfield •

Erie •   Ithaca •

        Jamestown •   Corning • Elmira • Binghamton •

• Meadville   • Warren   Poughkeepsie •

• Oil City   Newburgh •

                    Williamsport •   Scranton •
                                   Wilkes-Barre •

• New Castle   State College   Hazleton •   Stamford •
                                                              • Yonkers

P E N N S Y L V A N I A   Newark •
                                              New York

            Altoona •   Allentown • Bethlehem •
Pittsburgh •   Johnstown •   • New Brunswick

• Washington   Carlisle • Harrisburg • Reading •   NEW
                                              Trenton ◉   JERSEY
        Mt. Davis
        3,213 ft   York • Lancaster • Philadelphia •
        +979 m   Camden •

M A R Y L A N D   • Vineland

OHIO

Ohio

LAKE ERIE

Allegheny

Delaware

Susquehanna

Hudson

CO
Waterbu
New Ha
Bridgeport
Long

W E S T
V I R G I N I A   VIRGINIA   D.C.   DEL.

Potomac

• Atlantic City

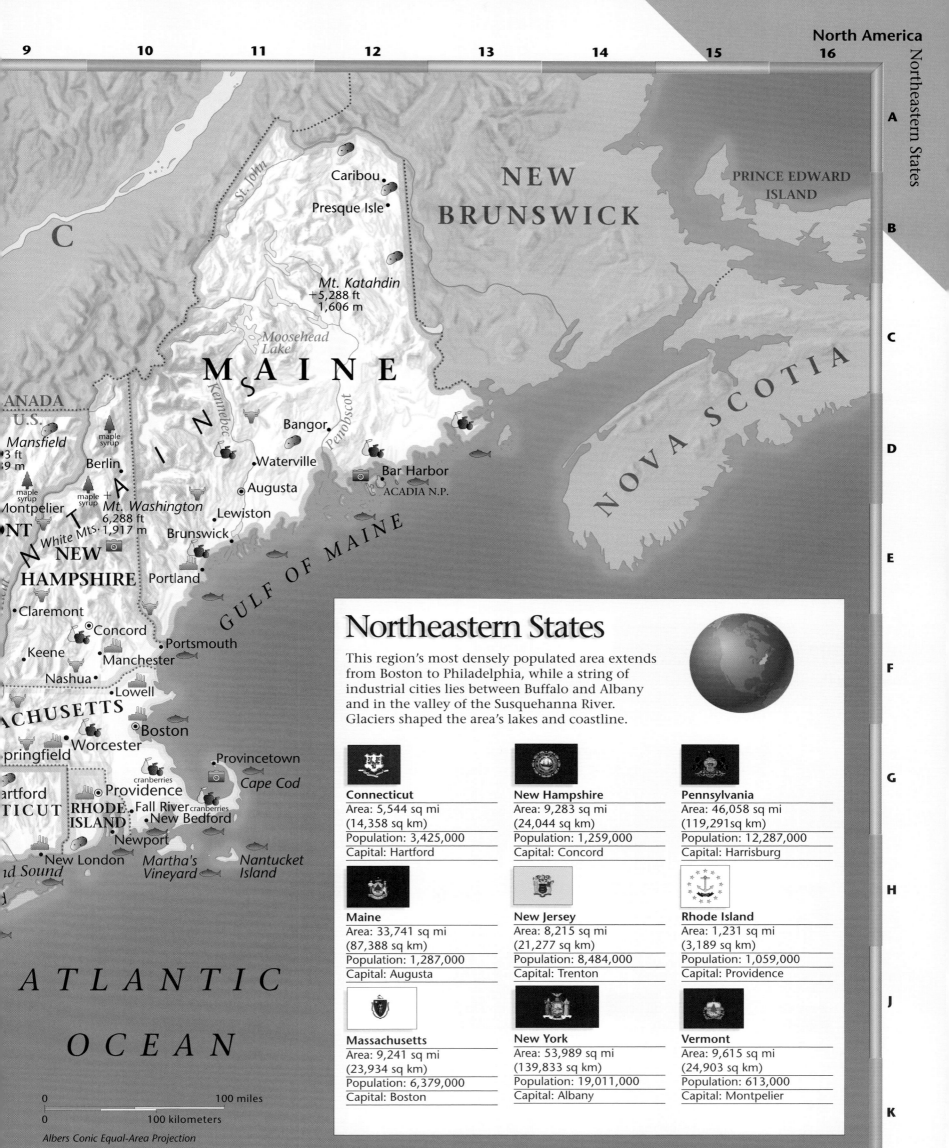

Northeastern States

This region's most densely populated area extends from Boston to Philadelphia, while a string of industrial cities lies between Buffalo and Albany and in the valley of the Susquehanna River. Glaciers shaped the area's lakes and coastline.

Connecticut
Area: 5,544 sq mi
(14,358 sq km)
Population: 3,425,000
Capital: Hartford

New Hampshire
Area: 9,283 sq mi
(24,044 sq km)
Population: 1,259,000
Capital: Concord

Pennsylvania
Area: 46,058 sq mi
(119,291sq km)
Population: 12,287,000
Capital: Harrisburg

Maine
Area: 33,741 sq mi
(87,388 sq km)
Population: 1,287,000
Capital: Augusta

New Jersey
Area: 8,215 sq mi
(21,277 sq km)
Population: 8,484,000
Capital: Trenton

Rhode Island
Area: 1,231 sq mi
(3,189 sq km)
Population: 1,059,000
Capital: Providence

Massachusetts
Area: 9,241 sq mi
(23,934 sq km)
Population: 6,379,000
Capital: Boston

New York
Area: 53,989 sq mi
(139,833 sq km)
Population: 19,011,000
Capital: Albany

Vermont
Area: 9,615 sq mi
(24,903 sq km)
Population: 613,000
Capital: Montpelier

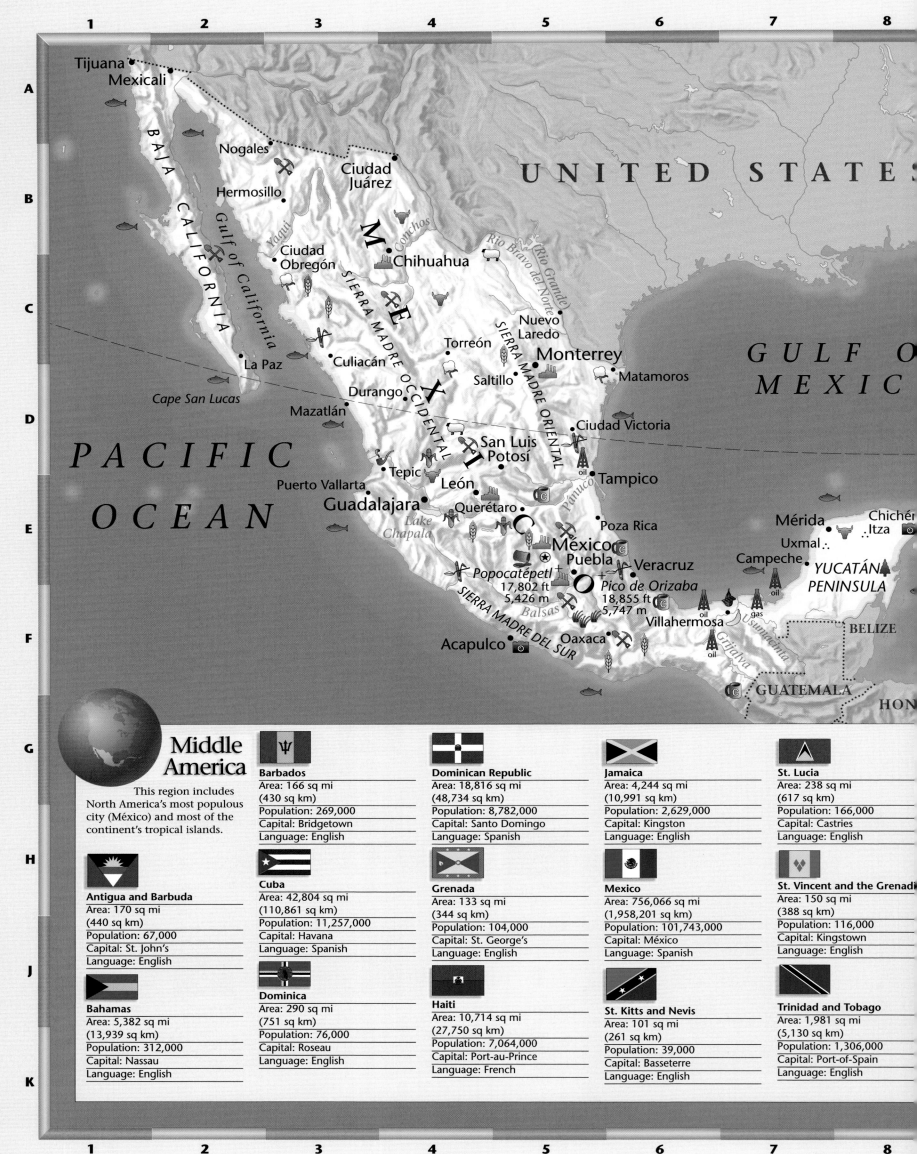

Map labels

Tijuana
Mexicali
Nogales
Hermosillo
Ciudad Juárez
BAJA CALIFORNIA
Gulf of California
Yaqui
Ciudad Obregón
Conchos
Chihuahua
UNITED STATES
La Paz
Cape San Lucas
Culiacán
Torreón
SIERRA MADRE OCCIDENTAL
SIERRA MADRE ORIENTAL
Nuevo Laredo
Rio Bravo del Norte
Rio Grande
Monterrey
Saltillo
Matamoros
Durango
Mazatlán
Ciudad Victoria
GULF OF MEXICO
San Luis Potosí
oil
Tepic
León
Puerto Vallarta
Pánuco
Tampico
Guadalajara
Lake Chapala
Querétaro
Poza Rica
Mérida
Chichén Itzá
Uxmal
Campeche
México
Puebla
Veracruz
YUCATÁN PENINSULA
Popocatépetl
17,802 ft
5,426 m
Pico de Orizaba
18,855 ft
5,747 m
oil
gas
PACIFIC OCEAN
SIERRA MADRE DEL SUR
Balsas
Villahermosa
oil
BELIZE
Acapulco
Oaxaca
Grijalva
Usumacinta
GUATEMALA
HON

Middle America

This region includes North America's most populous city (México) and most of the continent's tropical islands.

Barbados
Area: 166 sq mi (430 sq km)
Population: 269,000
Capital: Bridgetown
Language: English

Dominican Republic
Area: 18,816 sq mi (48,734 sq km)
Population: 8,782,000
Capital: Santo Domingo
Language: Spanish

Jamaica
Area: 4,244 sq mi (10,991 sq km)
Population: 2,629,000
Capital: Kingston
Language: English

St. Lucia
Area: 238 sq mi (617 sq km)
Population: 166,000
Capital: Castries
Language: English

Antigua and Barbuda
Area: 170 sq mi (440 sq km)
Population: 67,000
Capital: St. John's
Language: English

Cuba
Area: 42,804 sq mi (110,861 sq km)
Population: 11,257,000
Capital: Havana
Language: Spanish

Grenada
Area: 133 sq mi (344 sq km)
Population: 104,000
Capital: St. George's
Language: English

Mexico
Area: 756,066 sq mi (1,958,201 sq km)
Population: 101,743,000
Capital: México
Language: Spanish

St. Vincent and the Grenadines
Area: 150 sq mi (388 sq km)
Population: 116,000
Capital: Kingstown
Language: English

Bahamas
Area: 5,382 sq mi (13,939 sq km)
Population: 312,000
Capital: Nassau
Language: English

Dominica
Area: 290 sq mi (751 sq km)
Population: 76,000
Capital: Roseau
Language: English

Haiti
Area: 10,714 sq mi (27,750 sq km)
Population: 7,064,000
Capital: Port-au-Prince
Language: French

St. Kitts and Nevis
Area: 101 sq mi (261 sq km)
Population: 39,000
Capital: Basseterre
Language: English

Trinidad and Tobago
Area: 1,981 sq mi (5,130 sq km)
Population: 1,306,000
Capital: Port-of-Spain
Language: English

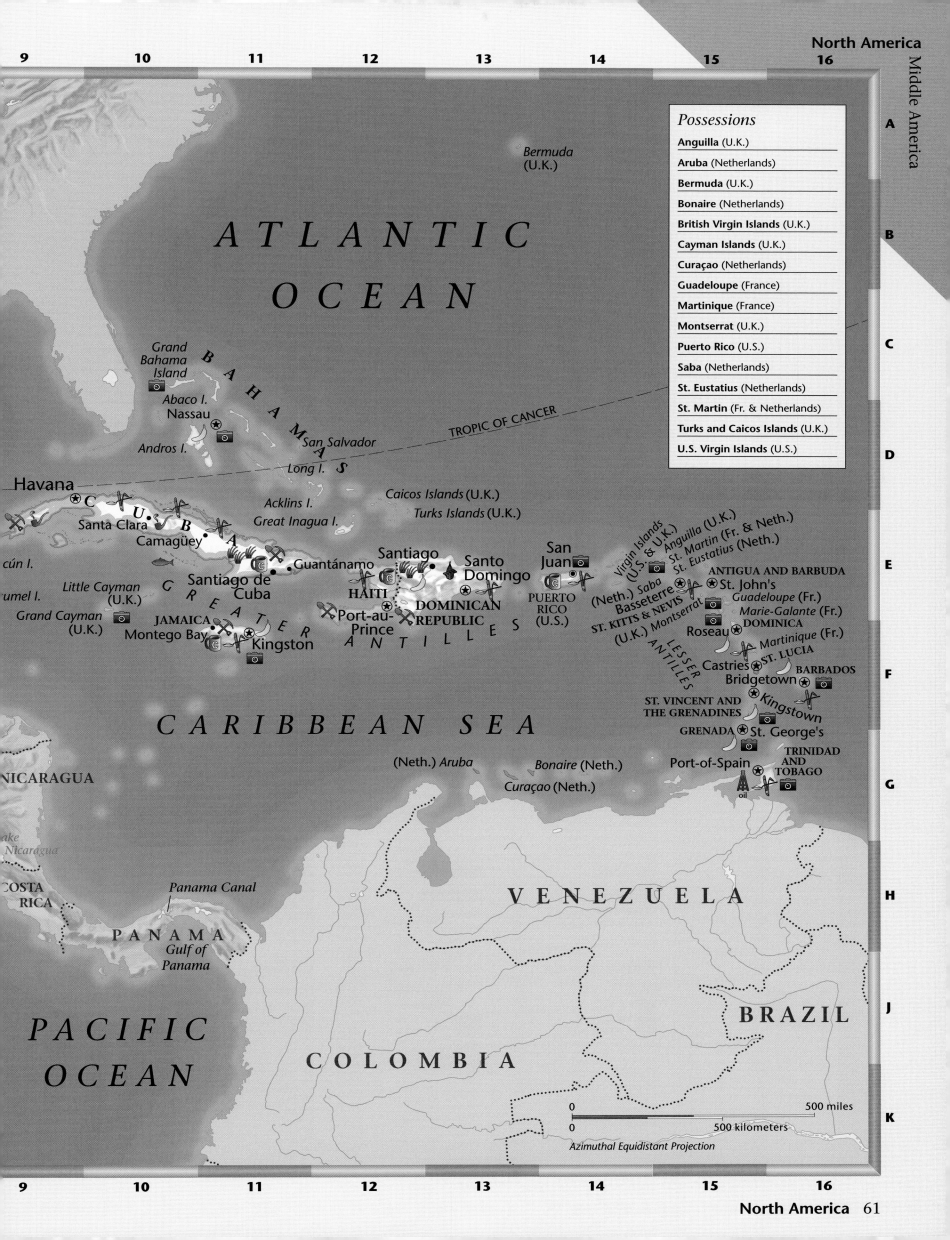

9 **10** **11** **12** **13** **14** **15** **16**

A

Possessions

Anguilla (U.K.)

Aruba (Netherlands)

Bermuda (U.K.)

Bonaire (Netherlands)

British Virgin Islands (U.K.)

Cayman Islands (U.K.)

Curaçao (Netherlands)

Guadeloupe (France)

Martinique (France)

Montserrat (U.K.)

Puerto Rico (U.S.)

Saba (Netherlands)

St. Eustatius (Netherlands)

St. Martin (Fr. & Netherlands)

Turks and Caicos Islands (U.K.)

U.S. Virgin Islands (U.S.)

Bermuda
(U.K.)

A T L A N T I C

O C E A N

B

*Grand
Bahama
Island*

Abaco I.
Nassau

Andros I.

San Salvador

TROPIC OF CANCER

C

Long I.

Havana

Caicos Islands (U.K.)

Acklins I.

Great Inagua I.

Turks Islands (U.K.)

D

Santa Clara

C   U   B   A

Camagüey

·Guantánamo

Santiago

cún I.

·Guantánamo

Santo
Domingo

San
Juan

*Virgin Islands
(U.S. & U.K.)*

Anguilla (U.K.)

St. Martin (Fr. & Neth.)

St. Eustatius (Neth.)

E

*Little Cayman
(U.K.)*

Santiago de
Cuba

HAITI

DOMINICAN
REPUBLIC

PUERTO
RICO
(U.S.)

(Neth.) Saba

Basseterre

ST. KITTS & NEVIS

(U.K.) *Montserrat*

ANTIGUA AND BARBUDA

St. John's

Guadeloupe (Fr.)

Marie-Galante (Fr.)

DOMINICA

umel I.

*Grand Cayman
(U.K.)*

JAMAICA

Montego Bay

Kingston

G R E A T E R   A N T I L L E S

Port-au-
Prince

Roseau

Martinique (Fr.)

F

Castries ★ **ST. LUCIA**

*L E S S E R
A N T I L L E S*

BARBADOS

Bridgetown

**ST. VINCENT AND
THE GRENADINES**

Kingstown

GRENADA St. George's

C A R I B B E A N   S E A

G

(Neth.) Aruba

Bonaire (Neth.)

Curaçao (Neth.)

Port-of-Spain

**TRINIDAD
AND
TOBAGO**

oil

NICARAGUA

H

*ake
Nicaragua*

V E N E Z U E L A

Panama Canal

**COSTA
RICA**

P A N A M A

*Gulf of
Panama*

J

B R A Z I L

PACIFIC

C O L O M B I A

OCEAN

K

0   500 miles

0   500 kilometers

Azimuthal Equidistant Projection

9 **10** **11** **12** **13** **14** **15** **16**

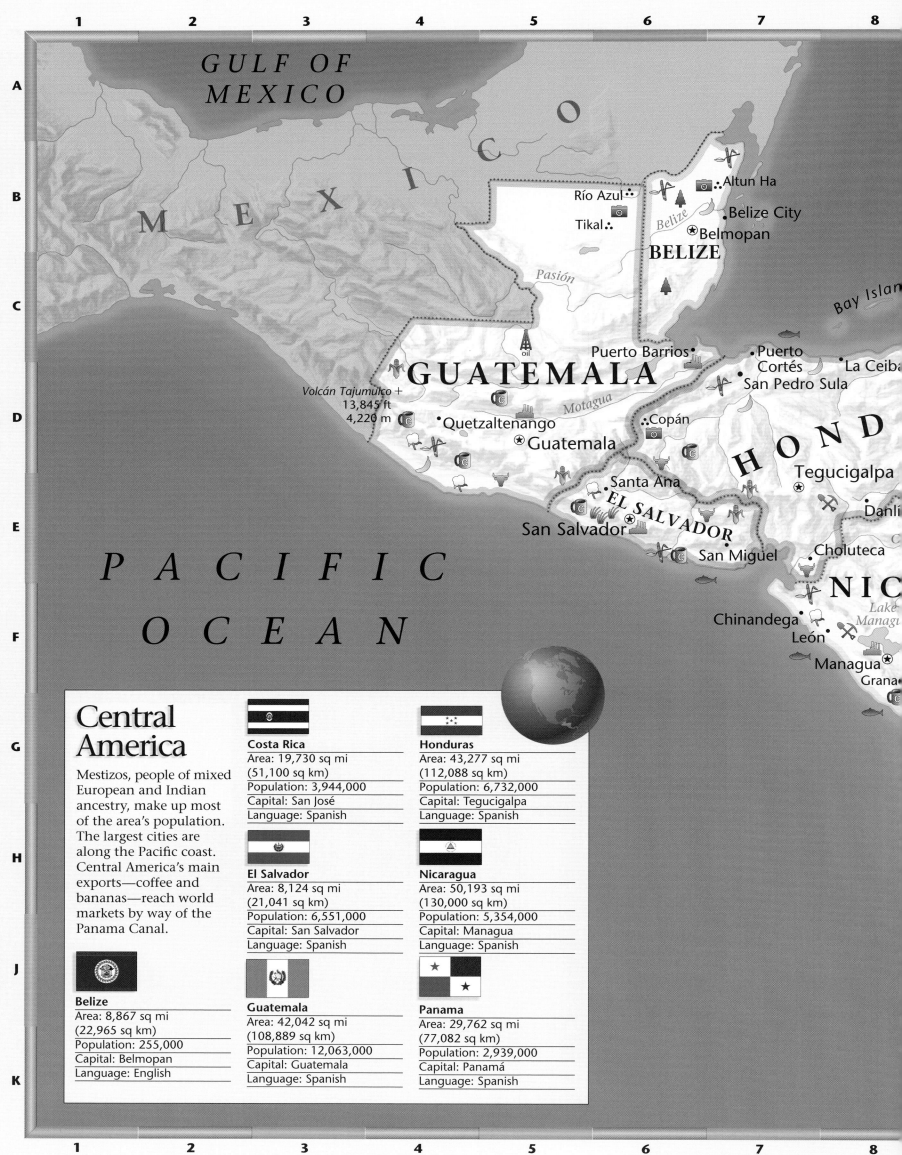

GULF OF MEXICO

M E X I C O

BELIZE

Río Azul
Altun Ha
Tikal
Belize City
★ Belmopan

Pasión

Belize

Bay Island

oil

GUATEMALA

Puerto Barrios

Puerto Cortés
La Ceiba

San Pedro Sula

Volcán Tajumulco +
13,845 ft
4,220 m

Motagua

Copán

H O N D

Quetzaltenango

★ Guatemala

Tegucigalpa

Santa Ana

EL SALVADOR

Danlí

San Salvador

San Miguel

Choluteca

NIC

Chinandega

Lake Managu

León

PACIFIC OCEAN

Managua

Grana

Central America

Mestizos, people of mixed European and Indian ancestry, make up most of the area's population. The largest cities are along the Pacific coast. Central America's main exports—coffee and bananas—reach world markets by way of the Panama Canal.

Costa Rica
Area: 19,730 sq mi
(51,100 sq km)
Population: 3,944,000
Capital: San José
Language: Spanish

Honduras
Area: 43,277 sq mi
(112,088 sq km)
Population: 6,732,000
Capital: Tegucigalpa
Language: Spanish

El Salvador
Area: 8,124 sq mi
(21,041 sq km)
Population: 6,551,000
Capital: San Salvador
Language: Spanish

Nicaragua
Area: 50,193 sq mi
(130,000 sq km)
Population: 5,354,000
Capital: Managua
Language: Spanish

Belize
Area: 8,867 sq mi
(22,965 sq km)
Population: 255,000
Capital: Belmopan
Language: English

Guatemala
Area: 42,042 sq mi
(108,889 sq km)
Population: 12,063,000
Capital: Guatemala
Language: Spanish

Panama
Area: 29,762 sq mi
(77,082 sq km)
Population: 2,939,000
Capital: Panamá
Language: Spanish

9 10 11 12 13 14 15 16

A

Grand Cayman
(U.K.)

JAMAICA

B

C

C A R I B B E A N

AS

Mosquito Cays

D

Mosquito Coast

Providence Island
(Colombia)

E

AGUA

San Andrés Islands
(Colombia)

S E A

Corn Islands
(Nicaragua)

F

Bluefields

Lake
Nicaragua

0   200 miles
0   200 kilometers

San Juan

Azimuthal Equidistant Projection

G

C O S T A
R I C A

Puerto Limón

Alajuela
San José

PANAMA CANAL

H

Cerro Chirripó
12,530 ft
3,819 m

Volcán Barú
11,400 ft
3,475 m

Colón

P A N A M A

Panamá

David

P A N A M A

J

Gulf of
Panama

Coiba Island

COLOMBIA

K

9 10 11 12 13 14 15 16

South Am

The coast of South America stretches straight to the horizon in this unusual view showing south at the top and west at the right edge of the page. Flowing along the coast is the cold Peru current, which creates rich fishing grounds. The hammerhead-shaped cape (far right) harbors the Chilean port of Antofagasta. The town exports nitrates and copper mined in the Atacama Desert (far right along the coast). East, under the puffed clouds, lie the Andean mountains, and beyond them the Pampas, the grassy lowlands of Argentina. South America—from the Atacama Desert to the enormous Amazon rain forest—has a vast range of landscapes. Much of the land is still wilderness.

Salt deposits stretch as far as the eye can see (below) in Chile's Atacama Desert, the world's driest place. A cold Pacific current brings fog but almost no rain to the desert.

CONNECTION: *You can find the southern tip of South America and the Atacama Desert on the maps on pages 66–67 and 78–79.*

erica

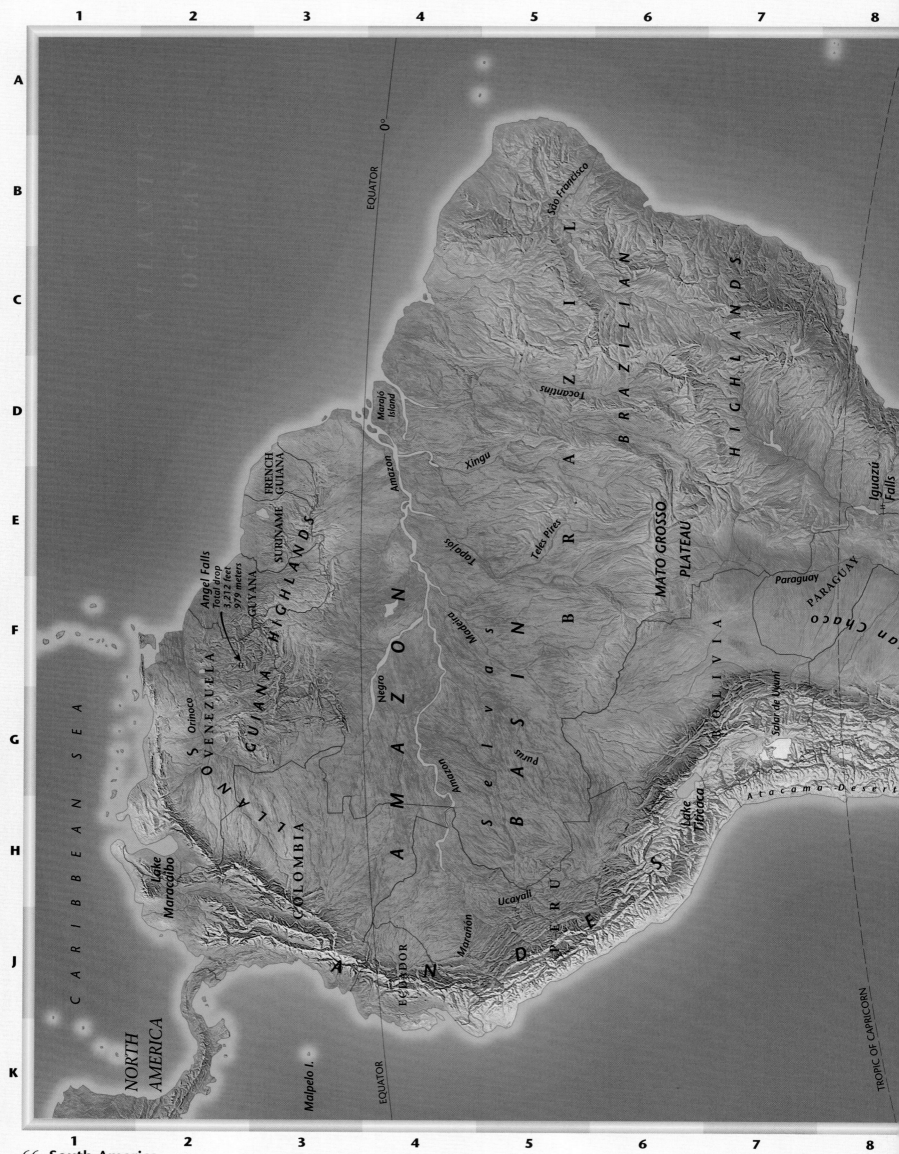

A
B
C
D
E
F
G
H
J
K

9 10 11 12 13 14 15 16

South America

Andes and Amazon

South America is a midsize continent that stretches far to the south. It runs from the warm Caribbean Sea, north of the Equator, almost to Antarctica, some 4,700 miles (7,560 kilometers) in all. The Andes, the Earth's longest continental mountain chain, run the length of the continent. The Atacama Desert is squeezed between the mountains and the Pacific Ocean. In the north, waters from the eastern slopes of the Andes drain into the mighty Amazon River and its tributaries. Moving south, the Amazon rain forest gives way to grassy plains called the Pampas. Even farther south, the dry plateau region of Patagonia lies in a rain shadow created by the Andes.

The Land

Area
6,880,454 sq mi
(17,819,000 sq km)

Highest mountain
Aconcagua (Argentina):
22,834 ft (6,960 m)

Lowest point
Valdés Peninsula (Argentina):
131 ft (40 m) below
sea level

Longest river
Amazon: 4,000 mi
(6,437 km)

Largest lake
Lake Titicaca (Bolivia-Peru):
3,200 sq mi (8,290 sq km)

Highest waterfall
Angel Falls (Venezuela):
3,212 ft (979 m)

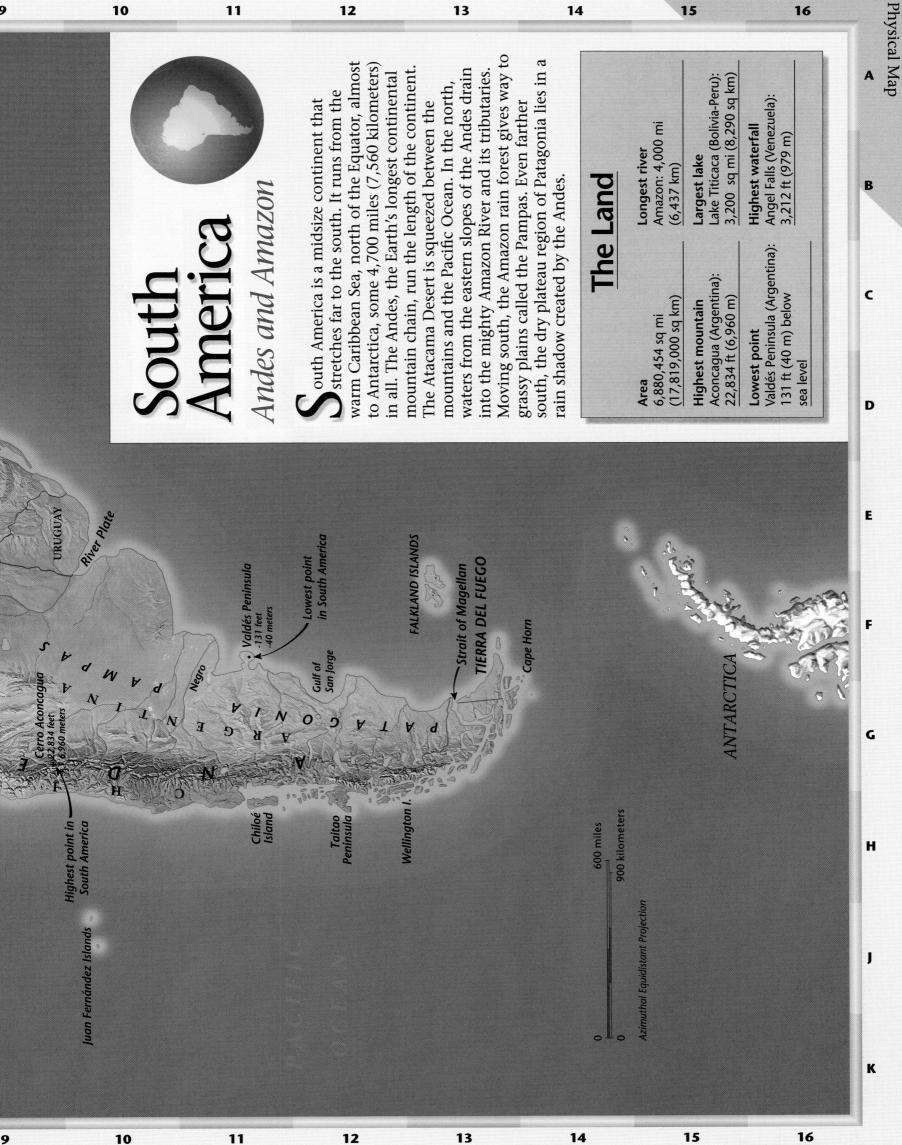

URUGUAY

River Plate

Negro

PAMPAS

ARGENTINA

PATAGONIA

Cerro Aconcagua
+22,834 feet
+6,960 meters

Highest point in
South America

Juan Fernández Islands

Chiloé
Island

Taitao
Peninsula

Wellington I.

Valdés Peninsula
-131 feet
-40 meters

Lowest point
in South America

Gulf of
San Jorge

FALKLAND ISLANDS

Strait of Magellan
TIERRA DEL FUEGO

Cape Horn

ANTARCTICA

600 miles
900 kilometers
0
0

Azimuthal Equidistant Projection

South America

A Mix of Old and New Worlds

Spanish conquistadors, searching for gold, arrived in what is now Peru in 1532. Determined to vanquish the native Inca, they found that much of their work had been done for them. Diseases brought from Europe had already killed so many Indians that a handful of Spaniards was able to conquer an entire empire. The ruins of ancient Indian cities today draw tourists from all over the world. Most present-day Indians still live in the Andes, although some seek jobs in the crowded cities.

Spain colonized most of the land except for Brazil, which was settled by the Portuguese. Colonists brought thousands of enslaved Africans to lands along the Atlantic coast. Most of South America's countries have been independent for almost 200 years. Today they reflect a diverse ethnic mix. Brazil, in particular, shows its African heritage in a rich array of music, dance, religion, and food.

South America is home to the Amazon rain forest, one of the most important ecosystems on Earth. Loggers, miners, and ranchers clear huge areas of forest every month. Alarmed governments and citizens worldwide are working to find ways to save this rain forest, its plants, and creatures.

▶ **GRACEFUL** *buildings from the early 19th century house modern businesses—including the stock exchange—in Santiago. The city is the capital and economic center of Chile.*

▲ **A BREAKFAST DRINK** *beloved around the globe will be brewed from this bucketful of Colombian coffee beans. Colombia and Brazil are the world's leading producers of coffee.*

▲ **GUARDED BY SUGAR LOAF** (*the high hill in the background*), *Rio de Janeiro glitters magically in the twilight. Rio is Brazil's second largest city. Although many of its people are very poor, the city is known for its lively, fun-loving culture.*

▼ **A THREE-TOED SLOTH** *cradles its young. Sloths live in tropical forests in Central and South America. In the wet climate algae grow in their fur, tinting it green.*

▲ **BUNDLES OF TOTORA** *reeds lashed together make a fishing boat on Lake Titicaca, in the Andes. At 12,500 feet (3,810 meters), the lake is the highest in the world that ships can navigate.*

▲ **DESCENDANT** of the ancient Inca, a Peruvian Indian carries her child and leads a llama. Llamas are traditional Andean beasts of burden.

▲ **THE QUICK**, graceful margay lives in the rain forest of South America. The tree-climbing wild cat, whose dappled fur helps it hide in the leafy shadows, is not much bigger than a small dog. Demand for the margay's handsome coat has helped make it a threatened species.

▶ **LOST CITY OF THE INCA** is the name visitors gave to Machu Picchu, discovered in 1911. These ruins high in the Peruvian Andes may once have been a place of worship.

◀ **LAYERS OF GREEN** *make up the lush Amazon rain forest. Different kinds of plants and animals have adapted to life at each layer. Home to nearly half of the Earth's plant and animal species, the Amazon is being cleared (above) to make room for people. Most of the region's more than 12 million people live in towns and cities built on cleared land.*

▶**THRILL-SEEKERS** *wearing parachutes dive from the top of Venezuela's Angel Falls, the world's highest waterfall. Ecotourism (visiting a place to see and help conserve its environment) is an important new business in South America.*

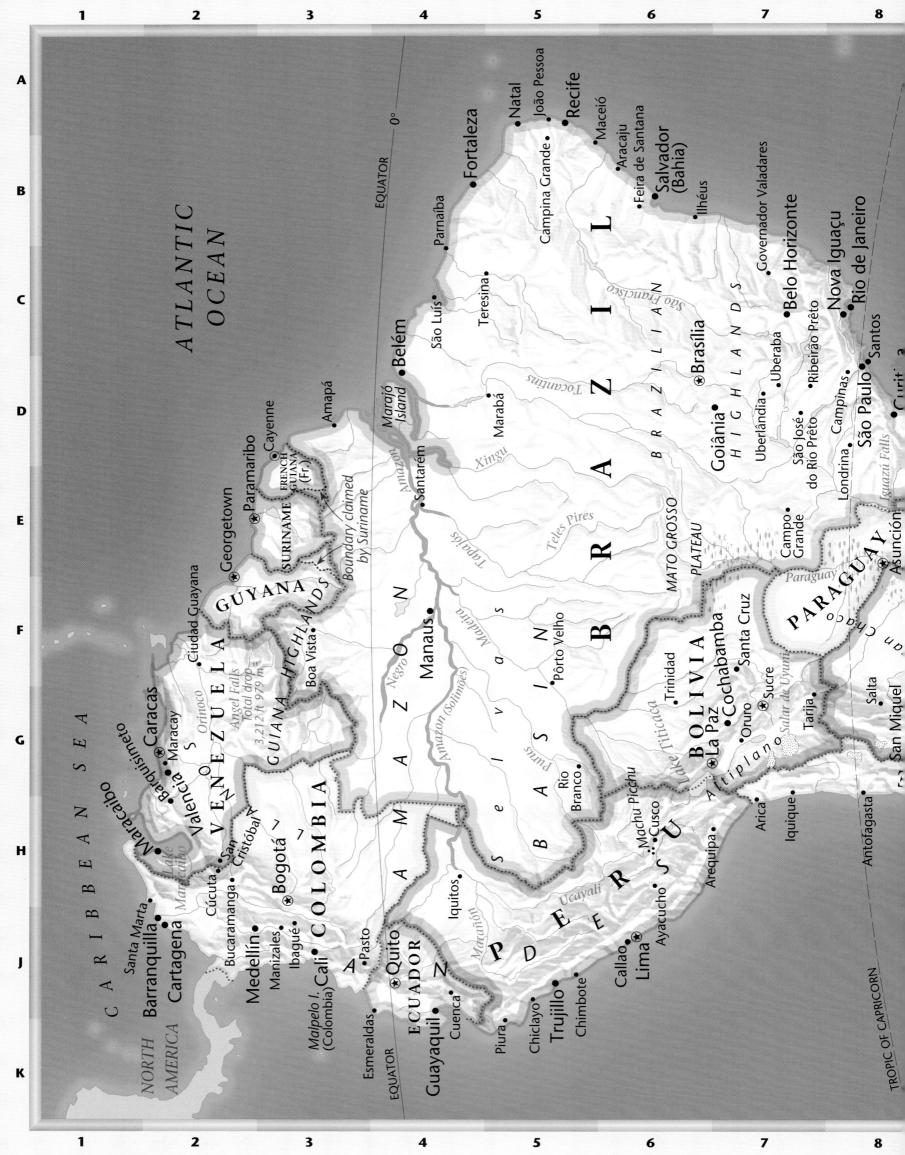

ATLANTIC
OCEAN

EQUATOR 0°

Natal
João Pessoa
Recife
Maceió
Fortaleza
Aracaju
Campina Grande
Feira de Santana
Salvador
(Bahia)
Ilhéus
Governador Valadares

Parnaíba
Belo Horizonte
Nova Iguaçu
Rio de Janeiro

Teresina
Ribeirão Prêto
Santos

B R A Z I L

São Luís
Belém
Brasília
Uberaba
São Paulo
Marajó
Island
Marabá
Goiânia HIGHLANDS
Uberlândia
São José
do Rio Prêto
Campinas
Londrina
Iguazú Falls
Curitiba

Amapá
Santarém
Xingu
Amazon
Teles Pires
Campo
Grande
PARAGUAY

Cayenne
FRENCH
GUIANA
(Fr.)
Boundary claimed
by Suriname

Paramaribo
SURINAME
MATO GROSSO
PLATEAU
Paraguay
Asunción

Georgetown
Tapajós
Negro
Manaus
Pôrto Velho
BRAZILIAN
Santa Cruz
Gran Chaco

GUYANA
Boa Vista
Trinidad
Cochabamba
San Miguel

Ciudad Guayana
A M A Z O N
Madeira
Purus
BOLIVIA
Sucre
Salta

Angel Falls
Total drop
3,212 ft 979 m
GUIANA HIGHLANDS
Rio
Branco
La Paz
Oruro
Tarija

VENEZUELA
Orinoco
B O L I V I A
Lake Titicaca
Altiplano
Salar de Uyuni

Caracas
Maracay
B A S I N
Machu Picchu
Cusco
Antofagasta

Valencia
Ucayali
P E R U
Arequipa
Arica
Iquique

Barquisimeto
San
Cristóbal
Cúcuta
Bucaramanga
COLOMBIA
Iquitos
Marañón
Ayacucho
Callao
Lima

Maracaibo
Lake
Maracaibo
Medellín
Manizales
Ibagué
Bogotá
Pasto
Quito
Chiclayo
Trujillo
Chimbote

Santa Marta
Barranquilla
Cartagena
Cali
A N D E S
Guayaquil
Cuenca
Piura

CARIBBEAN SEA
NORTH
AMERICA
Malpelo I.
(Colombia)
Esmeraldas
ECUADOR
EQUATOR

San
Cristóbal
TROPIC OF CAPRICORN

1   2   3   4   5   6   7   8
A
B
C
D
E
F
G
H
J
K

A B C D E F G H J K

South America

A Colonial Heritage

Just 12 countries—and a French dependency, French Guiana—make up all of South America. Brazil, alone, takes up half the continent and accounts for half its people. Brazil was the only part of South America that was not given to Spain by the Treaty of Tordesillas in 1494. Claimed by Portugal, it is now the world's largest Portuguese-speaking country. Spanish is the dominant language throughout the rest of the continent. After most of South America's countries became independent, many were governed by dictators who controlled national wealth. Development led to huge foreign debts and inflation. Today, democracy is taking hold and some economies, particularly Chile's and Brazil's, are improving.

The People

Population
354,082,000

Largest metropolitan areas
São Paulo, Brazil:
Pop. 17,900,000
Buenos Aires, Argentina:
Pop. 12,000,000

Largest country
Brazil: 3,286,488 sq mi
(8,511,965 sq km)

Most densely populated country
Ecuador: 119 people per sq mi

Economy
Farming: cattle, coffee, fruit
Industry: textiles, mining

Life expectancy
70 years

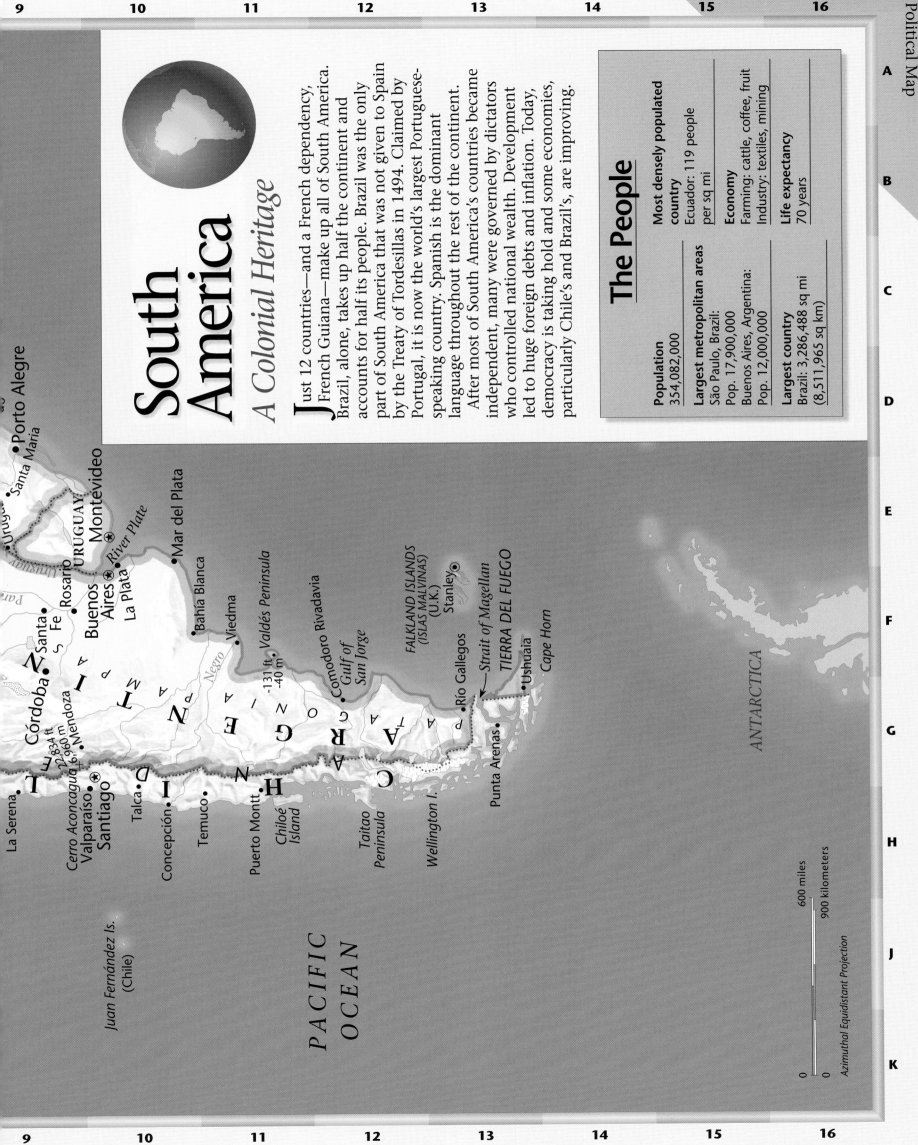

Porto Alegre
Santa Maria
Uruguay
URUGUAY
Montevideo
River Plate
Rosario
Santa Fe
Buenos Aires
La Plata
Mar del Plata
Bahía Blanca
Viedma
Valdés Peninsula
-131 ft -40 m
Río Negro
Comodoro Rivadavia
Gulf of San Jorge
FALKLAND ISLANDS (ISLAS MALVINAS) (U.K.)
Stanley
Río Gallegos
Strait of Magellan
TIERRA DEL FUEGO
Ushuaia
Cape Horn
Punta Arenas
ANTARCTICA

La Serena
Córdoba
Cerro Aconcagua 22,834 ft
Mendoza 6,960 m
Valparaíso
Santiago
Talca
Concepción
Temuco
Puerto Montt
Chiloé Island
Taitao Peninsula
Wellington I.
ARGENTINA
PATAGONIA

Juan Fernández Is. (Chile)

PACIFIC OCEAN

600 miles
900 kilometers
0
0
Azimuthal Equidistant Projection

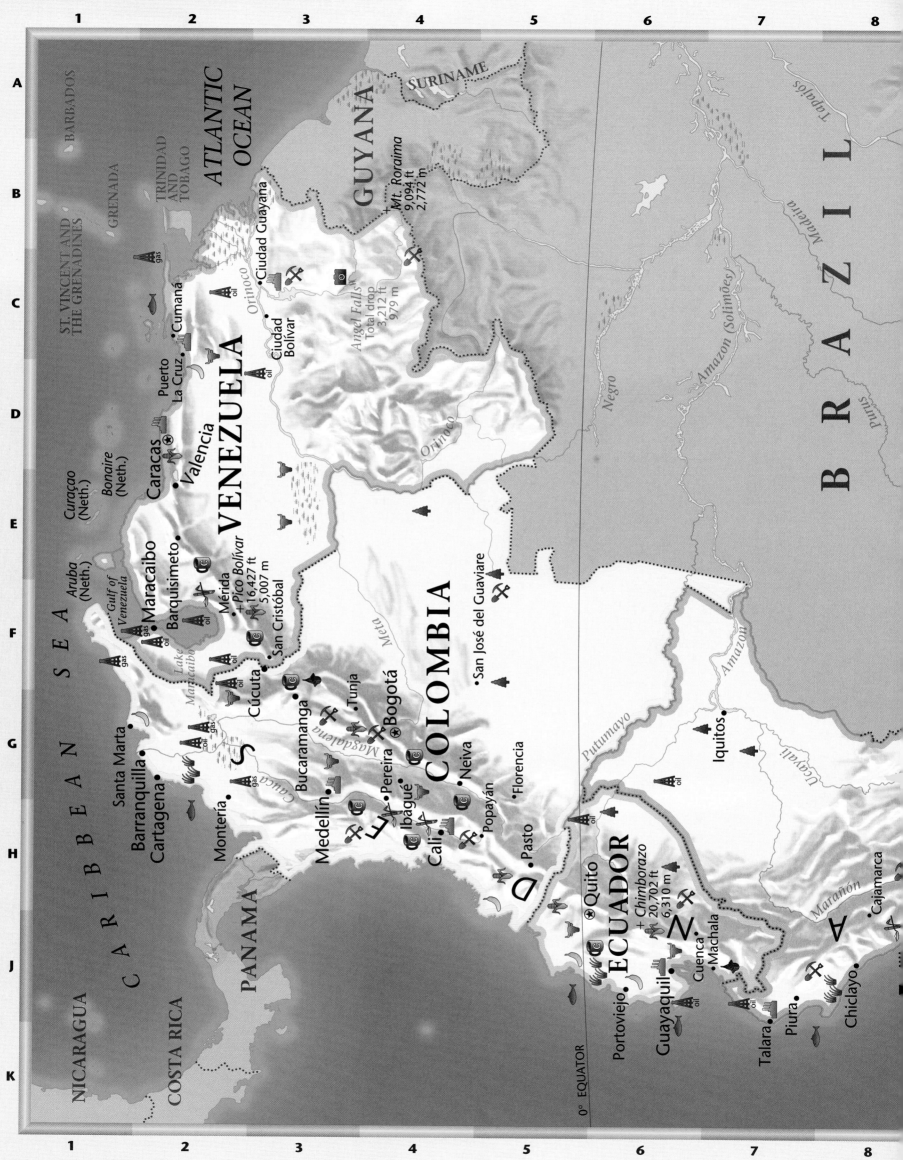

A | B | C | D | E | F | G | H | J | K

1 | 2 | 3 | 4 | 5 | 6 | 7 | 8

BARBADOS

ST. VINCENT AND
THE GRENADINES

GRENADA

TRINIDAD AND
TOBAGO

ATLANTIC
OCEAN

GUYANA

SURINAME

Mt. Roraima
9,094 ft
2,772 m

BRAZIL

Tapajós

Madeira

CARIBBEAN SEA

Curaçao (Neth.)

Bonaire (Neth.)

Aruba (Neth.)

Gulf of Venezuela

Lake Maracaibo

Orinoco

Ciudad Guayana

Cumaná

Puerto
La Cruz

Ciudad
Bolívar

Angel Falls
Total drop
3,212 ft
979 m

Negro

Amazon (Solimões)

VENEZUELA

Caracas

Valencia

Maracaibo

Barquisimeto

Mérida

Pico Bolívar
16,427 ft
5,007 m

San Cristóbal

Cúcuta

Santa Marta

Barranquilla

Cartagena

Montería

Medellín

Bucaramanga

Tunja

Bogotá

COLOMBIA

Meta

Orinoco

Magdalena

Cauca

San José del Guaviare

Putumayo

Amazon

Iquitos

Ucayali

NICARAGUA

COSTA RICA

PANAMA

Pereira

Ibagué

Cali

Neiva

Popayán

Florencia

Pasto

Quito

ECUADOR

Chimborazo
20,702 ft
6,310 m

Cuenca

Machala

Marañón

Cajamarca

Portoviejo

Guayaquil

Talara

Piura

Chiclayo

EQUATOR

0°

74   South America

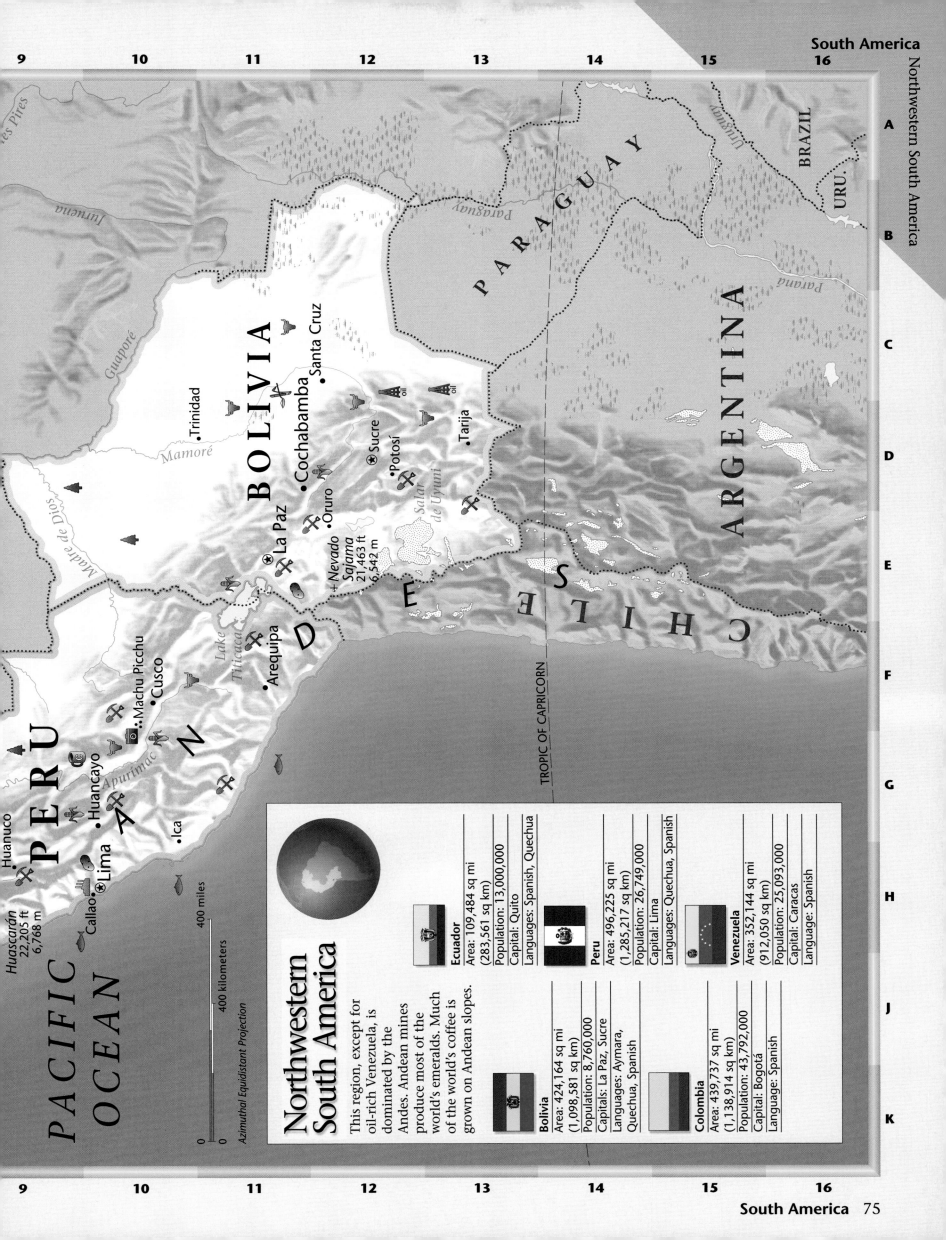

Map Labels

South America

- PARAGUAY
- URUGUAY
- BRAZIL
- URU.
- *Paraná*
- *Paraguay*
- PARAGUAY
- ARGENTINA
- BOLIVIA
- Santa Cruz
- Cochabamba
- Trinidad
- *Mamoré*
- *Guaporé*
- Sucre
- Potosí
- Oruro
- La Paz
- Tarija
- *Salar de Uyuni*
- *Nevado Sajama 21,463 ft 6,542 m*
- Arequipa
- *Lake Titicaca*
- Machu Picchu
- Cusco
- *Apurimac*
- Ica
- Huancayo
- Huánuco
- PERÚ
- ANDES
- CHILE
- D E S
- *Madre de Dios*
- *Tununa*
- *Los Pires*
- *Huascarán 22,205 ft 6,768 m*
- Callao
- Lima
- PACIFIC OCEAN
- TROPIC OF CAPRICORN

Scale

400 miles

400 kilometers

0

Azimuthal Equidistant Projection

Northwestern South America

This region, except for oil-rich Venezuela, is dominated by the Andes. Andean mines produce most of the world's emeralds. Much of the world's coffee is grown on Andean slopes.

Ecuador
Area: 109,484 sq mi
(283,561 sq km)
Population: 13,000,000
Capital: Quito
Languages: Spanish, Quechua

Peru
Area: 496,225 sq mi
(1,285,217 sq km)
Population: 26,749,000
Capital: Lima
Languages: Quechua, Spanish

Venezuela
Area: 352,144 sq mi
(912,050 sq km)
Population: 25,093,000
Capital: Caracas
Language: Spanish

Bolivia
Area: 424,164 sq mi
(1,098,581 sq km)
Population: 8,760,000
Capitals: La Paz, Sucre
Languages: Aymara, Quechua, Spanish

Colombia
Area: 439,737 sq mi
(1,138,914 sq km)
Population: 43,792,000
Capital: Bogotá
Language: Spanish

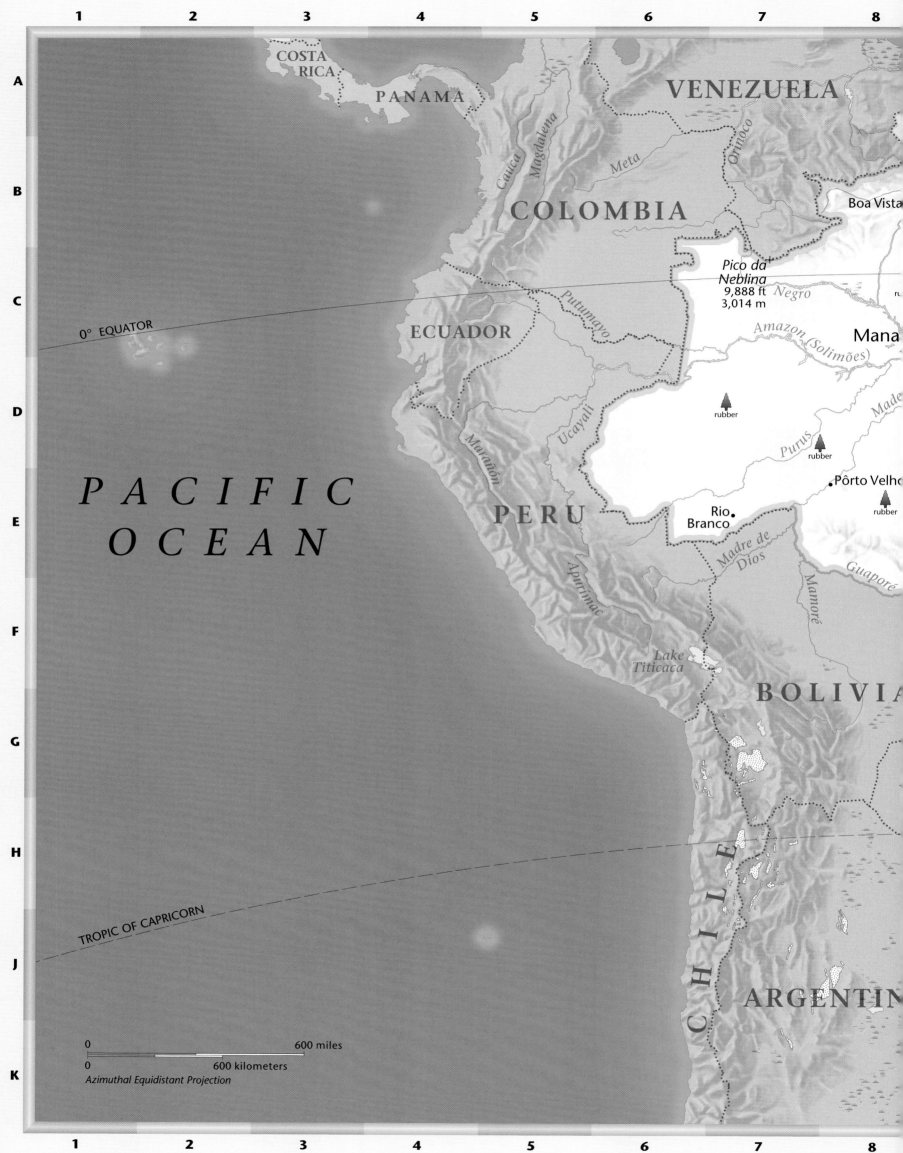

COSTA
RICA

PANAMA

VENEZUELA

COLOMBIA

Boa Vista

Cauca

Magdalena

Meta

Orinoco

Pico da
Neblina
9,888 ft
3,014 m

Negro

0° EQUATOR

ECUADOR

Putumayo

Amazon (Solimões)

Mana

PACIFIC
OCEAN

Marañón

Ucayali

Purus

rubber

Made

Pôrto Velho

PERU

Apurímac

Rio
Branco

Madre de
Dios

rubber

rubber

Mamoré

Guaporé

Lake
Titicaca

BOLIVIA

TROPIC OF CAPRICORN

CHILE

0   600 miles
0   600 kilometers
Azimuthal Equidistant Projection

ARGENTIN

9 10 11 12 13 14 15 16

A

GUYANA
Georgetown
Paramaribo
Cayenne
SURINAME
FRENCH
GUIANA
(France)

B

*Boundary claimed
by Suriname*

Macapá

C

rubber

Amazon

Santarém

*Marajó
Island*

Belém

São Luís

Parnaíba

Tapajós

Xingu

Marabá

Imperatriz

Teresina

Fortaleza

D

Natal

Araguaia

Tocantins

João Pessoa

Recife

B R A Z I L

São Francisco

Juàzeiro

Maceió

E

Teles Pires

Aracaju

Feira de Santana

Salvador (Bahia)

F

Cuiabá

Brasília

Vitória da Conquista

Goiânia

Governador
Valadares

G

Campo
Grande

Uberlândia

Ribeirão
Prêto

Belo Horizonte

Vitória

Paraná

Juiz de Fora

Londrina

São Paulo

Rio de Janeiro

H

São José dos Campos

Santos

*Iguazú
Falls*

Curitiba

Joinvile

Uruguay

Santa Maria

J

*Patos
Lagoon*

Porto Alegre

Pelotas

URUGUAY

A T L A N T I C

O C E A N

K

This region has
both the world's
largest rain forest
and its largest river by
volume, the Amazon.
Rich mines bring
wealth but threaten
local cultures and
the environment.

Brazil
Area: 3,286,488 sq mi
(8,511,965 sq km)
Population: 173,816,000
Capital: Brasília
Language: Portuguese

Guyana
Area: 83,000 sq mi
(214,969 sq km)
Population: 765,000
Capital: Georgetown
Language: English

Suriname
Area: 63,037 sq mi
(163,265 sq km)
Population: 436,000
Capital: Paramaribo
Languages: Dutch, English

French Guiana (France)

9 10 11 12 13 14 15 16

	9	10	11	12	13	14	15	16

Southern South America

This region has the continent's highest peak (Mount Aconcagua) and its lowest point (Valdés Peninsula). It stretches to within 600 miles (965 kilometers) of Antarctica.

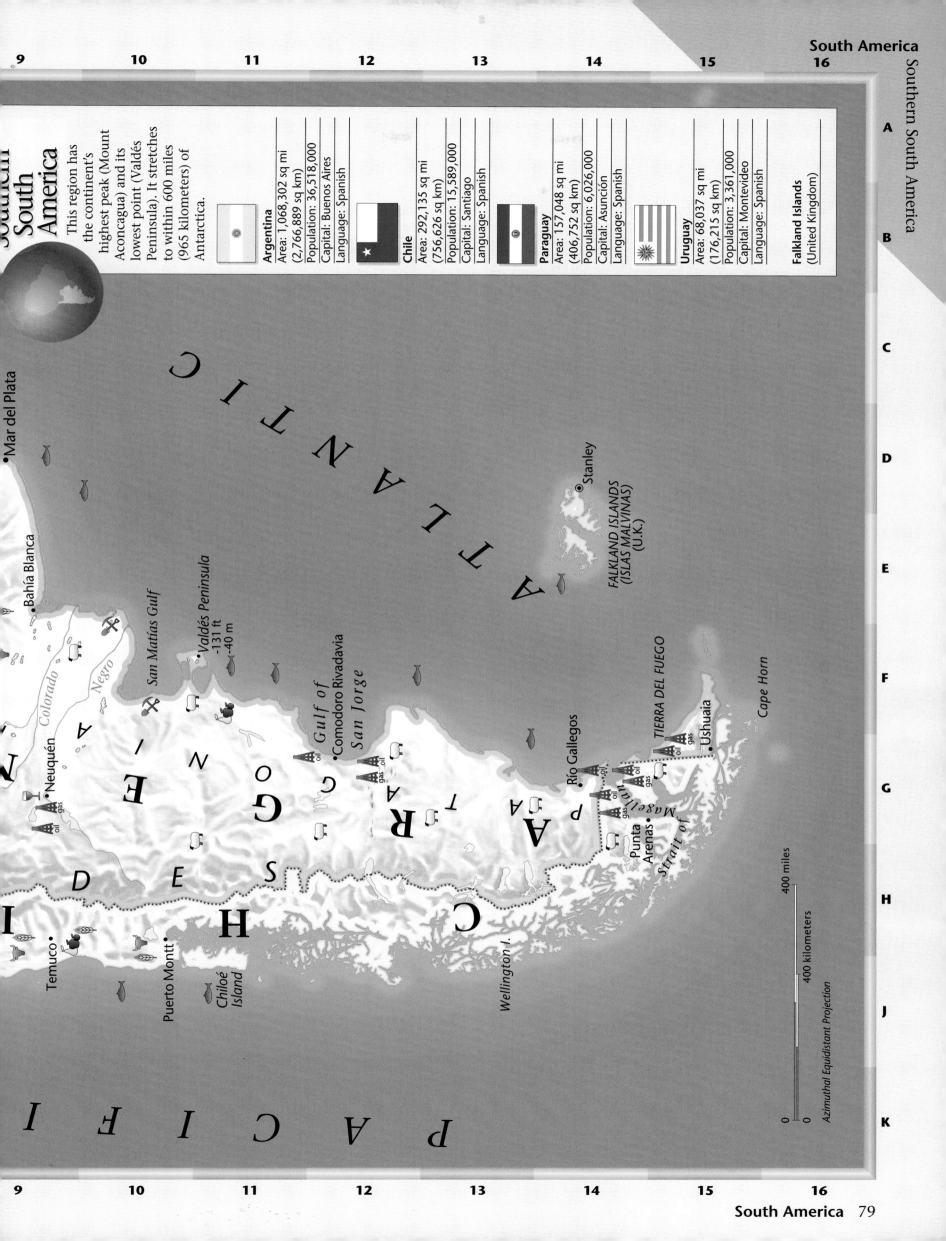

Argentina
Area: 1,068,302 sq mi
(2,766,889 sq km)
Population: 36,518,000
Capital: Buenos Aires
Language: Spanish

Chile
Area: 292,135 sq mi
(756,626 sq km)
Population: 15,589,000
Capital: Santiago
Language: Spanish

Paraguay
Area: 157,048 sq mi
(406,752 sq km)
Population: 6,026,000
Capital: Asunción
Language: Spanish

Uruguay
Area: 68,037 sq mi
(176,215 sq km)
Population: 3,361,000
Capital: Montevideo
Language: Spanish

Falkland Islands
(United Kingdom)

ATLANTIC

PACIFIC

Mar del Plata

Bahía Blanca

Colorado

Negro

Neuquén

San Matías Gulf

Valdés Peninsula
-131 ft
-40 m

Gulf of San Jorge

Comodoro Rivadavia
oil

gas
oil

Stanley

FALKLAND ISLANDS
(ISLAS MALVINAS)
(U.K.)

PATAGONIA

ANDES

Temuco

Puerto Montt

Chiloé Island

Wellington I.

Río Gallegos
oil
gas

Punta Arenas

Strait of Magellan

TIERRA DEL FUEGO

Ushuaia
oil
gas

Cape Horn

oil
gas
oil
gas

400 miles

400 kilometers

Azimuthal Equidistant Projection

Europe

The island of Sicily dwarfs the toe of the boot-shaped peninsula of Italy, which juts into the blue waters of the Mediterranean Sea. The Strait of Messina separates island from mainland. Just west of the strait on Sicily, a white plume of smoke reveals the location of the volcano Mount Etna. Long before geologists understood plate tectonics, Greek storytellers explained Etna's rumblings as roars from a monster, Typhon, imprisoned in the volcano by the god Zeus.

Although it is a relatively small continent, Europe has had an enormous influence on the rest of the world, culturally and politically. Because most countries border the sea along Europe's many peninsulas, these nations have ready access to the outside world.

Snow-covered Mount Etna lets off steam behind the elegant buildings of Taormina, in eastern Sicily. Etna is the highest active volcano in Europe.

CONNECTION: *You can find Sicily and the "boot" of Italy on the maps on pages 82–83 and 92–93.*

Europe

Land of Long Coasts

Europe is a small continent—only Australia is smaller—with a great range of landscapes. Its most marked feature is its irregular coastline, cut with inlets, bays, and peninsulas, great and small. Rocky highlands, scrubbed by glaciers, cover Europe's northwestern edge. The Alps form a chain across southern Europe, blocking cold northern winds from the mild Mediterranean region. In the east, the Ural Mountains separate Europe and Asia. The continent has a number of great navigable rivers, including the Danube, Rhine, Volga, and Rhône.

The Land

Area
3,837,000 sq mi
(9,938,000 sq km)

Highest mountain
El'brus (Russia): 18,510 ft
(5,642 m)

Lowest point
Caspian Sea: 92 ft (28 m)
below sea level

Longest river
Volga (Russia): 2,290 mi
(3,685 km)

Largest lake
Ladoga (Russia): 6,853 sq mi
(17,703 sq km)

Largest island
Great Britain: 84,215 sq mi
(218,100 sq km)

0 ——— 600 miles
0 ——— 900 kilometers
Azimuthal Equidistant Projection

Jan Mayen

ICELAND
Vatnajökull

Faroe Islands

NORWEGIAN SEA

Shetland Islands

Orkney Islands

Outer Hebrides

BRITISH ISLES

Highlands

NORTH SEA

UNITED

IRELAND

IRISH SEA

Great Britain

KINGDOM

Jutle
DEN

NETH.

N
O

BELGIUM

LUX.

Rhine

GERM

ATLANTIC OCEAN

English Channel

Brittany

Seine

Loire

Danube

FRANCE

Mont Blanc
15,771 feet
4,807 meters

SWITZ.
LIECH.

A L P

Bay of Biscay

Massif Central

Rhône

Po

Cantabrian Mountains

Pyrenees

MONACO

Riviera

SAN MARI

A
p
e

Douro

ANDORRA

Corsica

VATICAN
CITY

PORTUGAL

Tagus

IBERIAN

Ebro

SPAIN

PENINSULA

Sardinia

TYRRHE
SEA

Baetic Mountains

Balearic Islands

M

E

Sicily

Strait of Gibraltar

D

I

T

E

AFRICA

M

9 10 11 12 13 14 15 16

A

B

C

D

E

F

G

H

J

K

BARENTS SEA

North Cape

Kola Peninsula

Pechora

ARCTIC CIRCLE

URAL MOUNTAINS

Europe-Asia Boundary

WHITE SEA

Northern Dvina

Kama

Ural

RUSSIA

EUROPEAN PLAIN

Lake Region

Gulf of Bothnia

FINLAND

Lake Ladoga

Gulf of Finland

ESTONIA

Volga

Volga

SWEDEN

SCANDINAVIA

BALTIC SEA

LATVIA

Western Dvina

LITHUANIA

Oka

RUSSIA

CENTRAL

Ural

KAZAKHSTAN

Vistula

Dnieper

BELARUS

RUSSIAN

Volga

Oder

POLAND

UPLAND

Don

Caspian Depression

Elbe

CZECH REP.

UKRAINE

Dniester

Volga

Don

ASIA

Carpathian Mountains

SLOVAKIA

MOLDOVA

Dnieper

SEA OF AZOV

Highest point in Europe

Lowest point in Europe
-92 feet, -28 meters

CASPIAN SEA

Tisza

HUNGARY

Drava

Danube

ROMANIA

Crimea

El'brus
18,510 feet
5,642 meters

Caucasus Mountains

GEORGIA

AZERBAIJAN

CROATIA

Sava

Danube

BOSNIA & HERZG.

SERBIA

BLACK SEA

AZERB.

AND

BALKAN

Balkan Mountains

MONTENEGRO

BULGARIA

PENINSULA

MACED.

Bosporus

ADRIATIC SEA

ALBANIA

GREECE

TURKEY

ASIA

IONIAN SEA

Dardanelles

AEGEAN SEA

Peloponnesus

902 feet
23 meters

Crete

Rhodes

MEDITERRANEAN SEA

Europe
Cultural Colossus

Twenty-five hundred years ago in a tiny European city-state no bigger than Buffalo, New York, is today, an extraordinary flowering of the arts and sciences occurred. The place was Athens, in ancient Greece. The arts and sciences developed there and—along with later Roman additions—have had a deep influence on Western civilization as we know it today. Europe enjoyed a second period of enlightenment during the Renaissance. In that era, from the 14th to the 17th century, ideas from the ancient Greeks were revived, and arts and sciences had a rebirth.

Present-day Europe benefits from this cultural heritage. Many areas are like living museums. Beautiful old buildings bustle with people who live and work there, often in high-tech industries. Setting aside historic rivalries, many European nations have joined to become a united economic force: the European Union, established by treaty in 1993. Several former Eastern European communist countries are in the process of either becoming members or trying to qualify for full membership.

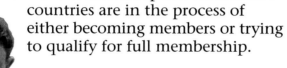

▼ **FOOTBALL EUROPEAN** *style is what's known as soccer in the United States and Canada.*

◀ **TALL RED PILLARS** and colorful domes mark ten chapels that together make up the Cathedral of St. Basil the Blessed. Standing in Moscow's Red Square, the church has been a Russian landmark since the 16th century.

▼ **GIRLS AT A WEDDING** in Bavaria, Germany's largest state, wear traditional dresses and floral wreaths.

▲ **BUILT FOR SPEED,** a Eurostar train waits in a Paris train station for its next trip to London. Eurostar trains travel between France and England via a tunnel—known as the Chunnel—under the English Channel. The high-speed trains can reach 100 miles per hour (160 kilometers per hour) during the three-hour journey.

▲ **ONE EURO, TWELVE COUNTRIES.** All but 3 of the 15 countries in the European Union have adopted the euro as their basic monetary unit. This currency has replaced traditional coins and bills such as the French franc and the German mark.

▲ **THE JAGGED PEAK** *of the Matterhorn towers above the town of Zermatt, in the Swiss Alps. Not conquered until 1865, the mountain has sent many climbers to their deaths. The Alps owe their sharp angles to glacial erosion and their geologic youth.*

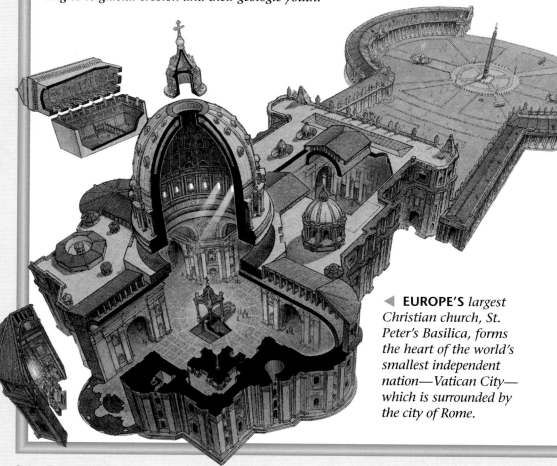

◄ **EUROPE'S** *largest Christian church, St. Peter's Basilica, forms the heart of the world's smallest independent nation—Vatican City— which is surrounded by the city of Rome.*

▲ **FLOWERS BLOOM** *on a barge in Amsterdam, capital of the Netherlands. Canals throughout the country provide watery highways and drain the land, most of which is at or below sea level.*

◀ **TREASURES OF THE ART WORLD** *grace the Uffizi Museum in Florence, the Italian city that is known as the birthplace of the Renaissance. Artists such as Michelangelo and Raphael created their masterpieces and inspired others during this period.*

▲ **TURRETS, TOWERS,** *and domes rise above Prague, the historic capital of the Czech Republic. Eastern European countries such as this one are changing and modernizing after years of communist rule.*

▶ **DRESSED FOR A FESTIVE** *occasion, this Greek boy wears his country's national costume instead of the more modern clothes he wears day-to-day.*

▲ **A BOUNTIFUL HARVEST** *of grapes fills a wagon in a vineyard in Tuscany, one of the 20 self-governing regions that make up Italy. Fertile soil and mild winters make parts of Italy and other Mediterranean countries ideal for farming.*

▲ **WEARING** *tall hats known as toques, a small army of chefs works furiously in a restaurant in Roanne, France. The French are known around the world for their fine cooking.*

▼ **A MYSTERIOUS STONE CIRCLE** *built in ancient times, Stonehenge is one of the most famous sites in England. Stonehenge may have been constructed as an early astronomical observatory.*

Europe

East Meets West Today

Europe is home to the world's third largest population: almost 728 million people live in 43 countries. The continent is commonly divided into eastern and western regions. Eastern Europe, which includes countries that were once part of or controlled by the former Soviet Union, extends roughly from Poland to Greece and east to the Caspian Sea and Ural Mountains. Western Europe, which includes the wealthy nations of the European Union and their neighbors, stretches to the Atlantic Ocean. No longer divided by political systems, the two regions can work together to solve common problems.

The People

Population
727,493,000

Largest metropolitan areas
Paris, France: Pop. 9,658,000
Moscow, Russia: Pop. 8,316,000
London, England: Pop. 7,640,000

Largest country (entirely in Europe)
Ukraine: 233,206 sq mi
(604,001 sq km)

Most densely populated country
Monaco: 34,000 people
in 0.7 sq mi

Economy
Farming: vegetables, fruit, grains
Industry: chemicals, machinery

Life expectancy
74 years

Jan Mayen
(Norway)

Ísafjördur

Akureyri

Reykjavík • **ICELAND** • Vopnafjördur

• Höfn

NORWEGI

FAROE ISLANDS
(Denmark) • Tórshavn

Ålesund

SHETLAND ISLANDS • Lerwick

Rockall
(U.K.)

ORKNEY ISLANDS

Bergen

Isle of Lewis

ATLANTIC OCEAN

Inverness •

Stavanger

UNITED • Aberdeen

Glasgow • **SCOTLAND**
◉ Edinburgh

North

Skag

**NORTHERN
IRELAND** ◉ Belfast

DENMA

IRELAND *Irish* **KINGDOM** *Sea*
Dublin ◉ *Sea*

Cork • Liverpool • Manchester

Hambu

WALES Birmingham

Celtic

Cardiff ◉ **ENGLAND**

NETH.

Land's End London ◉

The ◉ Amsterdar
Hague •

GEI

Sea Southampton

BELGIUM Bonn

English Channel Brussels ◉ Fran

Brest • Le Havre **LUX.**

• Rennes ◉ **Paris**

Nantes • Strasbourg •

Bay of
Biscay La Rochelle **FRANCE** **LIEC**

Zürich •

Limoges • Bern ◉ **SWITZ.**
Geneva

A Coruña • Bordeaux Lyon • A

Vigo • Santander • Turin • Ve

Oporto • Bilbao Donostia Milan

Coimbra • Valladolid San Sebastián **MONACO** Gend

PORTUGAL **ANDORRA** Nice **MAR**
Madrid ◉ • Zaragoza Marseille **ITA**

Lisbon ◉ **SPAIN** Toulouse Corsica **VATICA**
(France) **CI**

Cape • Córdoba Barcelona Ro
St. Vincent • Valencia

Cádiz • Seville • Murcia Palma • *Balearic* *Sardinia*
Islands (Sp.) (Italy)

(U.K.) **GIBRALTAR** • Málaga Cartagena Cagliari *Tyrrhe*

Strait of Gibraltar M E D I *Pale*
T

A F R I C A

9 10 11 12 13 14 15 16

A

Tobseda

URAL MOUNTAINS
Ob

Surgut

Barents Sea

North Cape
Hammerfest • Vadsø •Kirkenes
Tromsø • Pechenga
•Murmansk
Narvik • Ivalo
N Kirovsk
Kiruna • *Kola Peninsula*
Umba

Pechora •

ARCTIC CIRCLE

Khanty Mansiysk

B

Luleå
Namsos •
Åre • Umeå •Kemi
Trondheim •Oulu
Sundsvall • Vaasa •Kuopio

White Sea

Kem'
Arkhangel'sk
Severodvinsk

Syktyvkar •

Serov •
Nizhniy Tagil

C

Pori •Tampere
Turku • Helsinki
Stockholm • Uppsala
Göteborg Tallinn • St. Petersburg
Gotland ESTONIA

Lake Onega

Lake Ladoga

RUSSIA

Perm' •
Kirov •
Yekaterinburg
Chelyabinsk

EUROPE-ASIA BOUNDARY

D

Copenhagen •
Malmö Riga • LATVIA
Baltic Sea LITHUANIA Daugavpils
KALININGRAD Vitsyebsk
(Russia) Vilnius
Gdansk Kaunas • Minsk

Velikiy Novgorod
Tver'
Moscow

Yaroslavl' •
Nizhniy Novgorod
Samara •
Ryazan' • Penza •

Kazan'
Ufa •

Orenburg

Oral •

E

Berlin •
Bydgoszcz •Warsaw
POLAND Homyel'
Vroclaw • Lódz •

Smolensk

BELARUS

Bryansk •

Kursk •

Saratov •
Volga

Ural

KAZAKHSTAN

F

Prague • Kraków •
ZECH REP. L'viv
Vienna • SLOVAKIA *Carpathian Mts.*
Linz • Bratislava •
RIA Budapest
Ljubljana HUNGARY
SLOVENIA
Zagreb
CROATIA
Belgrade
BOSN. &
HERZG.
Sarajevo SERBIA &
MONTENEGRO

Chernihiy •
Sumy •
Kiev
UKRAINE Poltava
Vinnytsya
Dniester
Dnipropetrovs'k
MOLDOVA
Chisinau
Odesa

Kharkiv
Donets'k
Rostov

Volgograd •

Astrakhan' •

Atyrau •

CASPIAN SEA

G

ROMANIA
Bucharest
Constanta
Danube

Sea of Azov
Crimea Kerch
Simferopol'
Yalta
Sevastopol'

Stavropol' •

Caucasus Mountains
El'brus
18,510ft
5,642m
Groznyy •
GEORGIA
T'bilisi AZERBAIJAN
Gäncä

-92 ft
-28 m

Baku

H

Adriatic Sea
Tirana MACED.
ALBANIA
GREECE
Naples •
Messina •
Catania
Sicily
alletta LTA

Balkan Mts.
Varna
Sofia
BULGARIA
Skopje
Thessaloniki
Istanbul Bosporus
Dardanelles
Aegean Sea
Izmir
Pátrai
Peloponnesus
Athens
Kalamáta

BLACK SEA

Bat'umi
AZERB.

Trabzon
Samsun Erzurum
Zonguldak
Sivas
Bursa
Ankara
Eskisehir
TURKEY Kayseri
Konya Mardin
Adana

Bitlis •

J

Ionian Sea

Antalya Antioch

ASIA

K

Sea of Crete
Crete Irákleion
Rhodes

0 600 miles
0 900 kilometers

Azimuthal Equidistant Projection

SEA

9 10 11 12 13 14 15 16

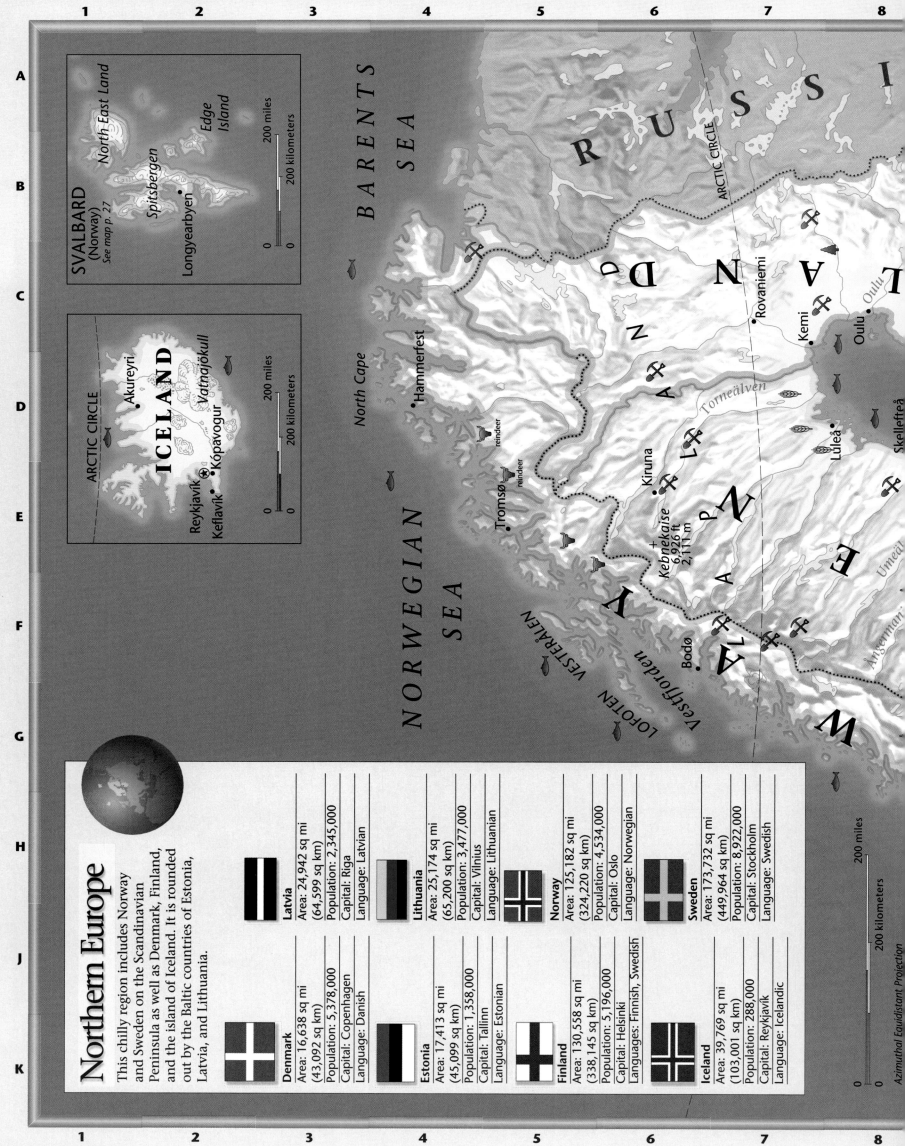

A 1 2 3 4 5 6 7 8

SVALBARD
(Norway)
See map p. 27

North East Land

Edge Island

Spitsbergen

Longyearbyen

200 miles

200 kilometers

ICELAND

ARCTIC CIRCLE

Akureyri

Vatnajökull

Reykjavik ⊛ Kópavogur
Keflavík

200 miles

200 kilometers

B A R E N T S

S E A

R U S S I

ARCTIC CIRCLE

F I N L A N D

Rovaniemi

Kemi

Oulu

Oulu

North Cape

Hammerfest

reindeer

reindeer

Tromsø

Kiruna

Torneälven

Luleå

Skellefteå

Kebnekaise
6,926 ft
2,111 m

Umeå

N O R W E G I A N

S E A

N O R W A Y

S W E

Bodø

Ångerman

LOFOTEN *VESTERÅLEN*

Vestfjorden

W

Northern Europe

This chilly region includes Norway and Sweden on the Scandinavian Peninsula as well as Denmark, Finland, and the island of Iceland. It is rounded out by the Baltic countries of Estonia, Latvia, and Lithuania.

Latvia
Area: 24,942 sq mi
(64,599 sq km)
Population: 2,345,000
Capital: Riga
Language: Latvian

Lithuania
Area: 25,174 sq mi
(65,200 sq km)
Population: 3,477,000
Capital: Vilnius
Language: Lithuanian

Norway
Area: 125,182 sq mi
(324,220 sq km)
Population: 4,534,000
Capital: Oslo
Language: Norwegian

Sweden
Area: 173,732 sq mi
(449,964 sq km)
Population: 8,922,000
Capital: Stockholm
Language: Swedish

Denmark
Area: 16,638 sq mi
(43,092 sq km)
Population: 5,378,000
Capital: Copenhagen
Language: Danish

Estonia
Area: 17,413 sq mi
(45,099 sq km)
Population: 1,358,000
Capital: Tallinn
Language: Estonian

Finland
Area: 130,558 sq mi
(338,145 sq km)
Population: 5,196,000
Capital: Helsinki
Languages: Finnish, Swedish

Iceland
Area: 39,769 sq mi
(103,001 sq km)
Population: 288,000
Capital: Reykjavík
Language: Icelandic

200 miles

200 kilometers

Azimuthal Equidistant Projection

1 2 3 4 5 6 7 8

A

Lake
Ladoga

RUSSIA

BELARUS

Joensuu

B

Kuopio

Lake
Saimaa

Mikkeli

Kotka

Narva

Lake
Peipus

Tartu

Western Dvina

Daugavpils

Jyväskylä

Lappeenranta

GULF OF FINLAND

Tallinn

ESTONIA

Riga

LATVIA

Vilnius

C

Lahti

Helsinki

Pärnu

Gulf of
Riga

Jelgava

Siauliai

LITHUANIA

Kaunas

Tampere

Turku

Hiiumaa

Saaremaa

Liepaja

Klaipeda

Neman

KALININGRAD
(Russia)

D

Vaasa

Pori

ALAND
ISLANDS

BALTIC SEA

POLAND

E

Örnsköldsvik

Sundsvall

Stockholm

Uppsala

Gotland

Visby

Öland

Bornholm

GULF OF BOTHNIA

Norrland

Liusnan

Falun

Svealand

Västerås

Mälaren

Norrköping

F

Östersund

S
W
E

Örebro

Linköping

Götaland

Jönköping

G

Karlstad

Vänern

Vättern

Göteborg

Borås

Helsingborg

Malmö

Klarälven

Glåma

N
O

Oslo

KATTEGAT

DENMARK

Copenhagen

ZEALAND

H

Trondheim

Trondhjemsfjorden

Galdhøpiggen
8,100 ft
+2,469 m

Drammen

Skien

Århus

Odense

Fyn

J

Ålesund

Bergen

Haugesund

Stavanger

Kristiansand

SKAGERRAK

NORTH
SEA

JUTLAND

Esbjerg

GERMANY

K

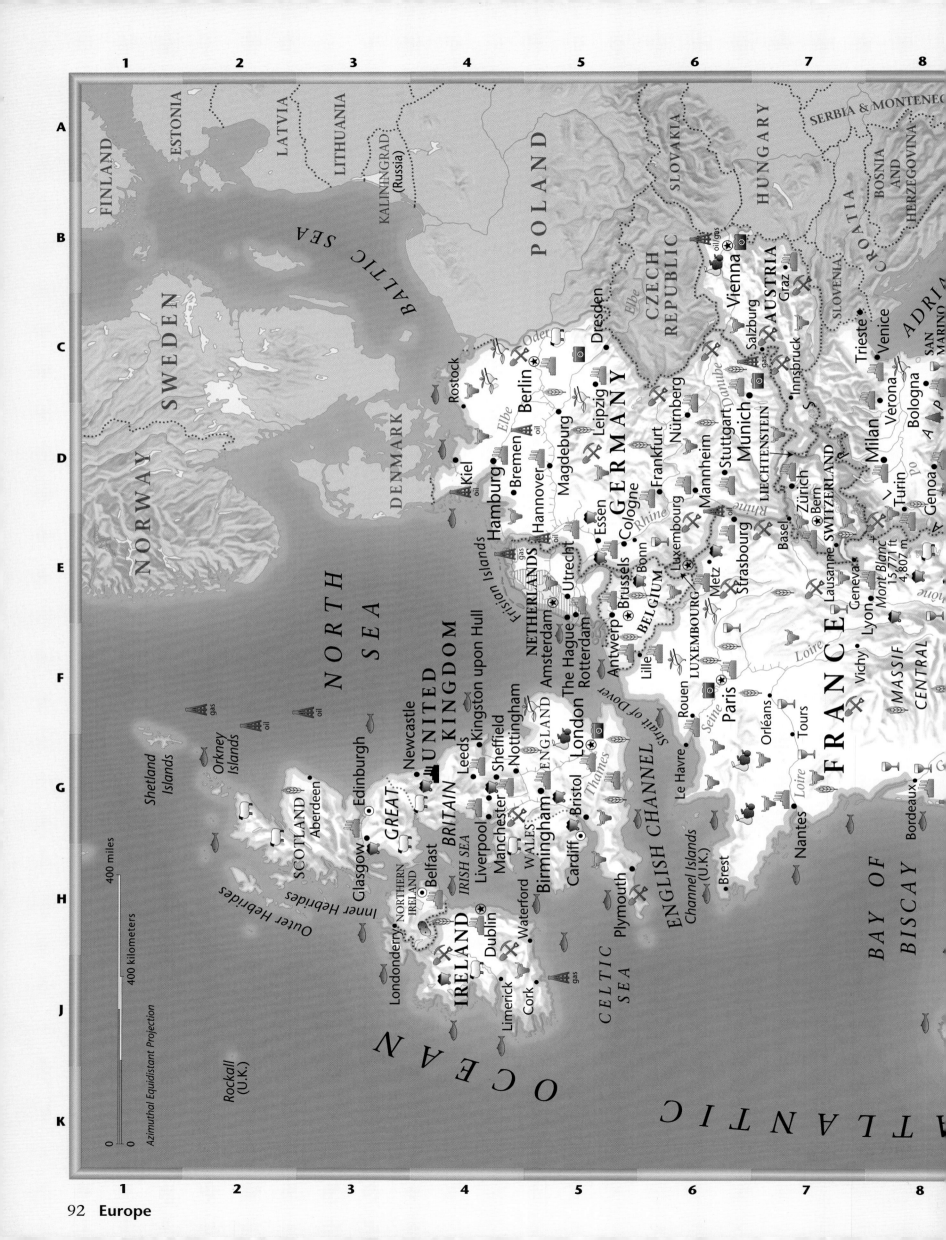

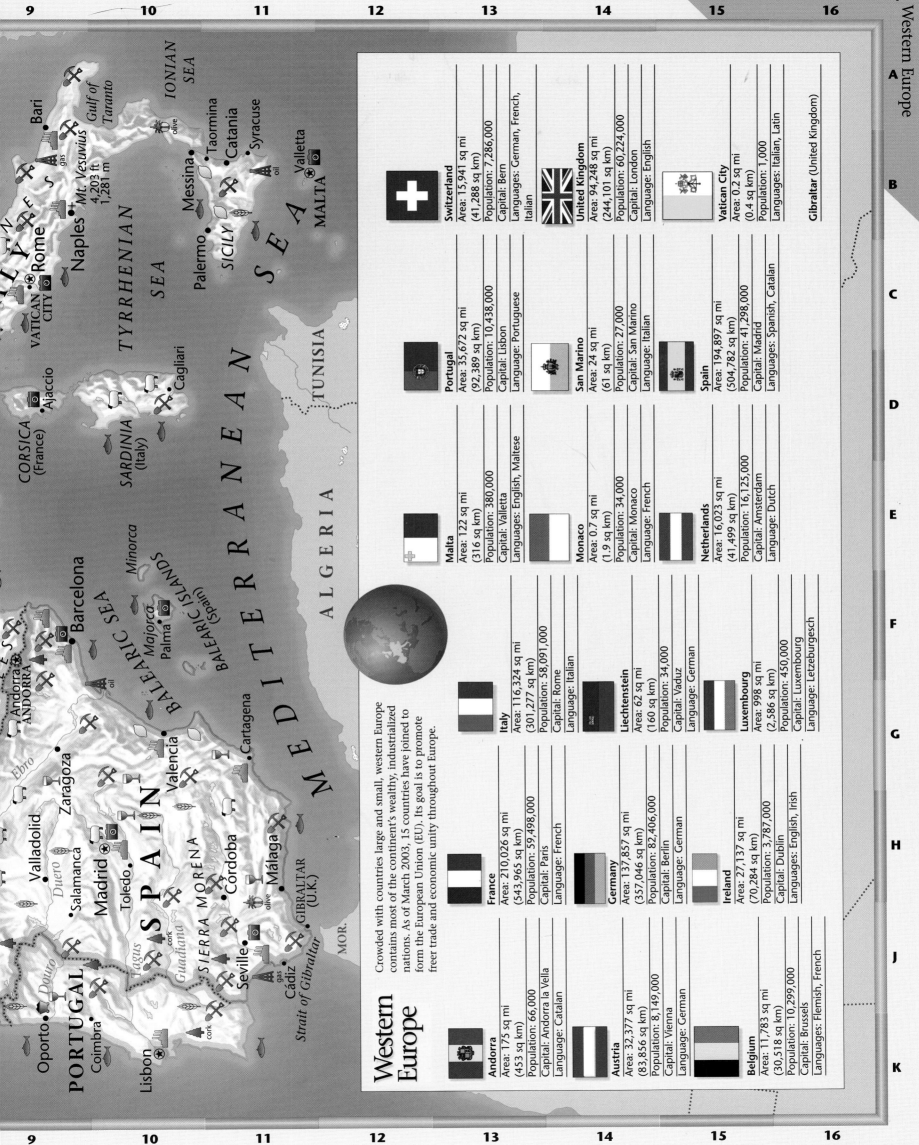

9   10   11   12   13   14   15   16

A
B
C
D
E
F
G
H
J
K

Map labels:

Bari
IONIAN SEA
Gulf of Taranto
olive
Taormina
Catania
Syracuse
Mt. Vesuvius
4,203 ft
1,281 m
Naples
Messina
Valletta
oil
Rome
VATICAN CITY
Palermo
SICILY
MALTA
VALLETTA
TYRRHENIAN SEA
TYRRHENIAN SEA
SEA

Ajaccio
Cagliari
CORSICA (France)
SARDINIA (Italy)
TUNISIA
MEDITERRANEAN SEA
ALGERIA

Barcelona
Minorca
Majorca
Palma
BALEARIC SEA
BALEARIC ISLANDS (Spain)

Andorra
ANDORRA
oil
Zaragoza
Valencia
Cartagena
Ebro
SPAIN
Valladolid
Salamanca
Madrid
Toledo
Córdoba
Málaga
Seville
Cádiz
GIBRALTAR (U.K.)
Strait of Gibraltar
gas
olive
cork
SIERRA MORENA
Duero
Tagus
Guadiana
Guadalquivir

Oporto
Coimbra
Lisbon
PORTUGAL
Douro
cork

MOR.

Western Europe

Crowded with countries large and small, western Europe contains most of the continent's wealthy, industrialized nations. As of March 2003, 15 countries have joined to form the European Union (EU). Its goal is to promote freer trade and economic unity throughout Europe.

Switzerland
Area: 15,941 sq mi
(41,288 sq km)
Population: 7,286,000
Capital: Bern
Languages: German, French, Italian

United Kingdom
Area: 94,248 sq mi
(244,101 sq km)
Population: 60,224,000
Capital: London
Language: English

Vatican City
Area: 0.2 sq mi
(0.4 sq km)
Population: 1,000
Languages: Italian, Latin

Gibraltar (United Kingdom)

Portugal
Area: 35,672 sq mi
(92,389 sq km)
Population: 10,438,000
Capital: Lisbon
Language: Portuguese

San Marino
Area: 24 sq mi
(61 sq km)
Population: 27,000
Capital: San Marino
Language: Italian

Spain
Area: 194,897 sq mi
(504,782 sq km)
Population: 41,298,000
Capital: Madrid
Languages: Spanish, Catalan

Malta
Area: 122 sq mi
(316 sq km)
Population: 380,000
Capital: Valletta
Languages: English, Maltese

Monaco
Area: 0.7 sq mi
(1.9 sq km)
Population: 34,000
Capital: Monaco
Language: French

Netherlands
Area: 16,023 sq mi
(41,499 sq km)
Population: 16,125,000
Capital: Amsterdam
Language: Dutch

Italy
Area: 116,324 sq mi
(301,277 sq km)
Population: 58,091,000
Capital: Rome
Language: Italian

Liechtenstein
Area: 62 sq mi
(160 sq km)
Population: 34,000
Capital: Vaduz
Language: German

Luxembourg
Area: 998 sq mi
(2,586 sq km)
Population: 450,000
Capital: Luxembourg
Language: Letzeburgesch

France
Area: 210,026 sq mi
(543,965 sq km)
Population: 59,498,000
Capital: Paris
Language: French

Germany
Area: 137,857 sq mi
(357,046 sq km)
Population: 82,406,000
Capital: Berlin
Language: German

Ireland
Area: 27,137 sq mi
(70,284 sq km)
Population: 3,787,000
Capital: Dublin
Languages: English, Irish

Andorra
Area: 175 sq mi
(453 sq km)
Population: 66,000
Capital: Andorra la Vella
Language: Catalan

Austria
Area: 32,377 sq mi
(83,856 sq km)
Population: 8,149,000
Capital: Vienna
Language: German

Belgium
Area: 11,783 sq mi
(30,518 sq km)
Population: 10,299,000
Capital: Brussels
Languages: Flemish, French

SWEDEN

DENMARK

B A L T I C   S E A

LATVIA

LITHUANIA

Gulf of Gdansk

Gdynia

KALININGRAD
(Russia)

Koszalin

Gdansk

Szczecin

Olsztyn

Hrodna

Mins

BE

Bydgoszcz

Bialystok

Baranav

GERMANY

Odra

Poznan

Vistula

P O L A N D

Warsaw

Brest

Pinsk

Pinsk M

Kalisz

Lódz

Legnica

Wroclaw

Walbrzych

Opole

Czestochowa

Kielce

Lublin

Luts'k

Liberec

Prague

Bytom

Rivne

Pilsen

C Z E C H
R E P U B L I C

Katowice

Kraków

Rzeszów

gas

oil

L'viv

U

Bielsko-
Biata

Ostrava

C A R P A T H I A N

oil

gas

Khmel'nyts'kyy

Brno

S L O V A K I A

Kam'yanets'-
Podil's'kyy

oil

Bratislava

Kosice

Uzhhorod

Chernivisti

Danube

AUSTRIA

Miskolc

M O U N T A I N S

Gyor

Budapest

Székesfehérvár

gas

ITALY

SLOVENIA

H U N G A R Y

gas

Drava

Pécs

Danube

Szeged

Tisza

A D R I A T I C   S E A

C R O A T I A

SERBIA

R O M A N I A

AND

BOSNIA AND
HERZEGOVINA

MONTENEGRO

Danube

Eastern Europe

Each of these countries was once controlled by the former Soviet Union. Belarus, Moldova, and Ukraine were Soviet republics. Poland, Hungary, and Czechoslovakia, which split into the Czech Republic and Slovakia, bordered the U.S.S.R.

Poland
Area: 120,725 sq mi
(312,677 sq km)
Population: 38,629,000
Capital: Warsaw
Language: Polish

Belarus
Area: 80,154 sq mi
(207,598 sq km)
Population: 9,936,000
Capital: Minsk
Language: Belorussian

Hungary
Area: 35,919 sq mi
(93,030 sq km)
Population: 10,146,000
Capital: Budapest
Language: Hungarian

Slovakia
Area: 18,921 sq mi
(49,006 sq km)
Population: 5,367,000
Capital: Bratislava
Language: Slovak

Czech Republic
Area: 30,450 sq mi
(78,864 sq km)
Population: 10,270,000
Capital: Prague
Language: Czech

Moldova
Area: 13,217 sq mi
(33,999 sq km)
Population: 4,258,000
Capital: Chisinau
Language: Moldovan

Ukraine
Area: 233,206 sq mi
(604,001 sq km)
Population: 48,225,000
Capital: Kiev
Language: Ukrainian

Kaliningrad (Russia)

Western Dvina

Vitsyebsk

Orsha

RUSSIA

Mahilyow

RUS

Babruysk

Homyel'

Dnieper

Mazyr

Chernihiv

Chornobyl'

Sumy

Zhytomyr

Kiev

Bila Tserkva

Kharkiv

Cherkasy

Poltava

RAINE

Kremenchuk

Slov'yans'k

Vinnytsya

Kramators'k

Luhans'k

Oleksandriya

Horlivka

Dnipropetrovs'k

Kirovohrad

Makiyivka

Dniprodzerzhyns'k

Donets'k

Kryvyy Rih

Zaporizhzhya

Dniester

Mariupol'

MOLDOVA

Melitopol'

Chisinau

Mykolayiv

Berdyans'k

Tiraspol

gas

Dnieper

Kherson

Odesa

SEA OF AZOV

CRIMEA

Kerch

Yevpatoriya

Simferopol'

Sevastopol'

BLACK SEA

0   200 miles
0   200 kilometers
Azimuthal Equidistant Projection

GERMANY

SLOVAKIA

SWITZERLAND

LIECHTENSTEIN

AUSTRIA

Danube

Tisza

HUNGARY

Satu Mare

Baia M

TRANSYL

Oradea

Cluj-Napoc

R O

Drava

Maribor

SLOVENIA

Ljubljana

oil

Zagreb

Sava

Drava

Subotica

Arad

Timisoara

Gulf of
Venice

Rijeka

CROATIA

Osijek

Novi Sad

Sava

gas

Belgrade

Resita

TRA

SAN
MARINO

Zadar

D
I
N
A
R
I
C

A
L
P
S

Banja Luka

BOSNIA

AND

SERBIA

*Iron G
Dam

Cra*

ITALY

A
D
R
I
A
T
I
C

S
E
A

D
A
L
M
A
T
I
A

Zenica

HERZEGOVINA

Sarajevo

Kragujevac

AND

Split

Mostar

Nis

B

CORSICA
(France)

Dubrovnik

Podgorica

MONTENEGRO

Pec

Pristina

Sofia

SARDINIA
(Italy)

TYRRHENIAN
SEA

Shkodër

Tetovo

Skopje

B
A

Durrës

Tirana

MACEDONIA

P
E
N
I

Elbasan

Bitola

ALBANIA

Thessaloníki

Strait of Otranto

Vlorë

Olympus
9,570 ft
2,917 m

SICILY

Corfu

GREECE

Lárissa

I
O
N
I
A
N

I
S
L
A
N
D
S

IONIAN
SEA

Pátrai

Athe

Corinth

Olympia

PELOPONNESUS

0   200 miles

0   200 kilometers

Sparta

olive

Azimuthal Equidistant Projection

TUNISIA

MALTA

Gulf of Messinia

M E D I T E R R A N E A N

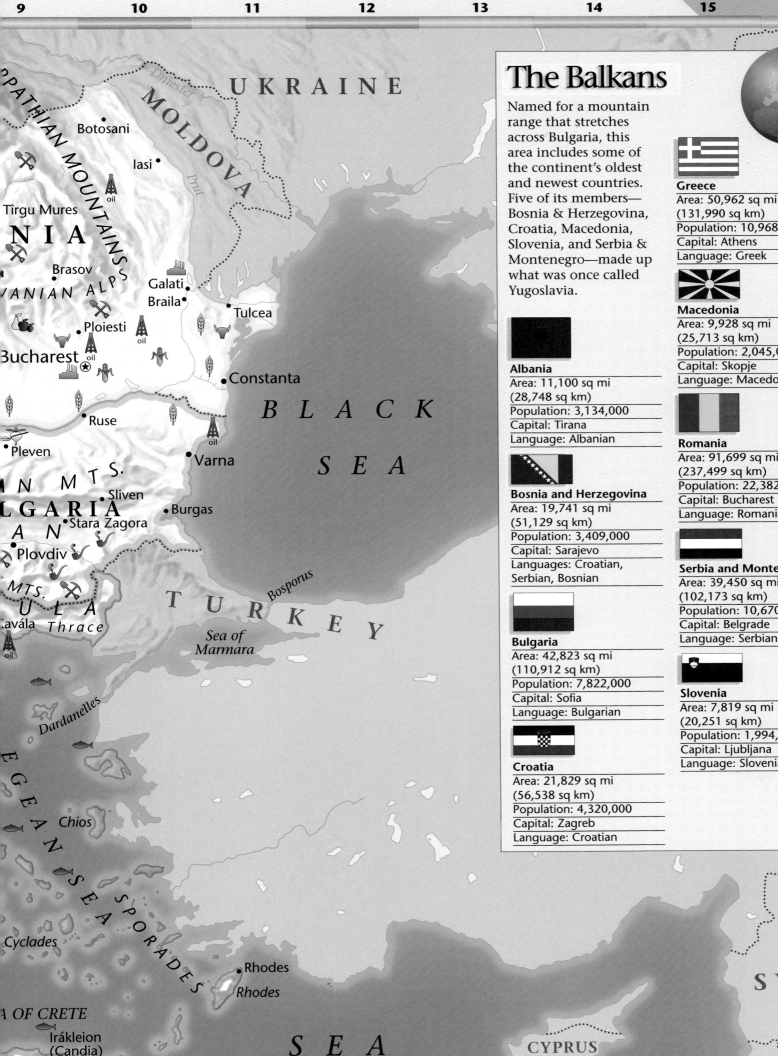

UKRAINE

MOLDOVA

Botosani

Iasi

CARPATHIAN MOUNTAINS

Tîrgu Mures

NIA

Brasov

VANIAN ALPS

Galati

Braila

Ploiesti

Bucharest

Tulcea

Constanta

Ruse

Pleven

Varna

N MTS.

Sliven

LGARIA

Stara Zagora

Burgas

AN

Plovdiv

MTS.

ULA

Kavála

Thrace

BLACK

SEA

Bosporus

TURKEY

Sea of
Marmara

Dardanelles

AEGEAN SEA

Chios

SPORADES

Cyclades

Rhodes

Rhodes

A OF CRETE

Irákleion
(Candia)

RETE

olive

SEA

CYPRUS

LEBANON

SYRIA

The Balkans

Named for a mountain range that stretches across Bulgaria, this area includes some of the continent's oldest and newest countries. Five of its members—Bosnia & Herzegovina, Croatia, Macedonia, Slovenia, and Serbia & Montenegro—made up what was once called Yugoslavia.

Greece
Area: 50,962 sq mi
(131,990 sq km)
Population: 10,968,000
Capital: Athens
Language: Greek

Macedonia
Area: 9,928 sq mi
(25,713 sq km)
Population: 2,045,000
Capital: Skopje
Language: Macedonian

Romania
Area: 91,699 sq mi
(237,499 sq km)
Population: 22,382,000
Capital: Bucharest
Language: Romanian

Serbia and Montenegro
Area: 39,450 sq mi
(102,173 sq km)
Population: 10,670,000
Capital: Belgrade
Language: Serbian

Slovenia
Area: 7,819 sq mi
(20,251 sq km)
Population: 1,994,000
Capital: Ljubljana
Language: Slovenian

Albania
Area: 11,100 sq mi
(28,748 sq km)
Population: 3,134,000
Capital: Tirana
Language: Albanian

Bosnia and Herzegovina
Area: 19,741 sq mi
(51,129 sq km)
Population: 3,409,000
Capital: Sarajevo
Languages: Croatian, Serbian, Bosnian

Bulgaria
Area: 42,823 sq mi
(110,912 sq km)
Population: 7,822,000
Capital: Sofia
Language: Bulgarian

Croatia
Area: 21,829 sq mi
(56,538 sq km)
Population: 4,320,000
Capital: Zagreb
Language: Croatian

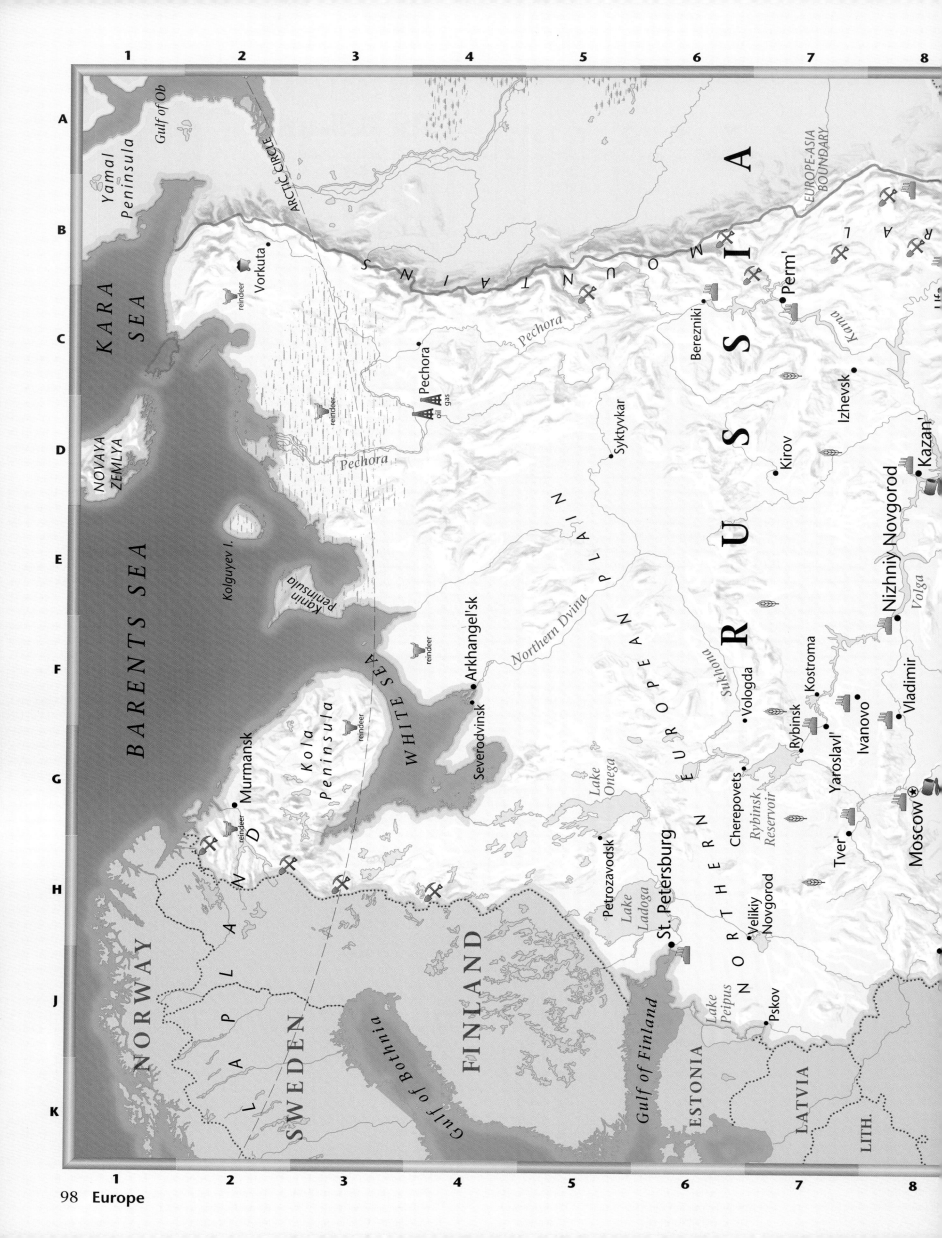

A

Gulf of Ob

Yamal
Peninsula

ARCTIC CIRCLE

EUROPE-ASIA
BOUNDARY

B

KARA

SEA

reindeer   Vorkuta

M O U N T A I N S

Pechora

Perm'

C

Berezniki

NOVAYA
ZEMLYA

Pechora

Pechora
oil   gas

Syktyvkar

Kirov

Izhevsk

D

Pechora

Kolguyev I.

Kanin
Peninsula

S
S
U
R

U

S
S
I
A

Nizhniy Novgorod

Kazan'

E

BARENTS SEA

Northern Dvina

Arkhangel'sk

Volga

F

WHITE SEA

Severodvinsk

reindeer

Sukhona

Vologda

Rybinsk   Kostroma

Yaroslavl'

Ivanovo

Vladimir

E
U
R
O
P
E
A
N

P
L
A
I
N

G

Murmansk

reindeer

Kola
Peninsula

*Lake
Onega*

Cherepovets

*Rybinsk
Reservoir*

Tver'

Moscow

H

reindeer

*Lake
Ladoga*

Petrozavodsk

St. Petersburg

Velikiy
Novgorod

N
O
R
T
H
E
R
N

NORWAY

L
A
P
L
A
N
D

J

SWEDEN

Gulf of Bothnia

FINLAND

Gulf of Finland

*Lake
Peipus*

Pskov

ESTONIA

LATVIA

K

LITH.

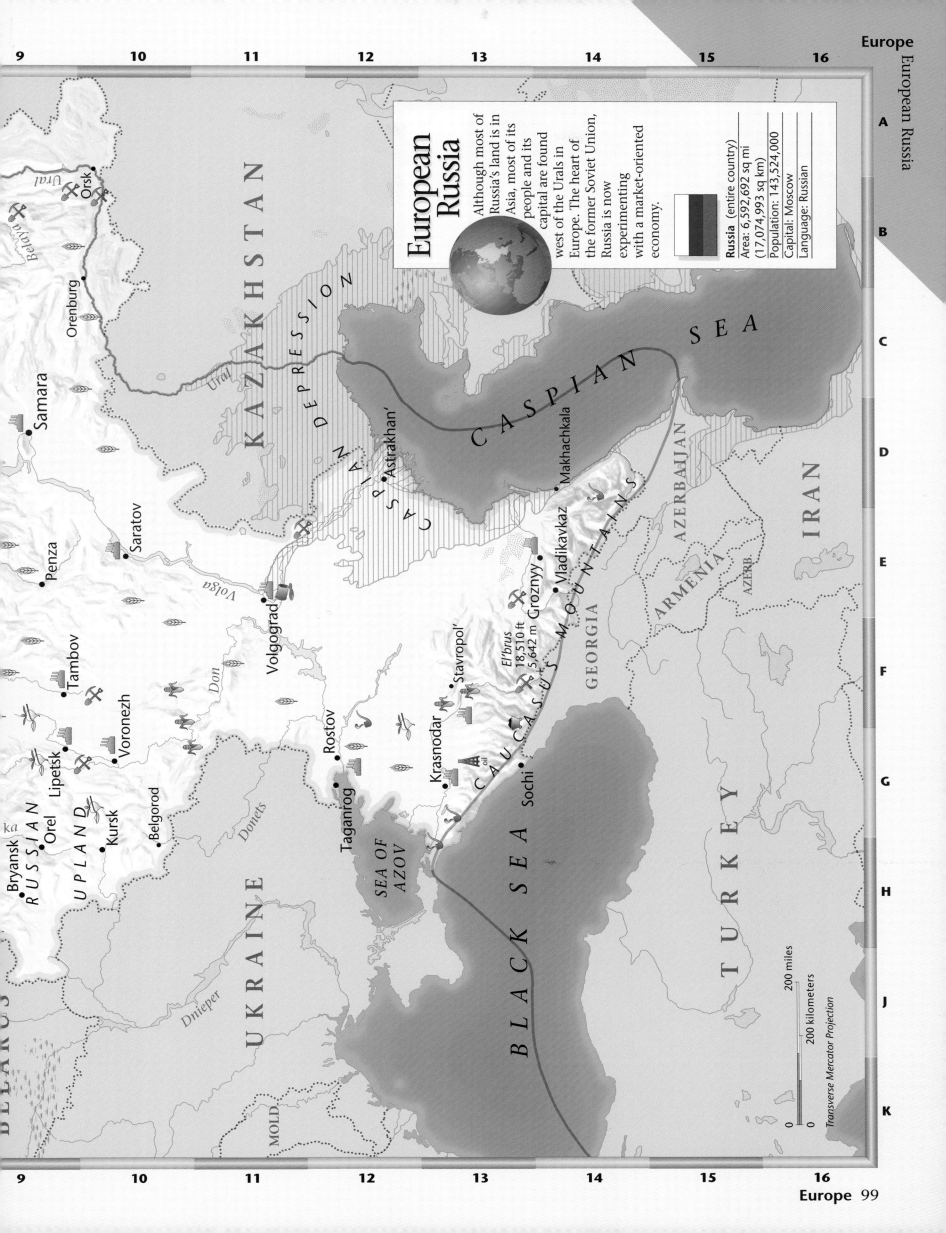

9 10 11 12 13 14 15 16

A
B
C
D
E
F
G
H
J
K

European Russia

Although most of Russia's land is in Asia, most of its people and its capital are found west of the Urals in Europe. The heart of the former Soviet Union, Russia is now experimenting with a market-oriented economy.

Russia (entire country)
Area: 6,592,692 sq mi (17,074,993 sq km)
Population: 143,524,000
Capital: Moscow
Language: Russian

KAZAKHSTAN

Orsk

Orenburg

Belaya

Ural

Ural

Samara

Saratov

Penza

CASPIAN DEPRESSION

Astrakhan'

CASPIAN

CASPIAN SEA

Makhachkala

AZERBAIJAN

ARMENIA

AZERB.

IRAN

Volga

Volgograd

Tambov

Voronezh

Don

Rostov

Stavropol'

Krasnodar

El'brus 18,510 ft 5,642 m

Grozny

Vladikavkaz

CAUCASUS MOUNTAINS

GEORGIA

Bryansk

RUSSIAN

UPLAND

Orel

Lipetsk

Kursk

Belgorod

ka

Donets

Taganrog

oil

Sochi

SEA OF AZOV

BLACK SEA

TURKEY

UKRAINE

BELARUS

Dnieper

MOLD.

200 miles

200 kilometers

0
0

Transverse Mercator Projection

Africa

The salty waters of the Red Sea (near right) and the Gulf of Aden (far right) fill the gap formed as geologic forces tear the Arabian Peninsula away from Africa. The rumpled-looking area at lower center is the Great Rift Valley, which rends East Africa like a pair of hatchet cuts. In about 50 million years, say geologists, a huge chunk of East Africa from Eritrea to Mozambique will break away from the rest of the continent, just as Madagascar broke away from what is now Mozambique millions of years ago.

Africa's position on the globe—straddling the Equator and lying almost entirely within the tropics—gives it the warmest average annual temperature of all the continents.

Radiant with color, schools of lyre-tailed goldfish swim among coral in the Red Sea. Although it is shallow along its shores, the sea plunges to a central trough more than 7,000 feet (2,134 meters) deep.

CONNECTION: *You can find East Africa and the Red Sea on the maps on pages 102–103 and 112–113.*

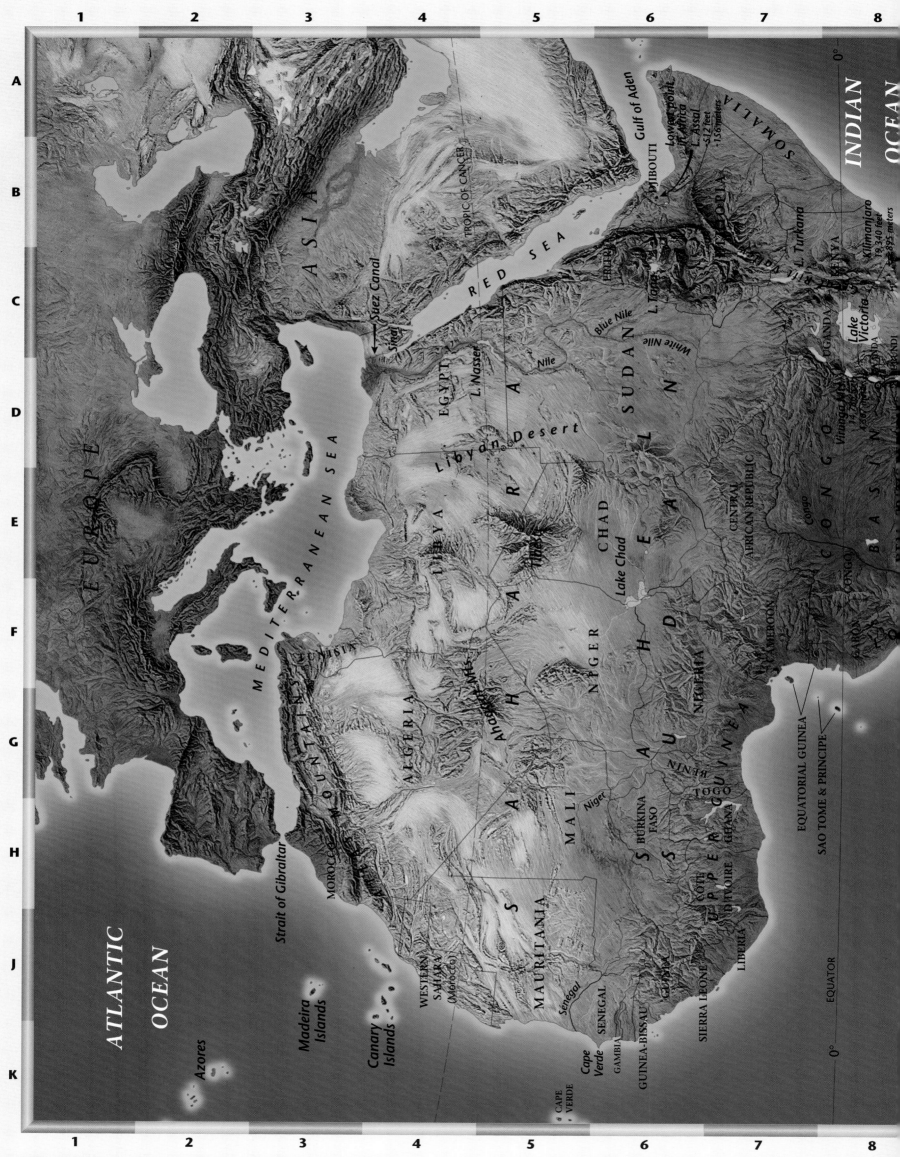

ATLANTIC
OCEAN

INDIAN
OCEAN

EUROPE

ASIA

MEDITERRANEAN SEA

RED SEA

Gulf of Aden

TROPIC OF CANCER

Suez Canal

Sinai

Strait of Gibraltar

Azores

Madeira
Islands

Canary
Islands

MOROCCO

ATLAS MOUNTAINS

TUNISIA

ALGERIA

LIBYA

EGYPT

L. Nasser

Nile

Blue Nile

White Nile

SUDAN

S A H A R A

Libyan Desert

Tibesti

Ahaggar Mts.

WESTERN
SAHARA
(Morocco)

MAURITANIA

MALI

NIGER

CHAD

Lake Chad

S A H E L

DJIBOUTI

ERITREA

SOMALIA

ETHIOPIA

Lower point
in Africa
L. Assal
-512 feet
-156 meters

Kilimanjaro
19,340 feet
895 meters

L. Turkana

UGANDA

Lake
Victoria

KENYA

Virunga Mts.

CONGO BASIN

Congo

CAMEROON

CENTRAL
AFRICAN REPUBLIC

GABON

EQUATORIAL GUINEA

SAO TOME & PRINCIPE

NIGERIA

BENIN

TOGO

GHANA

CÔTE
D'IVOIRE

UPPER GUINEA

LIBERIA

SIERRA LEONE

GUINEA

BURKINA
FASO

Niger

Senegal

SENEGAL

GAMBIA

GUINEA-BISSAU

Cape
Verde

CAPE
VERDE

EQUATOR

0°

0°

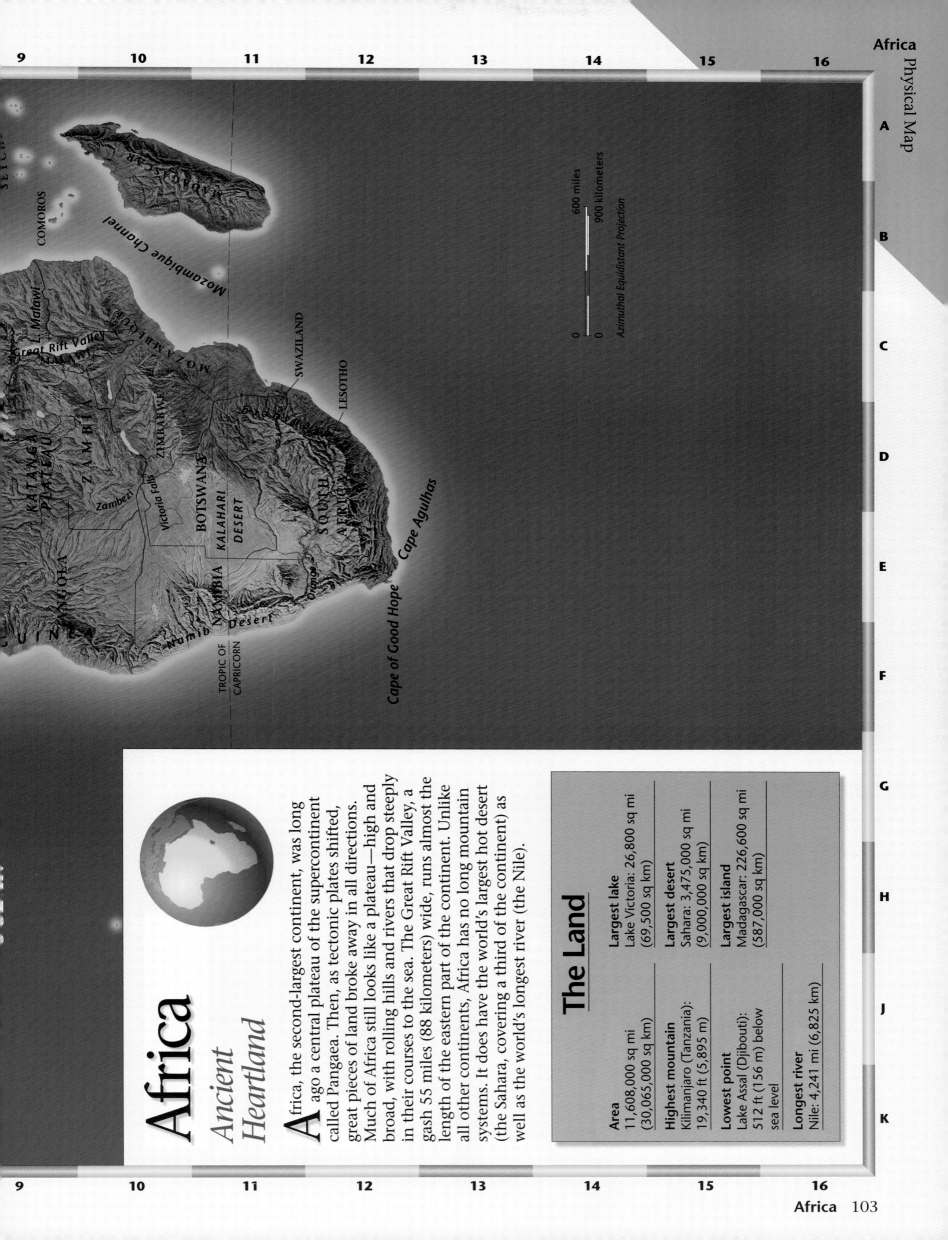

9   10   11   12   13   14   15   16

A

B

C

D

E

F

G

H

J

K

SEYCHELLES

COMOROS

MADAGASCAR

Mozambique Channel

L. Malawi

Great Rift Valley

MALAWI

MOZAMBIQUE

SWAZILAND

LESOTHO

ZIMBABWE

KATANGA PLATEAU

ZAMBIA

Zambezi

Victoria Falls

BOTSWANA

KALAHARI DESERT

South AFRICA

ANGOLA

NAMIBIA

Namib Desert

Orange

Cape of Good Hope

Cape Agulhas

TROPIC OF CAPRICORN

GUINEA

600 miles

900 kilometers

0

0

Azimuthal Equidistant Projection

Africa
Ancient Heartland

Africa, the second-largest continent, was long ago a central plateau of the supercontinent called Pangaea. Then, as tectonic plates shifted, great pieces of land broke away in all directions. Much of Africa still looks like a plateau—high and broad, with rolling hills and rivers that drop steeply in their courses to the sea. The Great Rift Valley, a gash 55 miles (88 kilometers) wide, runs almost the length of the eastern part of the continent. Unlike all other continents, Africa has no long mountain systems. It does have the world's largest hot desert (the Sahara, covering a third of the continent) as well as the world's longest river (the Nile).

The Land

Area
11,608,000 sq mi
(30,065,000 sq km)

Highest mountain
Kilimanjaro (Tanzania):
19,340 ft (5,895 m)

Lowest point
Lake Assal (Djibouti):
512 ft (156 m) below
sea level

Longest river
Nile: 4,241 mi (6,825 km)

Largest lake
Lake Victoria: 26,800 sq mi
(69,500 sq km)

Largest desert
Sahara: 3,475,000 sq mi
(9,000,000 sq km)

Largest island
Madagascar: 226,600 sq mi
(587,000 sq km)

9   10   11   12   13   14   15   16

Africa
Changing Continent

The roar of a lion. A river of wildebeests migrating across the plain. These images conjure up the traditional picture of Africa. It is a continent perhaps best known for its extraordinary natural heritage—abundant wildlife, grasslands, rain forests, and sculpted desert sands. It is here, on African soil, that early humans evolved. Today, in the fast-growing countries south of the Sahara, people desperately need land for farms and livestock. In many places, wildlife is squeezed onto shrinking habitat. Some countries hope to safeguard the future by setting aside huge national parks that would attract tourists. This could bring money into a continent where few nations are industrialized.

Africa saw more change in the 20th century than any other continent. Just 50 years ago, almost every country belonged to a European power. Today, only Spain still controls territory on the mainland. However, Africa's problems are far from over. Freedom brings the challenges of self-government, and ethnic and religious rivalries cause ongoing civil wars.

▼ **THE ELEPHANT'S NEED** *for habitat conflicts more and more with the human demand for land.*

▲ **A CITY OF LIGHTS** *at the southern tip of the African continent, Cape Town is one of South Africa's three capitals. A parliament, the country's governing body, meets in Cape Town to write national laws.*

▼ **DRILLS BITE INTO ROCK** *deep underground as miners set explosives in a South African gold mine. Mining is a major industry in several African countries. The continent is the source of much of the world's gold and diamonds.*

◀ **SERENELY SURVEYING**
*the savanna, a giraffe
trio towers above the
landscape. Africa's
wildlife draws visitors
from around the
world.*

◀ **BOLD**
*patterns and
brilliant colors
give a festive
air to a crowded
marketplace in
southern Africa.
At open-air markets
such as this one,
different ethnic groups
meet to trade.*

▲ **AS FAST AS A SPEEDING** *car, the cheetah can run at up to 70 miles per hour (113 kilometers per hour). Already extinct in India, this cat is becoming rare in Africa as well.*

▶ **A TUAREG** *nomad skirts the crest of a dune in the Sahara. The Sahara is the world's largest hot desert, covering an area about the size of the lower 48 U.S. states. Drought and overgrazing in the Sahel, a semiarid region bordering the Sahara, are expanding the desert.*

▲ **IMAGINATION CAN'T COMPARE** *with the terrifying reality children face in wartime. Here, young refugees in Mozambique use art as therapy to express their fears. Since 1950, almost every African nation has experienced war.*

▶ **NINGA TRIBAL DRUMMERS** *inspire a leaping dancer in Burundi. Hundreds of tribes speaking hundreds of languages live in Africa south of the Sahara.*

▶ **CRADLING THE WORDS** *of the Prophet Muhammad, a young Bedouin studies a lesson from the Koran, the sacred book of Islam. Bedouin are Arab nomads who traditionally roamed across North Africa on camels. Today, many Bedouin live a more settled existence.*

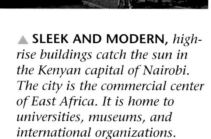

▲ **SLEEK AND MODERN,** *high-rise buildings catch the sun in the Kenyan capital of Nairobi. The city is the commercial center of East Africa. It is home to universities, museums, and international organizations.*

▲ **EGYPT'S**
ancient sands yield their secrets reluctantly. In 1922 archaeologists uncovered four treasure-filled rooms of the tomb of the teenage King Tutankhamun— also known as King Tut. Countless ancient tombs remain unexcavated beneath shifting desert sands.

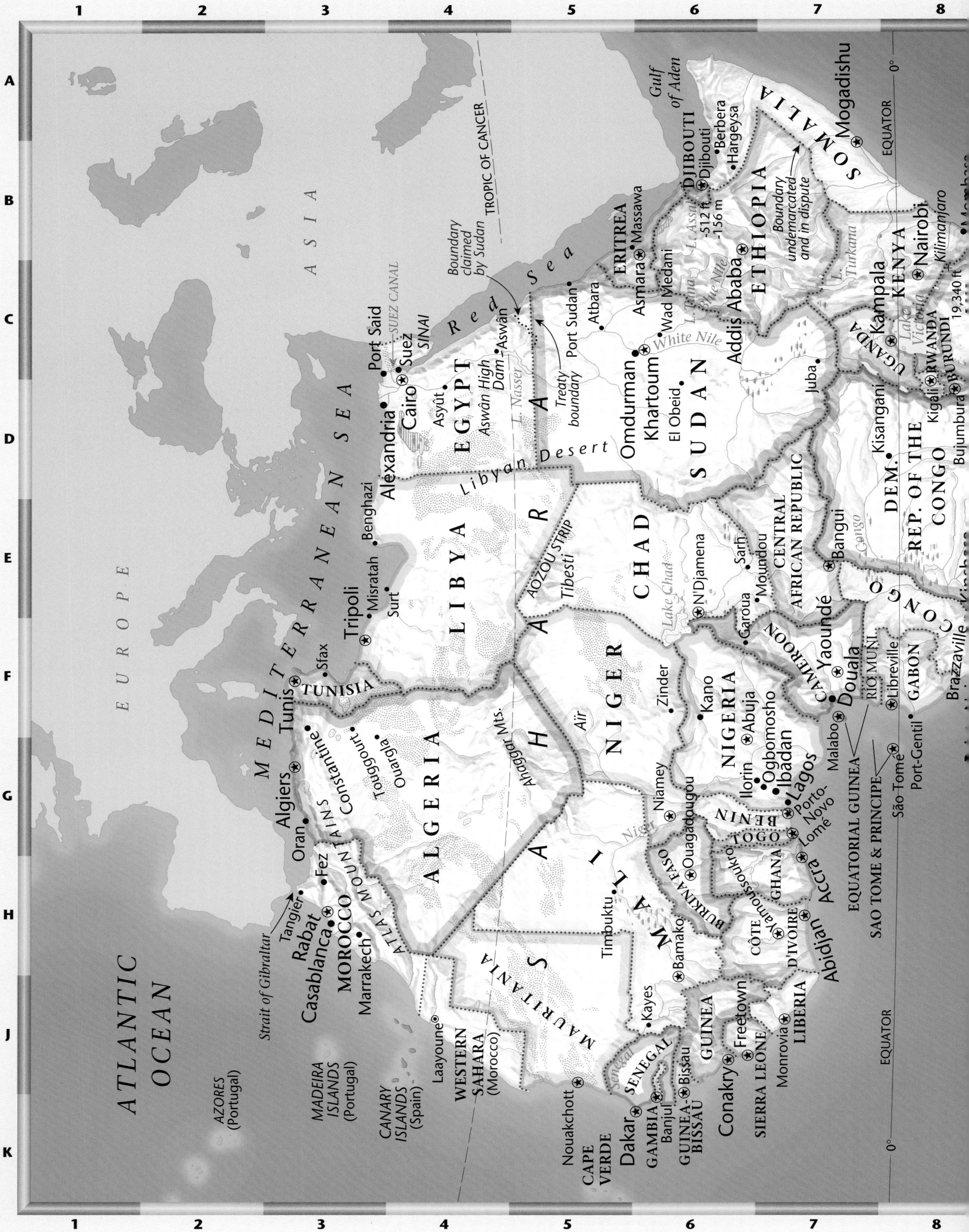

ATLANTIC OCEAN
EUROPE
ASIA
MEDITERRANEAN SEA
Red Sea
Gulf of Aden
TROPIC OF CANCER
EQUATOR
SAHARA
Libyan Desert
Strait of Gibraltar
ATLAS MOUNTAINS
Ahaggar Mts.
Aïr
Tibesti
AOZOU STRIP
SUEZ CANAL
SINAI
L. Nasser
Aswân High Dam
Boundary claimed by Sudan
Treaty boundary
Boundary undemarcated and in dispute
Lake Chad
L. Tana
Blue Nile
White Nile
L. Assal -512 ft. -156 m
L. Turkana
Lake Victoria
Kilimanjaro 19,340 ft.
Niger
Senegal
Congo
AZORES (Portugal)
MADEIRA ISLANDS (Portugal)
CANARY ISLANDS (Spain)
CAPE VERDE
WESTERN SAHARA (Morocco)
MOROCCO
ALGERIA
TUNISIA
LIBYA
EGYPT
SUDAN
ERITREA
DJIBOUTI
ETHIOPIA
SOMALIA
KENYA
UGANDA
RWANDA
BURUNDI
DEM. REP. OF THE CONGO
CONGO
GABON
CENTRAL AFRICAN REPUBLIC
CAMEROON
CHAD
NIGER
NIGERIA
BENIN
TOGO
GHANA
BURKINA FASO
CÔTE D'IVOIRE
LIBERIA
SIERRA LEONE
GUINEA
GUINEA-BISSAU
GAMBIA
SENEGAL
MAURITANIA
MALI
EQUATORIAL GUINEA
RIO MUNI
SAO TOME & PRINCIPE
Tangier
Rabat
Casablanca
Fez
Marrakech
Oran
Algiers
Constantine
Touggourt
Ouargla
Tunis
Sfax
Tripoli
Misratah
Surt
Benghazi
Alexandria
Cairo
Port Said
Suez
Asyût
Aswân
Port Sudan
Atbara
Omdurman
Khartoum
El Obeid
Wad Medani
Juba
Asmara
Massawa
Djibouti
Berbera
Hargeysa
Addis Ababa
Mogadishu
Nairobi
Kampala
Kigali
Bujumbura
Kisangani
Bangui
Brazzaville
Libreville
Port-Gentil
São Tomé
Malabo
Douala
Yaoundé
Garoua
Moundou
Sarh
N'Djamena
Zinder
Kano
Abuja
Ogbomosho
Ibadan
Ilorin
Lagos
Porto-Novo
Lomé
Accra
Yamoussoukro
Abidjan
Ouagadougou
Niamey
Timbuktu
Bamako
Kayes
Monrovia
Freetown
Conakry
Bissau
Banjul
Dakar
Nouakchott
Laayoune
1
2
3
4
5
6
7
8
A
B
C
D
E
F
G
H
J
K

A

B

C

D

E

F

G

H

J

K

Islands of Africa

EQUATOR 0°

MADEIRA IS. (PORTUGAL)

CANARY IS. (SPAIN)

CAPE VERDE

EQUATORIAL GUINEA

SAO TOME AND PRINCIPE

ASCENSION (UNITED KINGDOM)

ST. HELENA (UNITED KINGDOM)

A F R I C A

SEYCHELLES

COMOROS

MAURITIUS

RÉUNION (FRANCE)

SEYCHELLES

COMOROS
⊛Moroni

MADAGASCAR

⊛Antananarivo

Mozambique Channel

TROPIC OF CAPRICORN

Nampula

MOZAMBIQUE

Beira

Lake Malawi

MALAWI

Lilongwe⊛

Blantyre

Lusaka⊛

Harare⊛

ZIMBABWE

Bulawayo

Maputo⊛

Mbabane⊛

SWAZILAND

LESOTHO

Durban

Maseru⊛

Pretoria⊛

Johannesburg

Bloemfontein⊛

SOUTH AFRICA

Port Elizabeth

Lubumbashi

Kolwezi

Kitwe

Z A M B I A

Zambezi

Victoria Falls

BOTSWANA

Gaborone⊛

KALAHARI DESERT

NAMIBIA

Windhoek⊛

Etosha Pan

ANGOLA

Luanda⊛

Huambo

Lubango

Lobito

Namibe

Cape Town⊛

Cape of Good Hope

Cape Agulhas

ATLANTIC OCEAN

(U.K.)

0 600 miles

0 900 kilometers

Azimuthal Equidistant Projection

Africa

One Continent, Two Africas

Culturally and historically, there are two Africas. North Africa, including the Sahara, was conquered by Arabs from Asia in the seventh century. Today, most North Africans speak Arabic and follow Islam. In the second Africa, south of the Sahara, there are hundreds of diverse ethnic groups. In this region, most people are farmers and live in small villages, although many now are migrating to Africa's booming cities. The people of eastern and southern Africa speak more than a thousand different languages, including the ones introduced in the 1800s, when most of these countries were European colonies.

The People

Population
840,214,000

Largest country
Sudan: 963,600 sq mi
(2,495,712 sq km)

Largest metropolitan areas
Cairo, Egypt:
Pop. 9,586,000
Lagos, Nigeria:
Pop. 8,600,000

Most densely populated country
Mauritius: 1,520 people per sq mi

Economy
Farming: fruit, grains
Industry: chemicals, mining, cement

Life expectancy
53 years

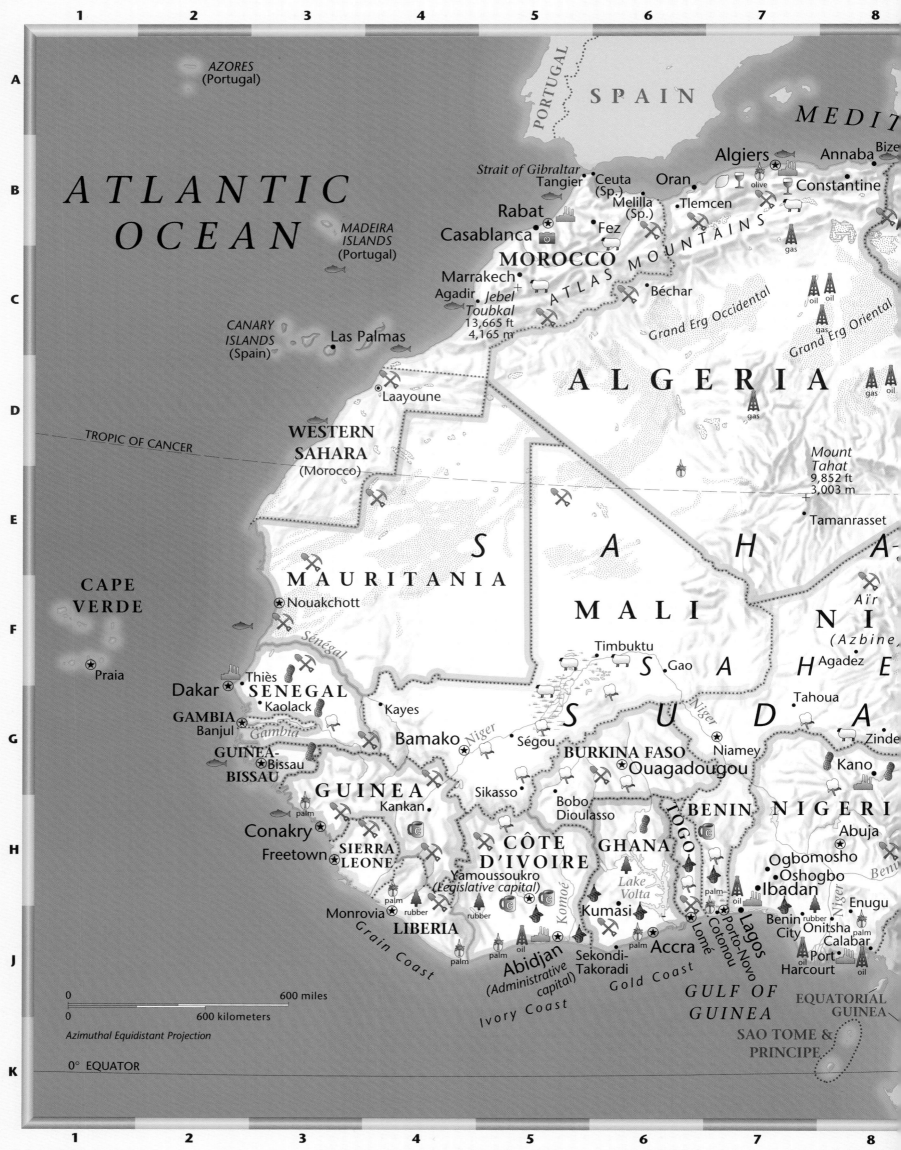

ATLANTIC
OCEAN

AZORES
(Portugal)

MADEIRA
ISLANDS
(Portugal)

SPAIN

MEDIT

PORTUGAL

Algiers Annaba Bize

Strait of Gibraltar Ceuta Oran Constantine
Tangier (Sp.) Tlemcen olive
Rabat Melilla
Casablanca (Sp.) gas
Fez
MOROCCO ATLAS MOUNTAINS
Marrakech
Agadir *Jebel* Béchar
Toubkal *Grand Erg Occidental* oil oil
13,665 ft *Grand Erg Oriental*
4,165 m gas
gas oil

CANARY **ALGERIA**
ISLANDS Las Palmas
(Spain)

Laayoune gas

TROPIC OF CANCER **WESTERN**
SAHARA
(Morocco)

Mount
Tahat
9,852 ft
3,003 m

CAPE **MAURITANIA** S Tamanrasset
VERDE
Nouakchott A *Aïr*
MALI **NI**
Praia *(Azbine)*

Sénégal Timbuktu S Agadez
Gao
Thiès *Niger* Tahoua
Dakar **SENEGAL** Kayes **SUD**
Kaolack
GAMBIA *Gambia* Bamako *Niger* Ségou Niamey Zinde
Banjul **BURKINA FASO** Kano
GUINEA- Bissau Ouagadougou
BISSAU
GUINEA Sikasso Bobo **BENIN** **NIGERI**
Kankan Dioulasso **TOGO** Abuja
Conakry **CÔTE** **GHANA** Ogbomosho
SIERRA **D'IVOIRE** Oshogbo
Freetown **LEONE** Yamoussoukro *Lake* Ibadan
(Legislative capital) *Volta* palm Benin Enugu
Monrovia rubber rubber Kumasi Lagos City Onitsha
LIBERIA Accra Lomé Porto-Novo Calabar
Grain Coast Abidjan Sekondi- Cotonou Port
palm *(Administrative* Takoradi *Gold Coast* Harcourt
capital) **GULF OF** **EQUATORIAL**
Ivory Coast **GUINEA** **GUINEA**

0 600 miles **SAO TOME &**
PRINCIPE
0 600 kilometers

Azimuthal Equidistant Projection

0° EQUATOR

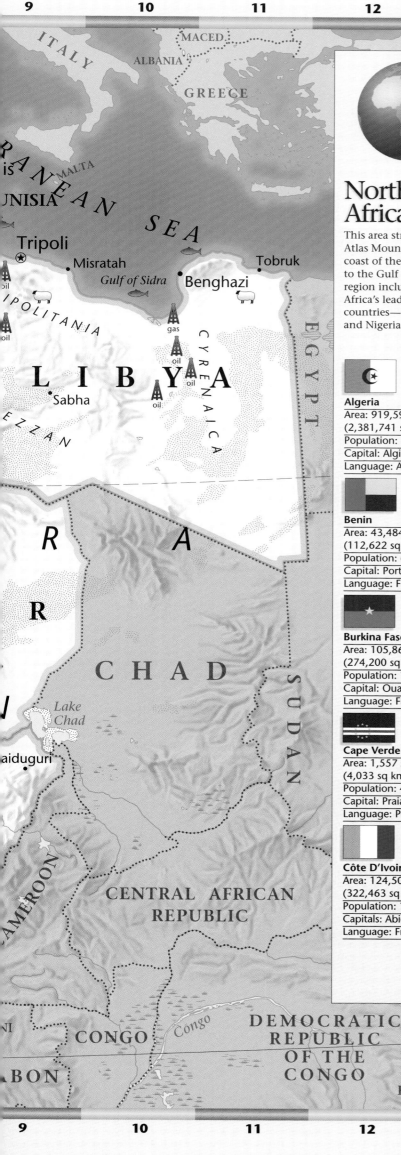

ITALY

ALBANIA

GREECE

MACED.

MALTA

is

UNISIA

RANEAN SEA

Tripoli

Misratah

Gulf of Sidra

Benghazi

Tobruk

oil

gas

IPOLITANIA

CYRENAICA

oil

oil

L I B Y A

oil

Sabha

oil

EGYPT

E Z Z A N

R

A

R

R

Lake Chad

CHAD

SUDAN

aiduguri

CAMEROON

CENTRAL AFRICAN REPUBLIC

ABON

CONGO

Congo

DEMOCRATIC REPUBLIC OF THE CONGO

UGANDA

Lake Victoria

KENYA

RWANDA

TANZANIA

Northwestern Africa

This area stretches from the Atlas Mountains along the coast of the Mediterranean Sea to the Gulf of Guinea. The region includes several of Africa's leading oil-producing countries—Algeria, Libya, and Nigeria.

Algeria
Area: 919,595 sq mi
(2,381,741 sq km)
Population: 31,382,000
Capital: Algiers
Language: Arabic

Benin
Area: 43,484 sq mi
(112,622 sq km)
Population: 6,629,000
Capital: Porto-Novo
Language: French

Burkina Faso
Area: 105,869 sq mi
(274,200 sq km)
Population: 12,603,000
Capital: Ouagadougou
Language: French

Cape Verde
Area: 1,557 sq mi
(4,033 sq km)
Population: 460,000
Capital: Praia
Language: Portuguese

Côte D'Ivoire
Area: 124,504 sq mi
(322,463 sq km)
Population: 16,805,000
Capitals: Abidjan, Yamoussoukro
Language: French

Gambia
Area: 4,361 sq mi
(11,295 sq km)
Population: 1,456,000
Capital: Banjul
Language: English

Ghana
Area: 92,100 sq mi
(238,537 sq km)
Population: 20,244,000
Capital: Accra
Language: English

Guinea
Area: 94,926 sq mi
(245,857 sq km)
Population: 8,381,000
Capital: Conakry
Language: French

Guinea-Bissau
Area: 13,948 sq mi
(36,125 sq km)
Population: 1,257,000
Capital: Bissau
Language: Portuguese

Liberia
Area: 43,000 sq mi
(111,369 sq km)
Population: 3,288,000
Capital: Monrovia
Language: English

Libya
Area: 679,362 sq mi
(1,759,540 sq km)
Population: 5,369,000
Capital: Tripoli
Language: Arabic

Mali
Area: 478,841 sq mi
(1,240,192 sq km)
Population: 11,340,000
Capital: Bamako
Language: French

Mauritania
Area: 397,955 sq mi
(1,030,700 sq km)
Population: 2,635,000
Capital: Nouakchott
Language: Arabic

Morocco
Area: 275,117 sq mi
(712,550 sq km)
Population: 29,662,000
Capital: Rabat
Language: Arabic

Niger
Area: 489,191 sq mi
(1,267,000 sq km)
Population: 11,641,000
Capital: Niamey
Language: French

Nigeria
Area: 356,669 sq mi
(923,768 sq km)
Population: 129,935,000
Capital: Abuja
Language: English

Senegal
Area: 75,955 sq mi
(196,722 sq km)
Population: 9,908,000
Capital: Dakar
Language: French

Sierra Leone
Area: 27,699 sq mi
(71,740 sq km)
Population: 5,615,000
Capital: Freetown
Language: English

Togo
Area: 21,925 sq mi
(56,785 sq km)
Population: 5,286,000
Capital: Lomé
Language: French

Tunisia
Area: 63,170 sq mi
(163,610 sq km)
Population: 9,782,000
Capital: Tunis
Language: Arabic

Western Sahara
Administered by Morocco, Western Sahara is a disputed area. A cease-fire in its struggle for independence has been in effect since 1991, but its status as a separate country is still undecided.

Northeastern Africa

This region is home to Africa's largest country, Sudan, as well as one of the world's oldest nations, Egypt. It also contains Africa's longest river (Nile), its largest lake (Victoria), and its highest peak (Kilimanjaro).

Somalia
Area: 246,201 sq mi
(637,657 sq km)
Population: 7,753,000
Capital: Mogadishu
Language: Somali

Sudan
Area: 963,600 sq mi
(2,495,712 sq km)
Population: 32,559,000
Capital: Khartoum
Language: Arabic

Tanzania
Area: 364,900 sq mi
(945,087 sq km)
Population: 37,188,000
Capitals: Dar es Salaam, Dodoma
Languages: English, Kiswahili

Uganda
Area: 91,134 sq mi
(236,036 sq km)
Population: 24,699,000
Capital: Kampala
Language: English

Eritrea
Area: 46,842 sq mi
(121,320 sq km)
Population: 4,466,000
Capital: Asmara
Language: Tigrinya

Ethiopia
Area: 424,934 sq mi
(1,100,574 sq km)
Population: 67,673,000
Capital: Addis Ababa
Language: Amharic

Kenya
Area: 228,861 sq mi
(592,747 sq km)
Population: 31,139,000
Capital: Nairobi
Languages: English, Kiswahili

Rwanda
Area: 10,169 sq mi
(26,338 sq km)
Population: 7,398,000
Capital: Kigali
Languages: French, Kinyarwanda, others

Burundi
Area: 10,747 sq mi
(27,834 sq km)
Population: 6,688,000
Capital: Bujumbura
Languages: French, Kirundi

Djibouti
Area: 8,958 sq mi
(23,200 sq km)
Population: 652,000
Capital: Djibouti
Languages: Arabic, French

Egypt
Area: 386,662 sq mi
(1,001,449 sq km)
Population: 71,244,000
Capital: Cairo
Language: Arabic

ROMANIA

SERBIA AND MONTENEGRO

BULGARIA

MACED.

GREECE

RUSSIA

GEORGIA

UKRAINE

BLACK SEA

TURKEY

SYRIA

IRAQ

LEBANON

CYPRUS

ISRAEL

JORDAN

MEDITERRANEAN SEA

OMAN

SAUDI ARABIA

RED SEA

Gulf of Aqaba

Port Said
Suez Canal
Sinai
Cairo
Suez
G. of Suez
oil
oil
oil

Alexandria
Tanta
El Gîza
El Faiyûm
El Minya
Asyût
Qattâra Depression
-436 ft
-133 m

EASTERN DESERT

WESTERN DESERT

LIBYAN DESERT

EGYPT

Nile
Thebes
Luxor
dates
1st Aswân
Aswân High Dam
Lake Nasser
2nd Cataract
3rd Cataract

Boundary claimed by Sudan
Treaty Boundary

NUBIAN DESERT

Port Sudan
dates
4th Cataract
5th Cataract
Merowe
Atbara

SAHARA

LIBYA

TROPIC OF CANCER

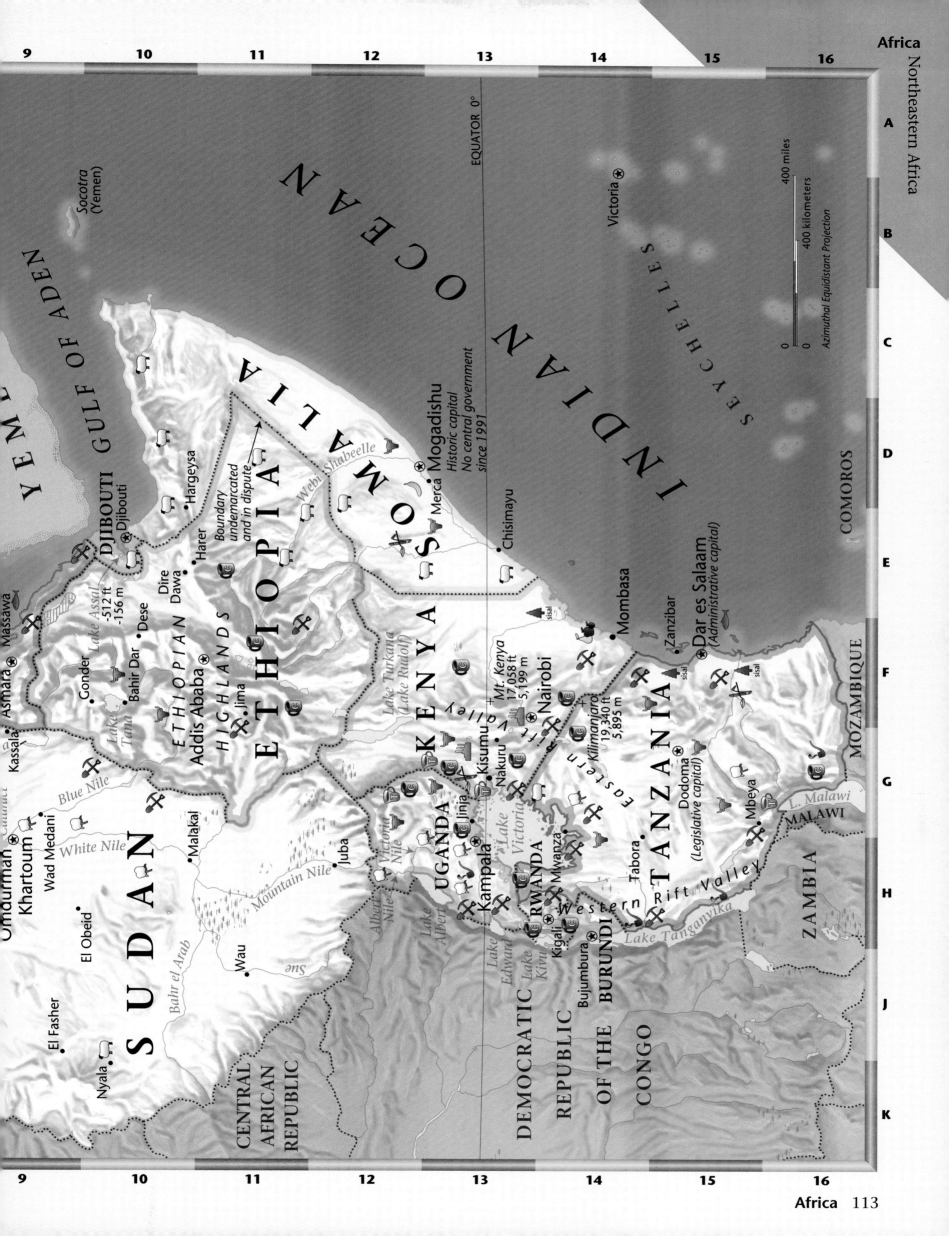

9 10 11 12 13 14 15 16

EQUATOR 0°

A

B

C

D

E

F

G

H

J

K

400 miles

400 kilometers

Azimuthal Equidistant Projection

INDIAN OCEAN

YEMEN

Socotra (Yemen)

GULF OF ADEN

Massawa

Asmara ⊛

Kassala

Gonder

Lake Tana

Bahir Dar

DJIBOUTI

Djibouti ⊛

Harer

Dire Dawa

Dese

ETHIOPIAN HIGHLANDS

Addis Ababa ⊛

Jima

ETHIOPIA

Hargeysa

Boundary undemarcated and in dispute

SOMALIA

Webi Shabeelle

Merca

Mogadishu
*Historic capital
No central government
since 1991*

Chisimayu

Lake Assal
-512 ft
-156 m

SUDAN

Omdurman

Khartoum

Wad Medani

Blue Nile

White Nile

El Obeid

El Fasher

Nyala

Malakal

Wau

Bahr el Arab

Sue

Mountain Nile

Juba

CENTRAL AFRICAN REPUBLIC

DEMOCRATIC REPUBLIC OF THE CONGO

KENYA

Lake Turkana
(Lake Rudolf)

Mt. Kenya
17,058 ft
5,199 m

Nairobi ⊛

Kisumu

Nakuru

Rift Valley

UGANDA

Victoria Nile

Kampala ⊛

Jinja

Lake Victoria

Mwanza

RWANDA

Kigali ⊛

BURUNDI

Bujumbura ⊛

Albert Nile

Lake Albert

Lake Edward

Lake Kivu

Western Rift Valley

Lake Tanganyika

TANZANIA

Kilimanjaro
19,340 ft
5,895 m

Eastern Rift Valley

Dodoma
(Legislative capital)

Tabora

Mbeya

Mombasa

Zanzibar

Dar es Salaam
(Administrative capital)

sisal

sisal

sisal

Victoria ⊛

SEYCHELLES

COMOROS

MOZAMBIQUE

L. Malawi

MALAWI

ZAMBIA

9 10 11 12 13 14 15 16

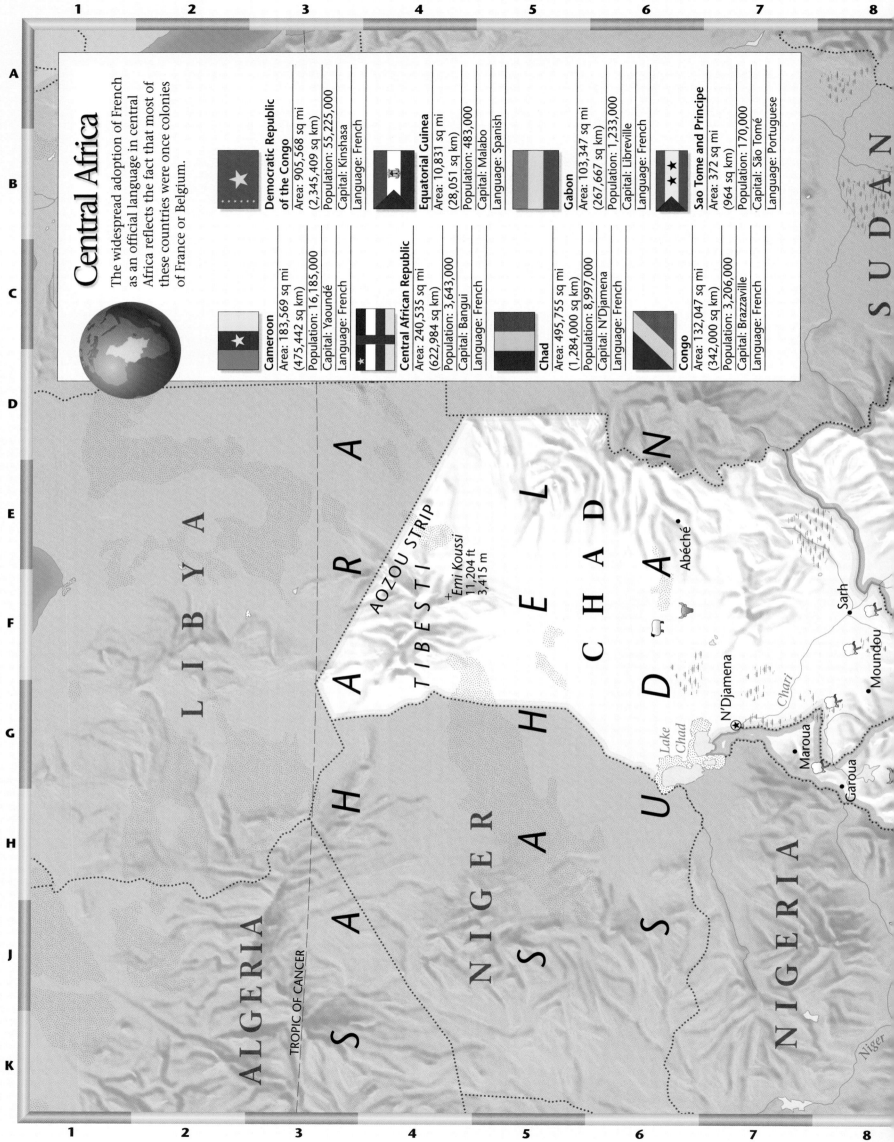

Central Africa

The widespread adoption of French as an official language in central Africa reflects the fact that most of these countries were once colonies of France or Belgium.

Democratic Republic of the Congo
Area: 905,568 sq mi
(2,345,409 sq km)
Population: 55,225,000
Capital: Kinshasa
Language: French

Equatorial Guinea
Area: 10,831 sq mi
(28,051 sq km)
Population: 483,000
Capital: Malabo
Language: Spanish

Gabon
Area: 103,347 sq mi
(267,667 sq km)
Population: 1,233,000
Capital: Libreville
Language: French

Sao Tome and Principe
Area: 372 sq mi
(964 sq km)
Population: 170,000
Capital: São Tomé
Language: Portuguese

Cameroon
Area: 183,569 sq mi
(475,442 sq km)
Population: 16,185,000
Capital: Yaoundé
Language: French

Central African Republic
Area: 240,535 sq mi
(622,984 sq km)
Population: 3,643,000
Capital: Bangui
Language: French

Chad
Area: 495,755 sq mi
(1,284,000 sq km)
Population: 8,997,000
Capital: N'Djamena
Language: French

Congo
Area: 132,047 sq mi
(342,000 sq km)
Population: 3,206,000
Capital: Brazzaville
Language: French

ALGERIA

LIBYA

SUDAN

S A H A R A

AOZOU STRIP

TIBESTI

+Emi Koussi
11,204 ft
3,415 m

C H A D

Abéché

Sarh

Moundou

Chari

N'Djamena

Lake
Chad

Maroua

Garoua

S A H E L

N I G E R

S U D A N

NIGERIA

TROPIC OF CANCER

Niger

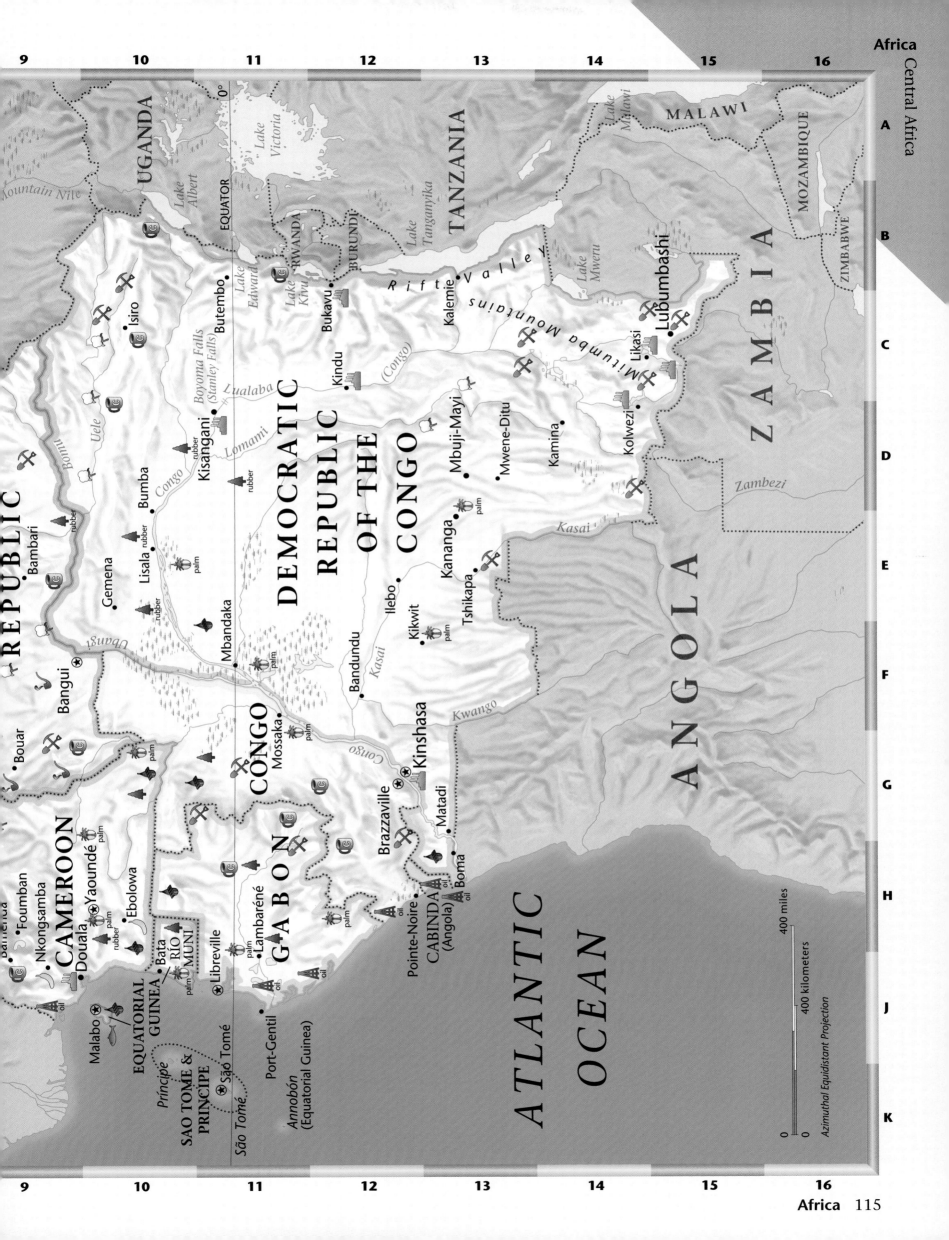

9 10 11 12 13 14 15 16

MALAWI

MOZAMBIQUE

ZIMBABWE

UGANDA

Lake Victoria

EQUATOR 0°

Mountain Nile

Lake Albert

TANZANIA

Lake Tanganyika

Lake Malawi

ZAMBIA

Lake Mweru

RWANDA

BURUNDI

Lake Edward

Lake Kivu

Bukavu

Kalemie

Rift Valley

Lubumbashi

Likasi

Mitumba Mountains

Kolwezi

Isiro

Butembo

Boyoma Falls
(Stanley Falls)

Lualaba

Kindu

(Congo)

Lomami

Kisangani

Congo

rubber

rubber

Bumba

DEMOCRATIC

REPUBLIC

OF THE

CONGO

Mbuji-Mayi

Mwene-Ditu

Kamina

Bambari

REPUBLIC

Gemena

Lisala rubber

rubber

Mbandaka

Kananga

palm

Kasai

Ilebo

Kikwit

Tshikapa

ANGOLA

Zambezi

Kasai

Bandundu

Kasai

Bangui

rubber

Bouar

CONGO

Mossaka palm

Ubangi

Brazzaville

Kinshasa

Kwango

Congo

Matadi

Boma

Pointe-Noire

CABINDA
(Angola) oil

ATLANTIC

OCEAN

CAMEROON

Foumban

Nkongsamba

Douala Yaoundé palm

Ebolowa

palm

GABON

Lambaréné

palm

RÍO

MUNI

Bata

Libreville

Port-Gentil

Annobón
(Equatorial Guinea)

EQUATORIAL
GUINEA

Malabo

Príncipe

SAO TOME &
PRINCIPE

São Tomé

São Tomé

oil

oil

400 miles

400 kilometers

Azimuthal Equidistant Projection

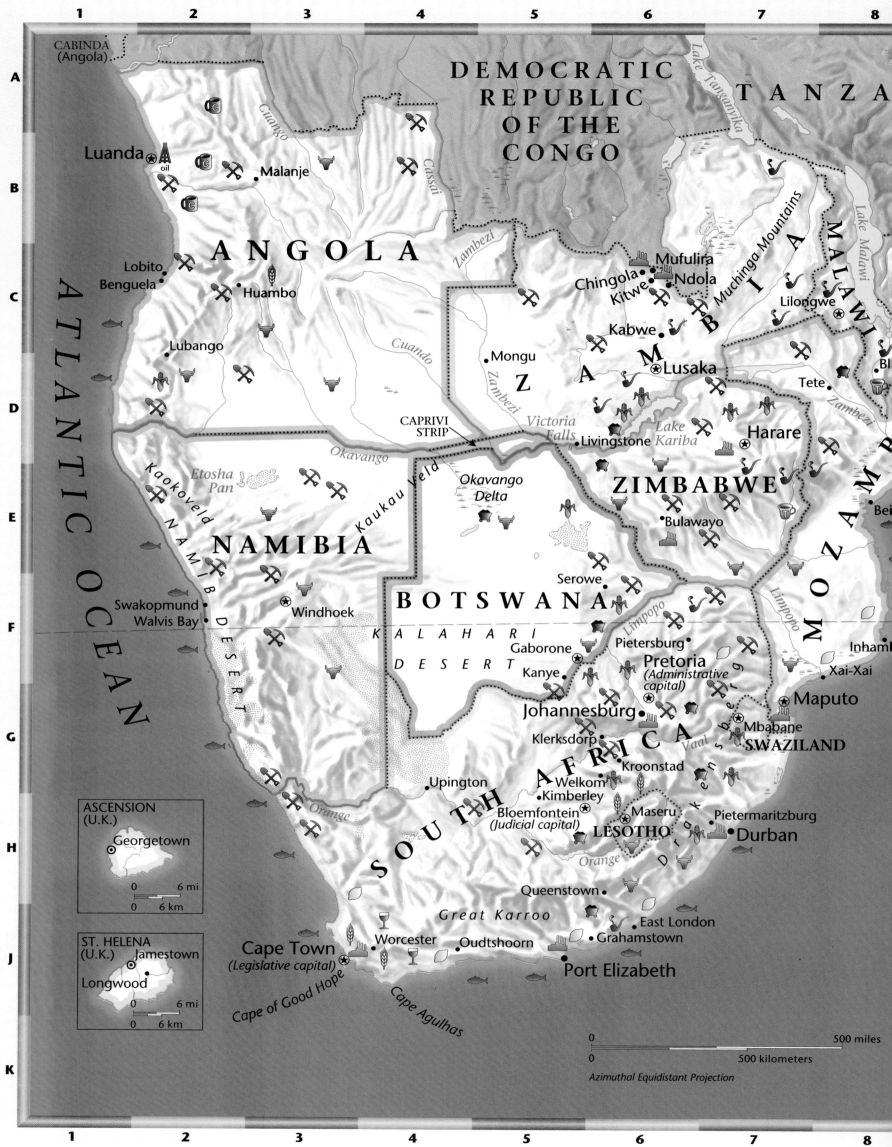

CABINDA
(Angola)

ATLANTIC OCEAN

Luanda
oil
Malanje

Lobito
Benguela
Huambo

Lubango

ANGOLA

Cuango

Cassai

Zambezi

Cuando

DEMOCRATIC REPUBLIC OF THE CONGO

TANZA

Lake Tanganyika

Mufulira
Chingola
Kitwe
Ndola

Kabwe

Z A M B I A

Muchinga Mountains

Lilongwe

M A L A W I

Lake Malawi

Bl

Mongu

Lusaka

Tete

Z A M

CAPRIVI STRIP

Okavango

Victoria Falls

Livingstone

Lake Kariba

Harare

Zambezi

M O Z A M B I

Etosha Pan

Kaokoveld

Kaukau Veld

Okavango Delta

ZIMBABWE

Bulawayo

Bei

NAMIBIA

NAMIB DESERT

Serowe

Limpopo

Swakopmund
Walvis Bay
Windhoek

BOTSWANA

K A L A H A R I   D E S E R T

Gaborone
Kanye

Pietersburg

Pretoria
(Administrative capital)

Limpopo

Xai-Xai

Maputo

Johannesburg

Klerksdorp

S O U T H

A F R I C A

Vaal

Mbabane

SWAZILAND

Upington

Welkom
Kimberley

Kroonstad

Bloemfontein
(Judicial capital)

Maseru

LESOTHO

Pietermaritzburg

Durban

Orange

Drakensberg

Orange

ASCENSION (U.K.)

⊙ Georgetown

0 ____ 6 mi
0 ____ 6 km

ST. HELENA (U.K.) Jamestown

Longwood

0 ____ 6 mi
0 ____ 6 km

Queenstown

Great Karroo

East London

Worcester
Oudtshoorn
Grahamstown

Cape Town
(Legislative capital)

Cape of Good Hope

Cape Agulhas

Port Elizabeth

0 _____ 500 miles
0 _____ 500 kilometers

Azimuthal Equidistant Projection

9 10 11 12 13 14 15 16

INDIAN OCEAN

SEYCHELLES

Îles Glorieuses
(France)

COMOROS
Moroni

Cap d'Ambre
• Antsiranana

Mayotte
(Fr.)

• Pemba

+ *Maromokotro*
9,436 ft
2,876 m

• Moçambique

• Nampula   Mahajanga •

Juan de Nova
(Fr.)

MOZAMBIQUE CHANNEL

• Toamasina

☆ Antananarivo

• Antsirabe

Bassas da India
(France)

• Fianarantsoa

Île Europa
(France)

Toliara •

TROPIC OF CAPRICORN

MADAGASCAR

Cap Ste. Marie

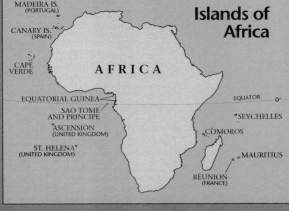

MADEIRA IS.
(PORTUGAL)

CANARY IS.
(SPAIN)

CAPE
VERDE

AFRICA

EQUATORIAL GUINEA

SAO TOME
AND PRINCIPE

ASCENSION
(UNITED KINGDOM)

ST. HELENA
(UNITED KINGDOM)

**Islands of
Africa**

EQUATOR   0°

• SEYCHELLES

COMOROS

MAURITIUS

RÉUNION
(FRANCE)

Southern
Africa

Rich in minerals and natural
beauty, the countries of
southern Africa range in size
from Angola, on the Atlantic
coast, to the Seychelles,
a tiny country in the
Indian Ocean.

Angola
Area: 481,354 sq mi
(1,246,700 sq km)
Population: 12,714,000
Capital: Luanda
Language: Portuguese

Botswana
Area: 231,805 sq mi
(600,372 sq km)
Population: 1,591,000
Capital: Gaborone
Language: English

Comoros
Area: 719 sq mi
(1,862 sq km)
Population: 614,000
Capital: Moroni
Languages: Arabic, French

Lesotho
Area: 11,720 sq mi
(30,355 sq km)
Population: 2,208,000
Capital: Maseru
Language: English

Madagascar
Area: 226,658 sq mi
(587,041 sq km)
Population: 16,913,000
Capital: Antananarivo
Language: French

Malawi
Area: 45,747 sq mi
(118,484 sq km)
Population: 10,917,000
Capital: Lilongwe
Languages: English, Chichewa

Mauritius
Area: 788 sq mi
(2,040 sq km)
Population: 1,213,000
Capital: Port Louis
Language: English

Mozambique
Area: 308,642 sq mi
(799,380 sq km)
Population: 19,608,000
Capital: Maputo
Language: Portuguese

Namibia
Area: 318,261 sq mi
(824,292 sq km)
Population: 1,821,000
Capital: Windhoek
Language: English

Seychelles
Area: 175 sq mi
(453 sq km)
Population: 85,000
Capital: Victoria
Languages: English, French

South Africa
Area: 471,445 sq mi
(1,221,037 sq km)
Population: 43,648,000
Capitals: Bloemfontein,
Cape Town, Pretoria,
Languages: Afrikaans,
English, others

Swaziland
Area: 6,704 sq mi
(17,364 sq km)
Population: 1,124,000
Capital: Mbabane
Languages: English, siSwati

Zambia
Area: 290,586 sq mi
(752,614 sq km)
Population: 9,959,000
Capital: Lusaka
Language: English

Zimbabwe
Area: 150,804 sq mi
(390,580 sq km)
Population: 12,341,000
Capital: Harare
Language: English

Ascunsion (United Kingdom)

Réunion (France)

St. Helena (United Kingdom)

9 10 11 12 13 14 15 16

Asia

From a great distance, the Zagros Mountains of Iran, in southwestern Asia, look like mere ripples of mud in a drying puddle. Yet the snowcapped northern peaks (bottom), reach 14,000 feet (4,267 meters). (In this image, south is at the top.) Land jutting in at the right pinches the Persian Gulf in two, forming the narrow Strait of Hormuz. Ships that pass through this strait carry much of the world's oil, pumped from under the sands around the Persian Gulf. The shallow waters north of the strait (far right) make up the Persian Gulf. To the south (top) lie the Gulf of Oman and the Arabian Sea. The world's largest continent, Asia occupies one-third of Earth's total landmass.

A Muslim prayer tower marks the skyline of Dubai, a deepwater port on the Persian Gulf. A trading center, Dubai is a port city in the United Arab Emirates, also known as the U.A.E.

CONNECTION: *You can find the Strait of Hormuz and Dubai on the maps on pages 120–121 and 134–135.*

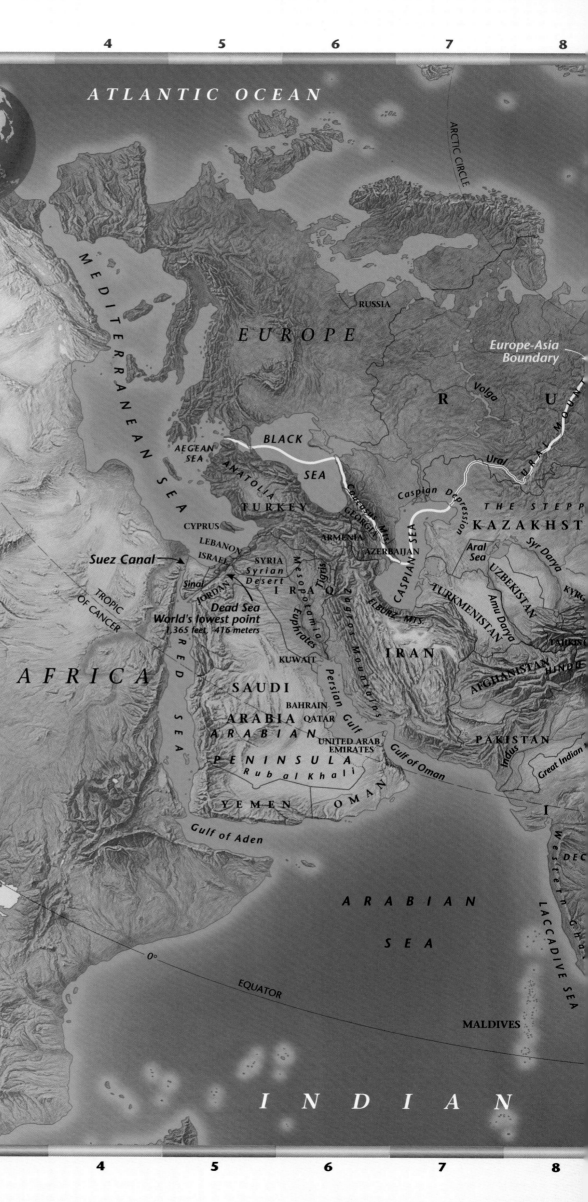

Asia
Land on a Grand Scale

Asia ranks as the world's biggest continent, and almost everything here is on a grand scale. It boasts not just Earth's highest peak, but the ten highest, all in the colossal Himalaya. On Asia's Arabian Peninsula, in the southwest, lies the lowest place on Earth's surface—the Dead Sea, too salty to support life. The world's largest expanse of tundra stretches across northern Asia. Southeast Asia offers a contrast: tropical forests drenched by monsoon rains. Rainwater and snowmelt feed into major rivers such as the Yangtze (Chang) and the Yellow (Huang).

The Land

Area
17,212,000 sq mi
(44,579,000 sq km)

Highest mountain
Everest: 29,035 ft (8,850 m)

Lowest point
Dead Sea: 1,365 ft (416 m)
below sea level

Longest river
Yangtze (Chang): 3,964 mi
(6,380 km)

Largest lake
Baikal: 12,200 sq mi
(31,500 sq km)

Largest island
Borneo: 280,100 sq mi
(725,100 sq km)

9   10   11   12   13   14   15   16

NORTH AMERICA

NORTH AMERICA

CHUKCHI
SEA

Bering Strait

Chukchi
Peninsula

BERING
SEA

ARCTIC OCEAN

Wrangel Island

EAST
SIBERIAN
SEA

ALEUTIAN ISLANDS

NEW SIBERIAN
ISLANDS

NORTH
LAND

LAPTEV
SEA

Commander
Islands

KAMCHATKA

KARA
SEA

Taymyr Peninsula

Cherskiy Range

Kolyma

Kolyma Range

Verkhoyansk Range

KAMCHATKA
PENINSULA

Gulf
of Ob

CENTRAL

SIBERIAN
PLATEAU

Lena

Aldan

SEA OF
OKHOTSK

600 miles

900 kilometers

Two-Point Equidistant Projection

Ob

SIBERIA

Yenisey   Angara

Lena

Amur

Sakhalin

KURIL ISLANDS

Lake
Baikal

Yablonovyy Range

Amur

Sikhote Alin Range

Ob

Yenisey

ALTAI MOUNTAINS

MONGOLIA   GOBI

Greater Khingan Range

Manchurian Plain

Hokkaido

J A P A N

NAMPO SHOTO

TROPIC
OF CANCER

khash

NORTH
KOREA

SEA OF
JAPAN
(EAST SEA)

Honshu

SHAN

SOUTH
KOREA

Shikoku

Kyushu

TAKLIMAKAN
DESERT

Yellow

Yellow

YELLOW
SEA

NLUN MOUNTAINS

Qaidam
Basin

C H I N A

North China plain

Yellow

EAST
CHINA
SEA

RYUKYU ISLANDS

MARIANA
ISLANDS

PLATEAU OF TIBET   Mekong

Yangtze

Yangtze

Sichuan
Basin

Yangtze

PACIFIC OCEAN

Mt. Everest
World's highest point
29,035 feet   8,850 meters

Salween

+ Gongga Shan
24,790 feet
7,556 meters

PHILIPPINE
SEA

NEPAL

BHUTAN

Taiwan

I N D I A

BANGLADESH

Ganges   Brahmaputra

SOUTH

CAROLINE ISLANDS

TEAU

n Ghats

MYANMAR
(BURMA)

Salween

Hainan

CHINA

Luzon

PHILIPPINE ISLANDS

BAY OF

Mekong

L A O S

VIETNAM

PHILIPPINES

ANDAMAN ISLANDS

THAILAND

CAMBODIA

Mindanao

EQUATOR   0°

BENGAL

NICOBAR
ISLANDS

MALAY PENINSULA

Gulf of
Thailand

SEA

SULU SEA

CELEBES
SEA

MOLUCCA

NEW GUINEA

SRI
LANKA

ANDAMAN SEA

BRUNEI

MALAYSIA

MALAYSIA

SINGAPORE

Borneo

Celebes

BANDA SEA

ARAFURA SEA

S U M A T R A

I N D O N E S I A

GREATER
SUNDA ISLANDS

JAVA SEA

Java

EAST TIMOR

Timor

TIMOR SEA

LESSER SUNDA ISLANDS

AUSTRALIA

CEAN

A   B   C   D   E   F   G   H   J   K

9   10   11   12   13   14   15   16

Asia
Ancient and Modern

Biggest, highest, most populous; to the superlatives Asia can boast of, add another: oldest culturally. Archaeologists believe that the world's first city-based civilization arose in the wide plain between the Tigris and Euphrates Rivers, in what is now Iraq, 55 centuries ago. Here, people learned how to bring water to their lands and plant grain. Cities grew up. Over the centuries, civilizations arose in other river valleys across Asia. These ancient cultures gave us writing, the wheel, astronomy, and mechanical printing, as well as all of the world's major religions.

In many parts of Asia—especially remote areas—people still live lives very similar to those of their ancestors. They depend on herding and traditional farming methods. They practice age-old crafts to make tools, clothes, and basic necessities. Other parts of Asia have entered the modern world in a big way. Huge cities have grown up, with the pollution and crowding that so often come with industrialization. Asian governments face the challenge the whole world faces—how to provide for their people and still protect the environment.

▲ **THE TIGER'S** *terrifying pounce can't protect it from the double threat it faces: illegal hunting, or poaching, and loss of habitat. Tigers live in the wild only in Asia.*

◄ **HANDLING** *her test tubes with care, a researcher in South Korea helps to develop new medicines.*

▶ **SKYSCRAPERS** *loom behind Singapore's deep harbor. This small country off the tip of the Malay Peninsula provides a major port for ships traveling between the Indian and Pacific Oceans.*

▲ **BUDDHIST MONKS** *climb the ancient steps of The Bayon, a temple in Angkor Thom, a Cambodian city built in about the year 1200. King Jayavarman VII, feeling that Hindu gods had not protected him, dedicated the new city to the Buddha instead.*

▶ **EAGER TO LEARN,** *an Afghan girl raises her hand. For more than five years, Afghanistan's Taliban government kept girls out of schools. When the Taliban fell in 2001, female students were allowed to return, although still only three out of ten school-children are girls.*

▼ **STUDENTS** *attend a class taught in Hebrew at a Jewish school in Israel. Arab students attend separate schools where classes are taught in Arabic—Israel's other official language.*

▶ **MEMBERS OF EARTH'S** *most populous nation—China—commute on the country's most popular vehicle: the bicycle.*

▶ **A PERFECT CONE** *framed by cherry blossoms, Mount Fuji is sacred to followers of Shinto, a religion that has its origins in Japan. The volcanic mountain is the highest in Japan.*

▼ **ALL HER EGGS** *in two baskets, a woman in China shoulders a delicate burden. Most Asians make a living by farming or herding.*

▼ **EAST AND WEST MEET** *in Istanbul, Turkey, which straddles the Bosporus. It is the only major world city located on two continents—Europe and Asia. Although most of its people are Muslims, Turkey's laws, education, and politics show a strong European influence.*

▶ **A TOWERING** *gold-and-bronze Buddha fills a temple in Nara, a former capital of Japan. Buddhism arose in India and spread across much of Asia. It is practiced by millions today.*

▶ **DASHING THROUGH THE SNOW,** *a pair of reindeer pull a sled across the tundra of Siberia, in Russia. Reindeer play a central role in the lives of many people who are native to Russia's Arctic regions. They provide food, shelter, clothing, and transportation.*

Asia

Home to Half the World

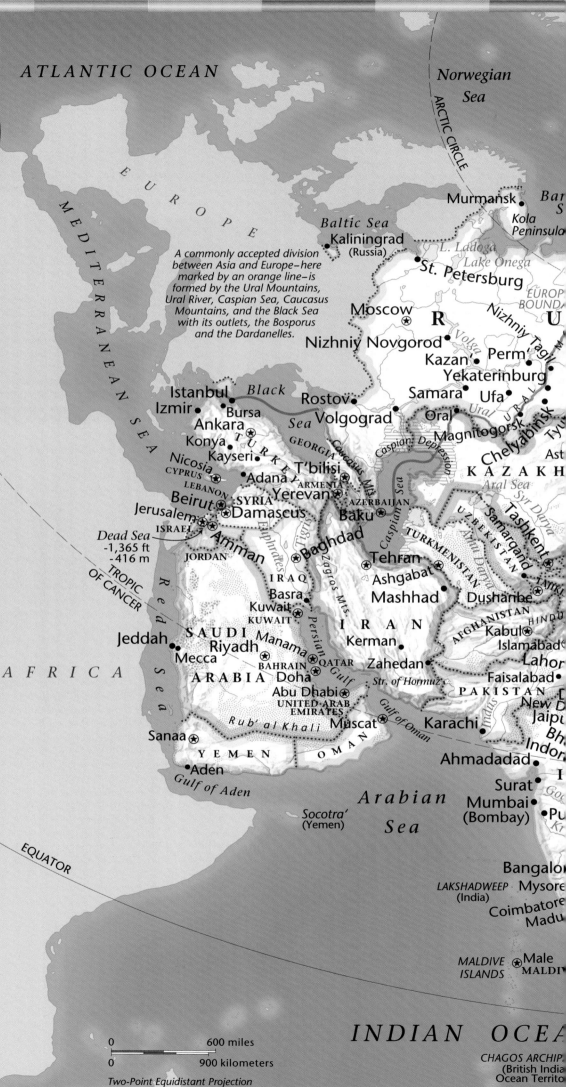

Forty-six countries make up Asia. China and India contain almost two-thirds of the continent's population. Because so much of Asia is uninhabitable—too high, too dry, or too cold—a majority of the population lives in coastal areas and river valleys. Although most Asians make their living farming or fishing, a growing number are finding work in factories and service industries. Japan has been Asia's leader in developing a modern industrialized economy. Many other countries, especially along the Pacific Rim, are now following Japan's example.

The People

Population
3,765,711,000

Largest metropolitan area
Tokyo, Japan:
Pop. 26,546,000

Largest country
China: 3,705,820 sq mi
(9,598,032 sq km)

Most densely populated country
Singapore: 17,746 people
per sq mi

Economy
Farming: rice, wheat
Industry: petroleum, electronics

Life expectancy
67 years

A commonly accepted division between Asia and Europe–here marked by an orange line–is formed by the Ural Mountains, Ural River, Caspian Sea, Caucasus Mountains, and the Black Sea with its outlets, the Bosporus and the Dardanelles.

ATLANTIC OCEAN

Norwegian Sea

ARCTIC CIRCLE

Murmansk

Kola Peninsula

E U R O P E

Baltic Sea

Kaliningrad (Russia)

L. Ladoga

Lake Onega

St. Petersburg

EUROPE BOUNDA

M E D I T E R R A N E A N   S E A

Moscow

Nizhniy Tagil

R U

Nizhniy Novgorod

Volga

Perm

Kazan

Yekaterinburg

Istanbul

Black

Rostov

Samara

Ufa

Izmir

Bursa

Volgograd

Oral

Magnitogorsk

URAL

Ankara

Sea

Tyu

Konya

T U R K E Y

GEORGIA

Caucasus Mts.

Caspian Depression

Chelyabinsk

Kayseri

Ast

Nicosia

T'bilisi

Aral Sea

K A Z A K H

CYPRUS

Adana

ARMENIA

Caspian Sea

Syr Darya

LEBANON

Yerevan

AZERBAIJAN

Baku

UZBEKISTAN

Tashkent

Beirut

SYRIA

Damascus

TURKMENISTAN

Samarqand

Jerusalem

Amman

Baghdad

Tehran

TAJIK

ISRAEL

Euphrates

Tigris

Ashgabat

Dushanbe

Dead Sea
-1,365 ft
-416 m

JORDAN

IRAQ

Zagros Mts.

Mashhad

AFGHANISTAN

HINDU

TROPIC OF CANCER

Basra

Kerman

Kabul

Kuwait

I R A N

Islamabad

KUWAIT

Persian Gulf

Lahor

Jeddah

SAUDI

Manama

Zahedan

Faisalabad

Mecca

Riyadh

BAHRAIN

QATAR

Str. of Hormuz

PAKISTAN

ARABIA

Doha

Abu Dhabi

Gulf

New D

UNITED ARAB EMIRATES

Jaipu

A F R I C A

Rub' al Khali

Muscat

Gulf of Oman

Karachi

Bh

Red Sea

OMAN

Indus

Sanaa

Indor

Y E M E N

Ahmadadad

Aden

Surat

Gulf of Aden

Mumbai (Bombay)

Goa

Socotra' (Yemen)

A r a b i a n

S e a

0°

EQUATOR

Bangalor

LAKSHADWEEP (India)

Mysore

Coimbatore

Madu

MALDIVE ISLANDS

Male MALDIV

0   600 miles

INDIAN OCEA

0   900 kilometers

CHAGOS ARCHIP.
(British India
Ocean Territo

Two-Point Equidistant Projection

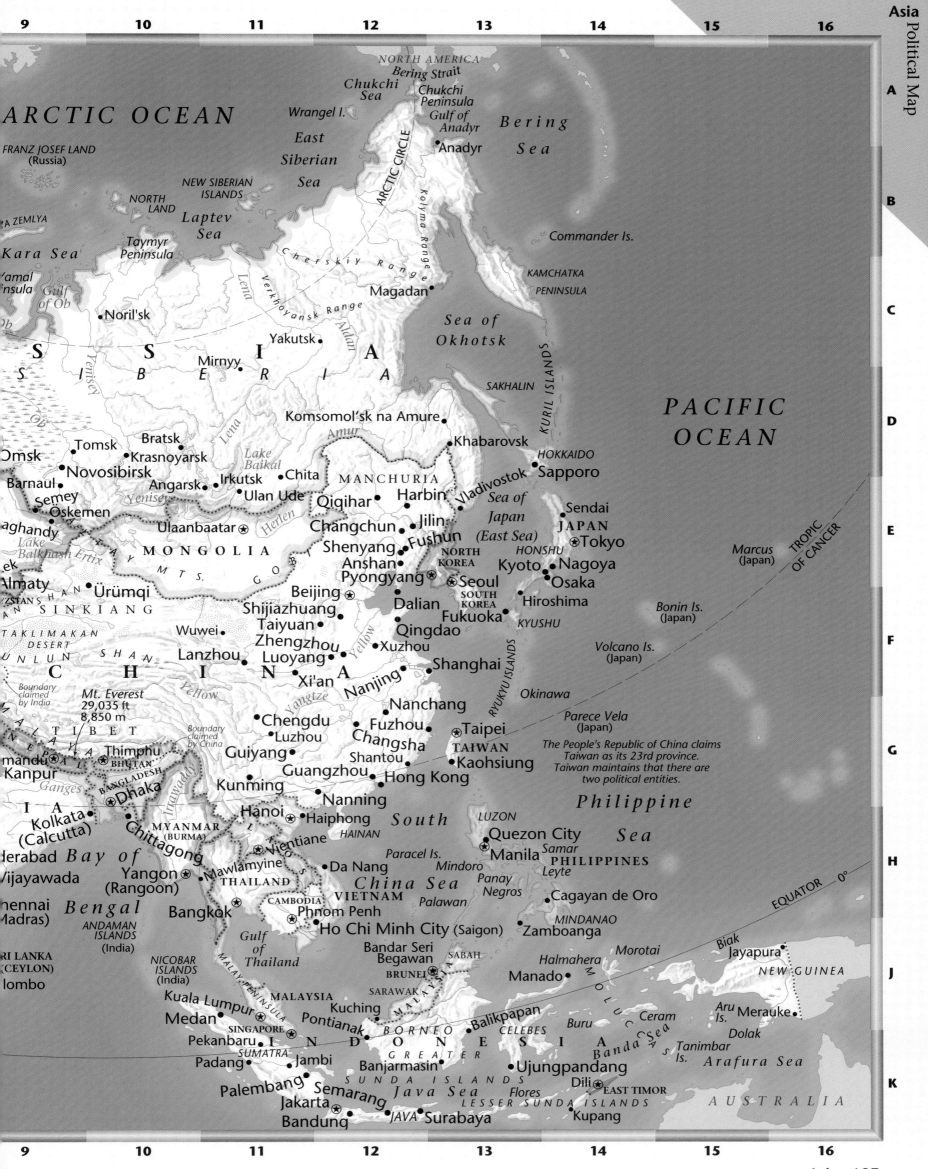

9   10   11   12   13   14   15   16

ARCTIC OCEAN

NORTH AMERICA
Bering Strait
Chukchi Sea
Wrangel I.
FRANZ JOSEF LAND
(Russia)
Chukchi Peninsula
Gulf of Anadyr
Bering Sea

A

A ZEMLYA
East Siberian Sea
Anadyr

B

Kara Sea
NORTH LAND
NEW SIBERIAN ISLANDS
ARCTIC CIRCLE
Commander Is.

Yamal nsula
Gulf of Ob
Laptev Sea
Taymyr Peninsula
Cherskiy Range
Kolyma Range
KAMCHATKA PENINSULA

C

Ob
Noril'sk
Yenisey
Yakutsk
Aldan
Magadan
Sea of Okhotsk

D

Omsk
Tomsk
Bratsk
Lake Baikal
Mirnyy
Lena
Komsomol'sk na Amure
SAKHALIN
KURIL ISLANDS
PACIFIC OCEAN

Novosibirsk
Krasnoyarsk
Amur
Khabarovsk
HOKKAIDO

Barnaul
Angarsk
Irkutsk
Chita
MANCHURIA
Vladivostok
Sapporo

Semey
Yenisey
Ulan Ude
Qiqihar
Harbin
Sea of Japan (East Sea)
Sendai
JAPAN

E

Oskemen
Herlen
Ulaanbaatar
Changchun
Jilin
HONSHU
Tokyo
Marcus (Japan)
TROPIC OF CANCER

aghandy
Lake Balkhash
Ertix
MONGOLIA
MTS.
Shenyang
Fushun
NORTH KOREA
Kyoto
Nagoya

ek
Almaty
Ürümqi
GOBI
Anshan
Pyongyang
Seoul
Osaka

ZSTAN'S
SHAN
SINKIANG
Beijing
Dalian
SOUTH KOREA
Hiroshima

F

SHAN
TAKLIMAKAN DESERT
Shijiazhuang
Fukuoka
KYUSHU
Bonin Is. (Japan)

UNLUN
SHAN
Wuwei
Taiyuan
Qingdao
Volcano Is. (Japan)

Lanzhou
Zhengzhou
Yellow
Xuzhou

CHINA
Luoyang
Shanghai

G

Boundary claimed by India
Mt. Everest 29,035 ft 8,850 m
Xi'an
Nanjing
Yangtze
RYUKYU ISLANDS
Okinawa

TIBET
Boundary claimed by China
Chengdu
Fuzhou
Nanchang
Parece Vela (Japan)

mandu
Thimphu
Luzhou
Changsha
Taipei
The People's Republic of China claims Taiwan as its 23rd province. Taiwan maintains that there are two political entities.

Kanpur
BHUTAN
Guiyang
Shantou
TAIWAN
Kaohsiung

Ganges
BANGLADESH
Kunming
Guangzhou
Hong Kong

I A
Kolkata (Calcutta)
Dhaka
Nanning
Philippine Sea

H

erabad
Bay of
Chittagong
Hanoi
Haiphong
South
LUZON
Quezon City

Vijayawada
Yangon (Rangoon)
MYANMAR (BURMA)
Irrawaddy
Vientiane
HAINAN
Paracel Is.
Manila
Samar
PHILIPPINES
Leyte

hennai (Madras)
Bengal
Mawlamyine
THAILAND
Da Nang
Mindoro
Panay
Negros
Cagayan de Oro
EQUATOR 0°

LANKA (CEYLON)
CAMBODIA
VIETNAM
China Sea
Palawan
MINDANAO

ombo
Bangkok
Phnom Penh
Ho Chi Minh City (Saigon)
Zamboanga

ANDAMAN ISLANDS (India)
Gulf of Thailand
Bandar Seri Begawan
SABAH
Morotai
Biak
Jayapura

J

NICOBAR ISLANDS (India)
BRUNEI
Halmahera
NEW GUINEA

Kuala Lumpur
MALAY PENINSULA
MALAYSIA
Kuching
SARAWAK
Buru
Ceram
Aru Is.
Merauke

Medan
Pontianak
BORNEO
Balikpapan
CELEBES
Dolak

SINGAPORE
INDONESIA
Tanimbar Is.
Arafura Sea

Pekanbaru
SUMATRA
GREATER
Banjarmasin
Ujungpandang
Banda Sea

K

Padang
Jambi
SUNDA ISLANDS
Dili
Kupang
AUSTRALIA

Palembang
Semarang
Java Sea
Flores
EAST TIMOR

Jakarta
Bandung
JAVA
Surabaya
LESSER SUNDA ISLANDS
Kupang

9   10   11   12   13   14   15   16

Central Asia

The countries of central Asia are marked by mountains and steppes. They also include some of Asia's biggest deserts, including the Gobi and the Kara Kum.

Kyrgyzstan
Area: 76,834 sq mi
(198,999 sq km)
Population: 4,994,000
Capital: Bishkek
Languages: Kirghiz, Russian

Tajikistan
Area: 55,213 sq mi
(143,001 sq km)
Population: 6,326,000
Capital: Dushanbe
Language: Tajik

Uzbekistan
Area: 172,588 sq mi
(447,001 sq km)
Population: 25,400,000
Capital: Tashkent
Language: Uzbek

Kazakhstan
Area: 1,049,039 sq mi
(2,716,998 sq km)
Population: 14,809,000
Capital: Astana
Languages: Kazakh, Russian

Mongolia
Area: 604,250 sq mi
(1,565,000 sq km)
Population: 2,400,000
Capital: Ulaanbaatar
Language: Khalkha Mongolian

Turkmenistan
Area: 188,418 sq mi
(488,000 sq km)
Population: 5,567,000
Capital: Ashgabat
Language: Turkmen

Asian Russia
Russia sprawls across the northern part of two continents: Europe and Asia. The Ural Mountains divide European Russia from Asian Russia. Statistics for Russia are found on page 99 in the Europe section.

CZECH REP.
POLAND
SLOVAKIA
HUNG.
ROMANIA
MOLDOVA
BELARUS
UKRAINE
BULG.
FINLAND
ESTONIA
LITHUANIA
LATVIA
RUSSIA
BLACK SEA
GEORGIA
TURKEY
ARMENIA
AZERB.
AZERBAIJAN
SYRIA
IRAQ
SAUDI ARABIA
KUWAIT
IRAN
AFGHANISTAN
PAK.

Moscow
Volga
EUROPE-ASIA BOUNDARY
Caspian Depression
Ural
Oral
Atyrau oil
CASPIAN SEA
oil
oil
TURKMENISTAN
Kara Kum
Ashgabat
Mary gas
gas
Bukhara
Samarqand
UZBEKISTAN
Kyzyl Kum
Syr Darya
Amu Darya
Tashkent
Namangan
Dushanbe gas
TAJIKISTAN
Communism Peak 24,590 ft 7,495 m

BARENTS SEA
NOVAYA ZEMLYA
KARA SEA
Yamal Peninsula gas
Gulf of Ob
Nor
gas
gas
gas
Ob
R U S S I A
URAL MOUNTAINS
Nizhniy Tagil
Yekaterinburg
Chelyabinsk
Magnitogorsk
Surgut
oil
WEST
SIBERIAN
PLAIN
Tyumen'
Kurgan
Petropavl
Kökshetau
Omsk
Novosibirsk
Kemerovo
Tom
Prokop'yevsk
Barnaul
Novokuznetsk
THE STEPPES
Aqtöbe
Astana
Pavlodar
Rubtsovsk
Semey
Öskemen
ARAL SEA
Qaraghandy
KAZAKHSTAN
Lake Balkhash
Taldyqorghan
Shymkent
Taraz
Bishkek
Almaty
KYRGYZSTAN
TIAN SHAN
Victory Peak 24,406 ft 7,439 m

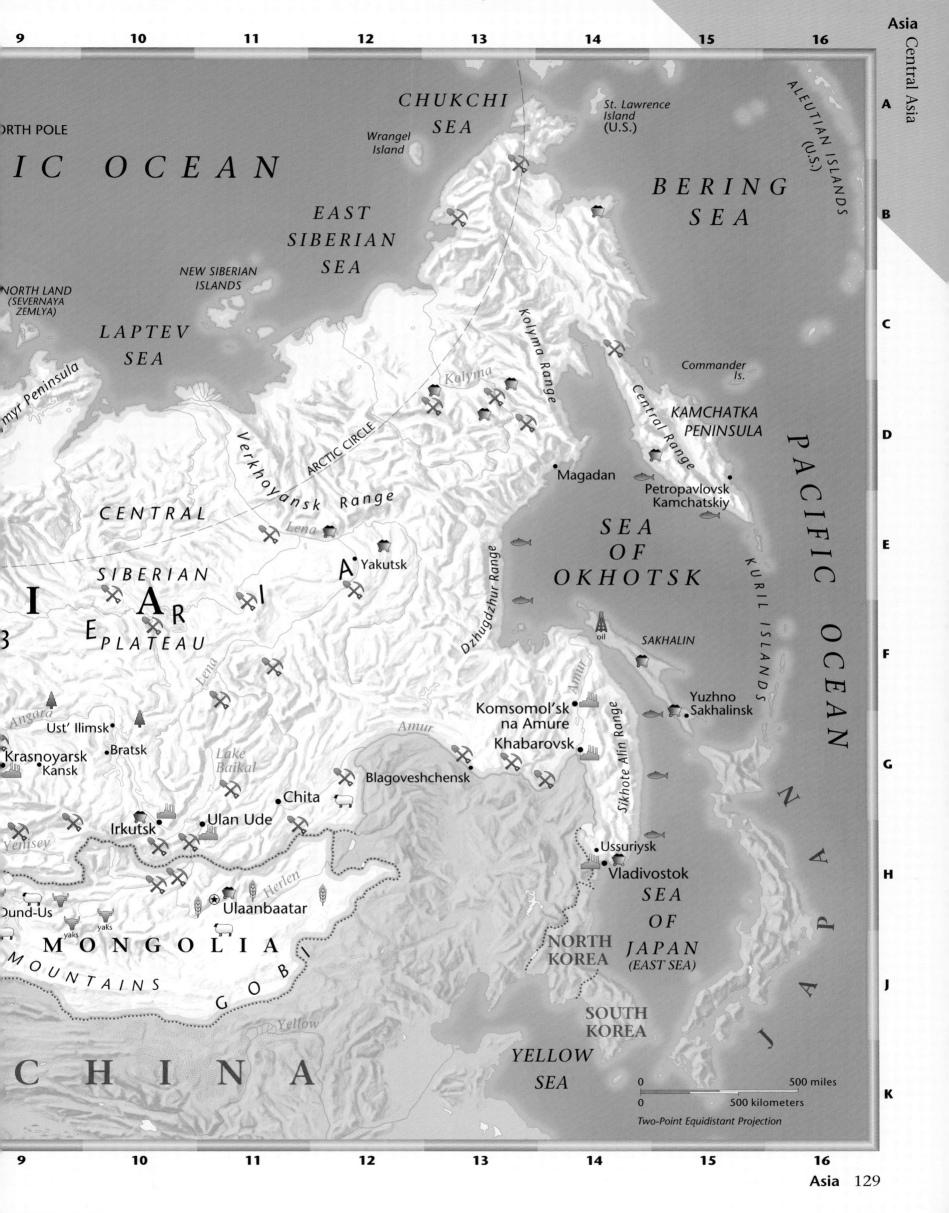

NORTH POLE

ARCTIC OCEAN

CHUKCHI SEA

Wrangel Island

EAST SIBERIAN SEA

NEW SIBERIAN ISLANDS

St. Lawrence Island (U.S.)

ALEUTIAN ISLANDS (U.S.)

BERING SEA

NORTH LAND (SEVERNAYA ZEMLYA)

LAPTEV SEA

Taimyr Peninsula

Kolyma

Kolyma Range

Commander Is.

KAMCHATKA PENINSULA

Central Range

PACIFIC OCEAN

Verkhoyansk Range

ARCTIC CIRCLE

Lena

Magadan

Petropavlovsk Kamchatskiy

SEA OF OKHOTSK

CENTRAL

SIBERIAN

PLATEAU

A R E A

Yakutsk

Dzhugdzhur Range

oil

SAKHALIN

KURIL ISLANDS

Lena

Angara

Ust' Ilimsk

Bratsk

Krasnoyarsk

Kansk

Amur

Amur

Komsomol'sk na Amure

Khabarovsk

Sikhote Alin Range

Yuzhno Sakhalinsk

Yenisey

Lake Baikal

Irkutsk

Ulan Ude

Chita

Blagoveshchensk

Ussuriysk

Vladivostok

SEA OF JAPAN (EAST SEA)

J A P A N

Herlen

Dund-Us

yaks

yaks

★ Ulaanbaatar

M O N G O L I A

M O U N T A I N S

G O B I

Yellow

NORTH KOREA

SOUTH KOREA

YELLOW SEA

C H I N A

0   500 miles

0   500 kilometers

Two-Point Equidistant Projection

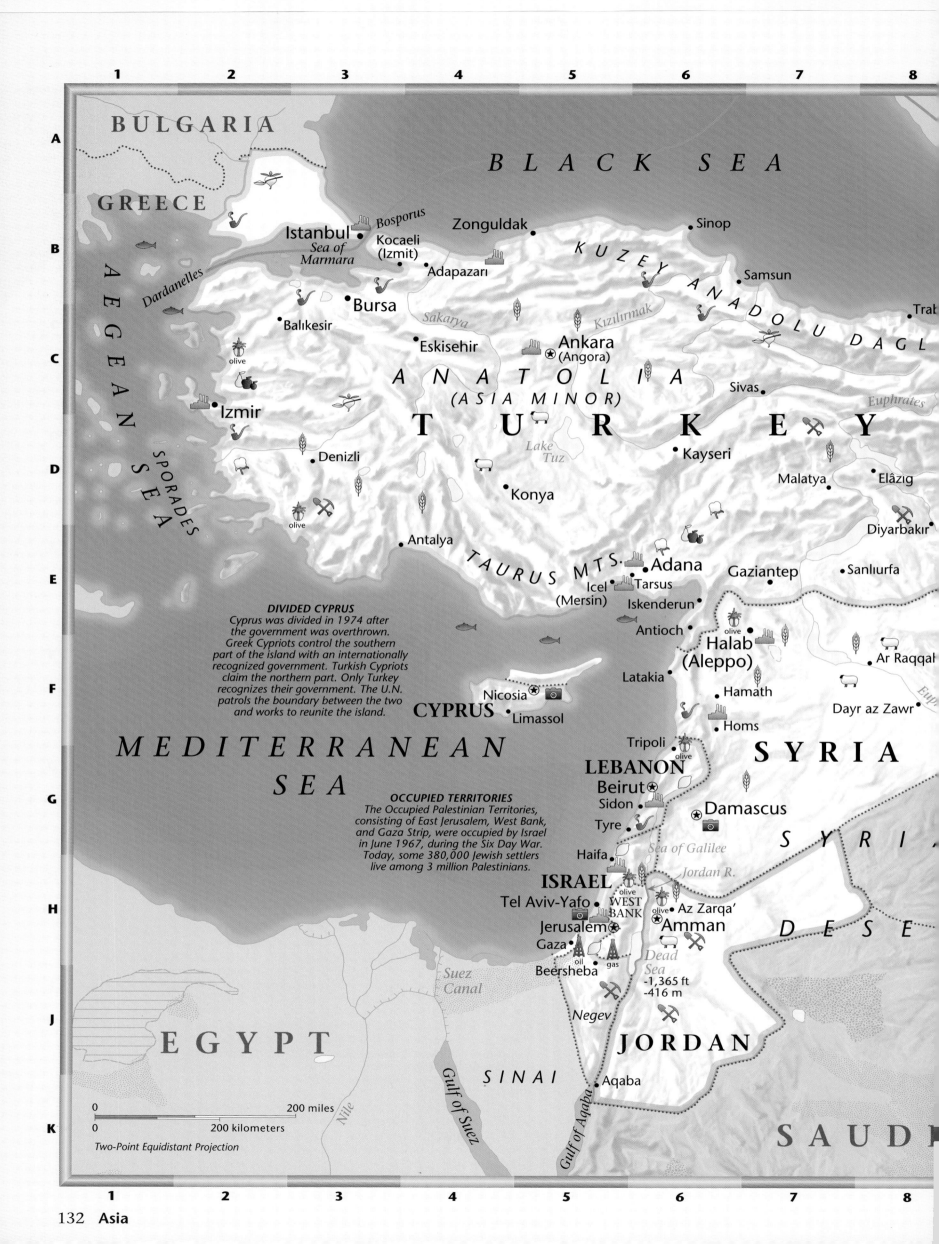

BULGARIA

GREECE

BLACK SEA

Zonguldak • Sinop

Istanbul • Kocaeli
(Izmit)

Bosporus

Sea of Marmara

Adapazarı

Dardanelles

KUZEY ANADOLU DAĞL

Samsun

Trab

Bursa

Balıkesir
Eskisehir

Ankara
(Angora)

Sakarya

Kızılırmak

Euphrates

A N A T O L I A
(ASIA MINOR)

Sivas

olive

Izmir

T U R K E Y

Lake Tuz

Kayseri

Malatya • Elâzig

AEGEAN SEA

SPORADES SEA

Denizli

olive

Diyarbakır

Antalya

Konya

TAURUS MTS.

Adana

Gaziantep • Sanlıurfa

Icel
(Mersin)

Tarsus

Iskenderun

olive

Halab
(Aleppo)

Ar Raqqah

DIVIDED CYPRUS
Cyprus was divided in 1974 after the government was overthrown. Greek Cypriots control the southern part of the island with an internationally recognized government. Turkish Cypriots claim the northern part. Only Turkey recognizes their government. The U.N. patrols the boundary between the two and works to reunite the island.

Antioch

Latakia

S Y R I A

Nicosia

CYPRUS

Limassol

Hamath

Dayr az Zawr

Euph

Homs

M E D I T E R R A N E A N

S E A

Tripoli

olive

OCCUPIED TERRITORIES
The Occupied Palestinian Territories, consisting of East Jerusalem, West Bank, and Gaza Strip, were occupied by Israel in June 1967, during the Six Day War. Today, some 380,000 Jewish settlers live among 3 million Palestinians.

LEBANON

Beirut

Sidon

Damascus

S Y R I A

Tyre

Sea of Galilee

Jordan R.

Haifa

ISRAEL

Tel Aviv-Yafo

olive

WEST BANK

olive

Az Zarqa'

DESE

Jerusalem

Gaza

Amman

oil

gas

Dead Sea
-1,365 ft
-416 m

Beersheba

Suez Canal

Negev

JORDAN

E G Y P T

SINAI

Aqaba

Nile

Gulf of Suez

Gulf of Aqaba

S A U D I

0 — 200 miles
0 — 200 kilometers

Two-Point Equidistant Projection

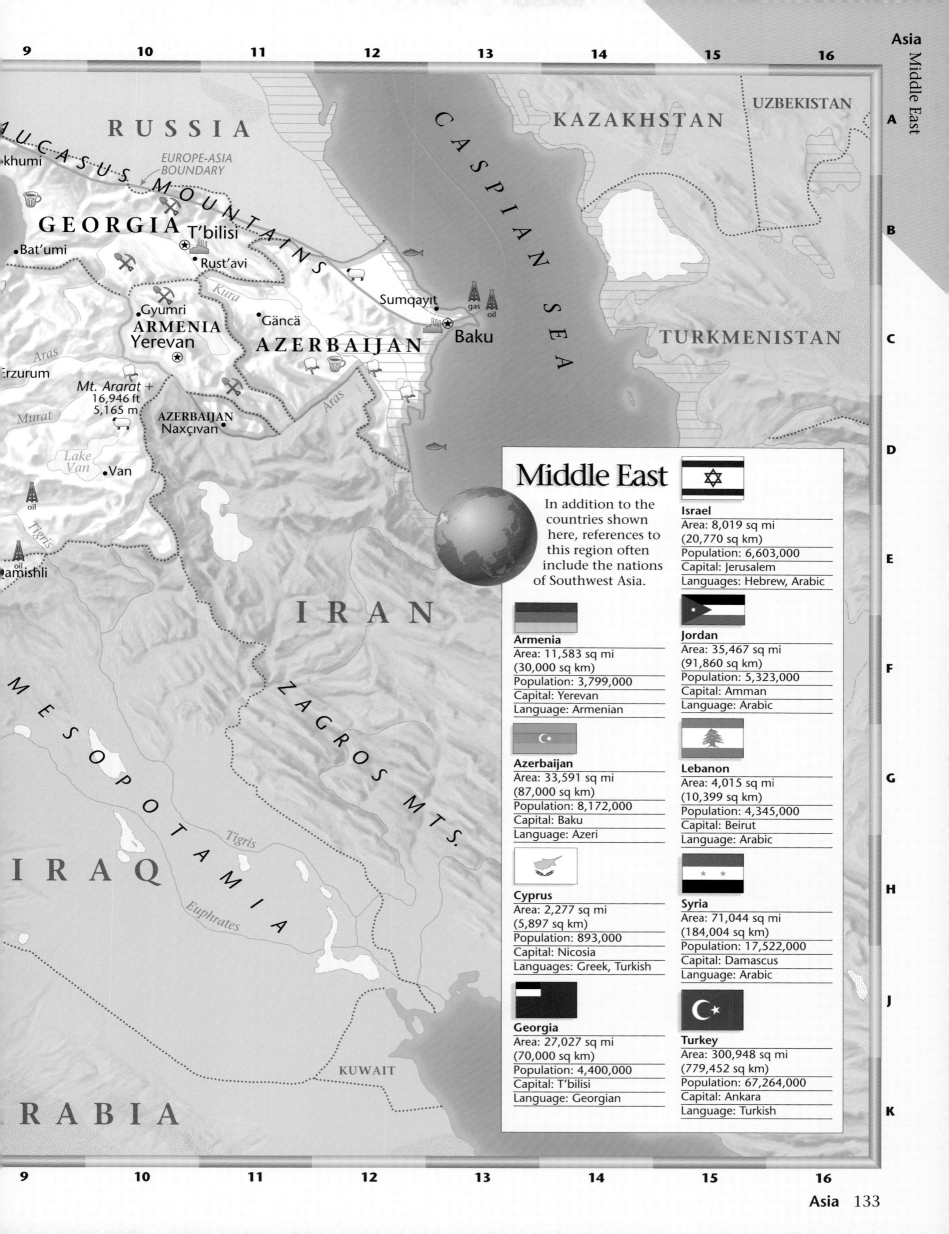

RUSSIA

CAUCASUS MOUNTAINS

EUROPE-ASIA
BOUNDARY

khumi

GEORGIA   T'bilisi

• Bat'umi

• Rust'avi

Kura

• Gyumri

ARMENIA   • Gäncä

Yerevan

AZERBAIJAN

Sumqayıt •

gas   oil

Baku

KAZAKHSTAN

UZBEKISTAN

C A S P I A N   S E A

TURKMENISTAN

Aras

Erzurum

Mt. Ararat +
16,946 ft
5,165 m

AZERBAIJAN
Naxçıvan •

Aras

Murat

Lake
Van

• Van

oil

Tigris

IRAN

ZAGROS MTS.

amishli

oil

M E S O P O T A M I A

I R A Q

Tigris

Euphrates

KUWAIT

RABIA

Middle East

In addition to the countries shown here, references to this region often include the nations of Southwest Asia.

Israel
Area: 8,019 sq mi
(20,770 sq km)
Population: 6,603,000
Capital: Jerusalem
Languages: Hebrew, Arabic

Armenia
Area: 11,583 sq mi
(30,000 sq km)
Population: 3,799,000
Capital: Yerevan
Language: Armenian

Jordan
Area: 35,467 sq mi
(91,860 sq km)
Population: 5,323,000
Capital: Amman
Language: Arabic

Azerbaijan
Area: 33,591 sq mi
(87,000 sq km)
Population: 8,172,000
Capital: Baku
Language: Azeri

Lebanon
Area: 4,015 sq mi
(10,399 sq km)
Population: 4,345,000
Capital: Beirut
Language: Arabic

Cyprus
Area: 2,277 sq mi
(5,897 sq km)
Population: 893,000
Capital: Nicosia
Languages: Greek, Turkish

Syria
Area: 71,044 sq mi
(184,004 sq km)
Population: 17,522,000
Capital: Damascus
Language: Arabic

Georgia
Area: 27,027 sq mi
(70,000 sq km)
Population: 4,400,000
Capital: T'bilisi
Language: Georgian

Turkey
Area: 300,948 sq mi
(779,452 sq km)
Population: 67,264,000
Capital: Ankara
Language: Turkish

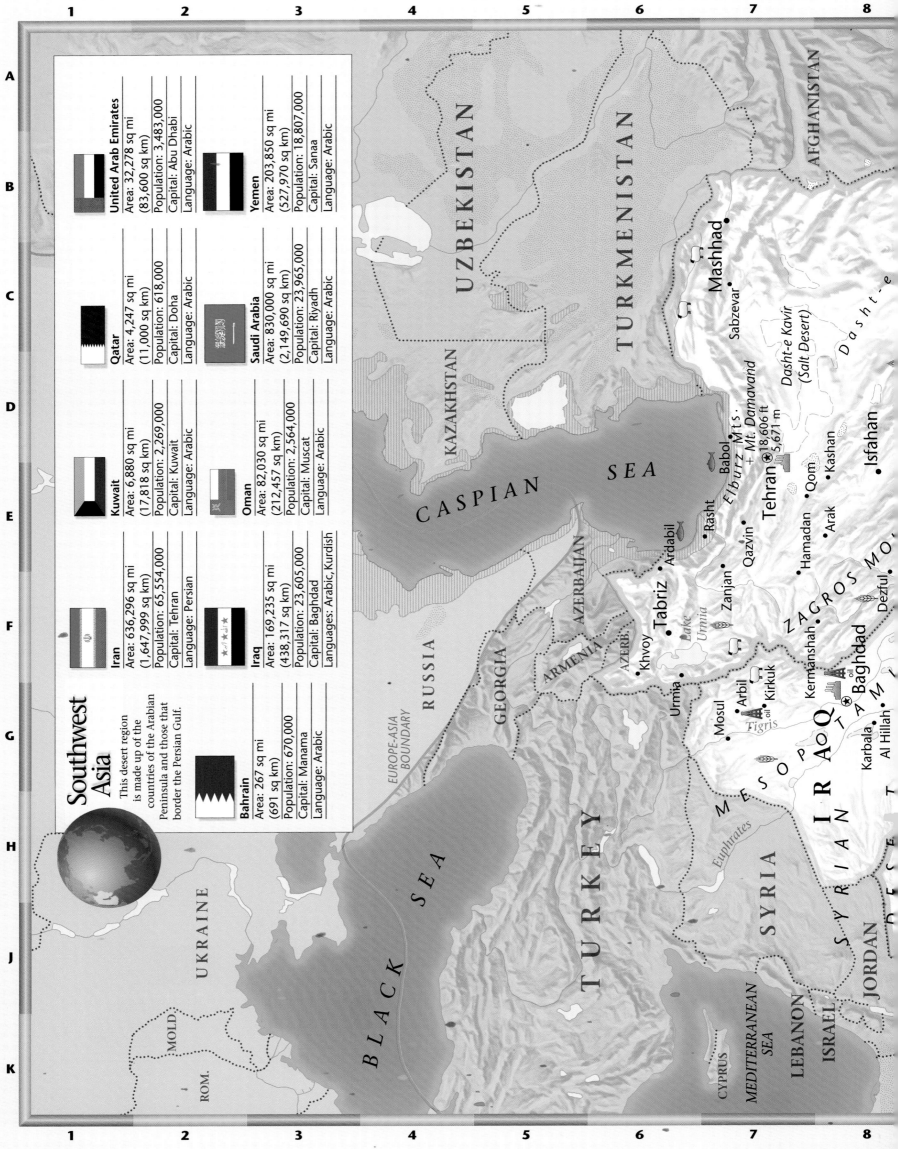

Southwest Asia

This desert region is made up of the countries of the Arabian Peninsula and those that border the Persian Gulf.

United Arab Emirates
Area: 32,278 sq mi (83,600 sq km)
Population: 3,483,000
Capital: Abu Dhabi
Language: Arabic

Yemen
Area: 203,850 sq mi (527,970 sq km)
Population: 18,807,000
Capital: Sanaa
Language: Arabic

Qatar
Area: 4,247 sq mi (11,000 sq km)
Population: 618,000
Capital: Doha
Language: Arabic

Saudi Arabia
Area: 830,000 sq mi (2,149,690 sq km)
Population: 23,965,000
Capital: Riyadh
Language: Arabic

Kuwait
Area: 6,880 sq mi (17,818 sq km)
Population: 2,269,000
Capital: Kuwait
Language: Arabic

Oman
Area: 82,030 sq mi (212,457 sq km)
Population: 2,564,000
Capital: Muscat
Language: Arabic

Iran
Area: 636,296 sq mi (1,647,999 sq km)
Population: 65,554,000
Capital: Tehran
Language: Persian

Iraq
Area: 169,235 sq mi (438,317 sq km)
Population: 23,605,000
Capital: Baghdad
Languages: Arabic, Kurdish

Bahrain
Area: 267 sq mi (691 sq km)
Population: 670,000
Capital: Manama
Language: Arabic

UZBEKISTAN

TURKMENISTAN

AFGHANISTAN

KAZAKHSTAN

Mashhad

Sabzevar

Dasht-e Kavir (Salt Desert)

Dasht-e

CASPIAN SEA

Babol

Elburz Mts.

Mt. Damavand
18,606 ft
5,671 m

Tehran

Isfahan

Qom · Kashan

Rasht

Ardabil

Hamadan

Arak

Qazvin

Zanjan

AZERBAIJAN

Tabriz

Lake Urmia

ZAGROS MO.

Dezful

RUSSIA

AZERB.

Khvoy

Kermanshah

oil

ARMENIA

GEORGIA

Urmia

Arbil

Kirkuk

Baghdad

EUROPE-ASIA BOUNDARY

Mosul

Tigris

oil

I R A Q

oil

MESOPO

Karbala

Al Hillah

BLACK SEA

TURKEY

SYRIA

SYRIAN

Euphrates

JORDAN

LEBANON

ISRAEL

oil

UKRAINE

MOLD.

ROM.

CYPRUS

MEDITERRANEAN SEA

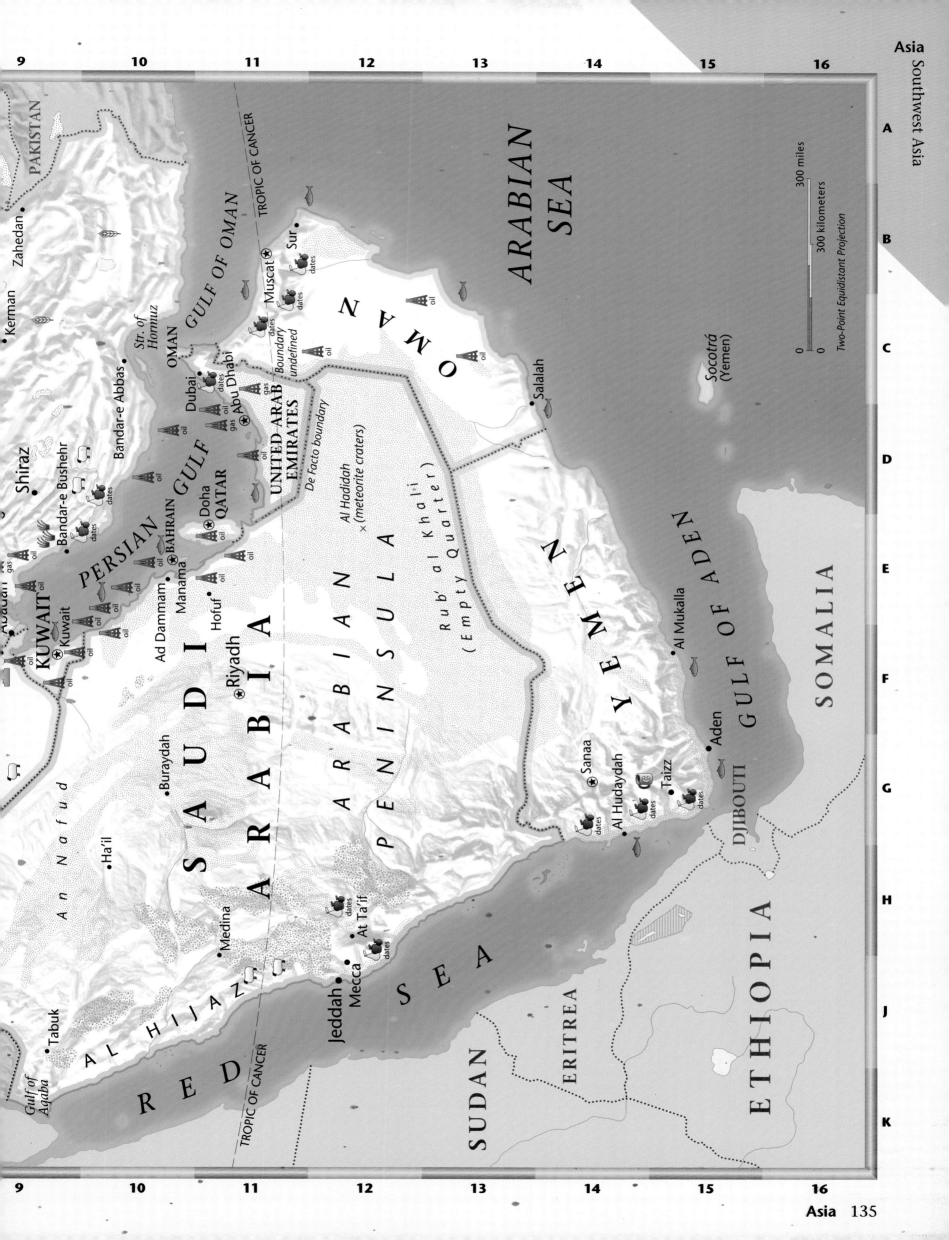

9 10 11 12 13 14 15 16

A

B

C

D

E

F

G

H

J

K

9 10 11 12 13 14 15 16

PAKISTAN

Zahedan

Kerman

Shiraz

Bandar-e Abbas

Str. of Hormuz

Bandar-e Bushehr

GULF OF OMAN

TROPIC OF CANCER

Sur

Muscat

dates

dates

oil

OMAN

Boundary
undefined

oil

oil

oil

O M A N

Salalah

**ARABIAN
SEA**

Socotrá
(Yemen)

300 miles

300 kilometers

0

0

Two-Point Equidistant Projection

Dubai
oil

Abu Dhabi
dates

gas

gas

**UNITED ARAB
EMIRATES**

De Facto boundary

Al Hadidah
× (meteorite craters)

PERSIAN

Doha
QATAR

oil

oil

BAHRAIN

oil

oil

GULF

dates

oil

oil

Manama

Ad Dammam

Hofuf

oil

oil

Rub' al Khali

(Empty Quarter)

KUWAIT
oil

Kuwait

oil

oil

oil

oil

oil

SAUDI

Riyadh

Bur_aydah

A R A B I A

A R A B I A N

P E N I N S U L A

Y E M E N

Al Mukalla

Aden

GULF OF ADEN

SOMALIA

An Nafud

Ha'il

Medina

Sanaa

Al Hudaydah
dates

Taizz
dates

DJIBOUTI

dates

Mecca

Jeddah

At Ta'if
dates

dates

AL HIJAZ

Tabuk

Gulf
of Aqaba

R E D

S E A

SUDAN

ERITREA

ETHIOPIA

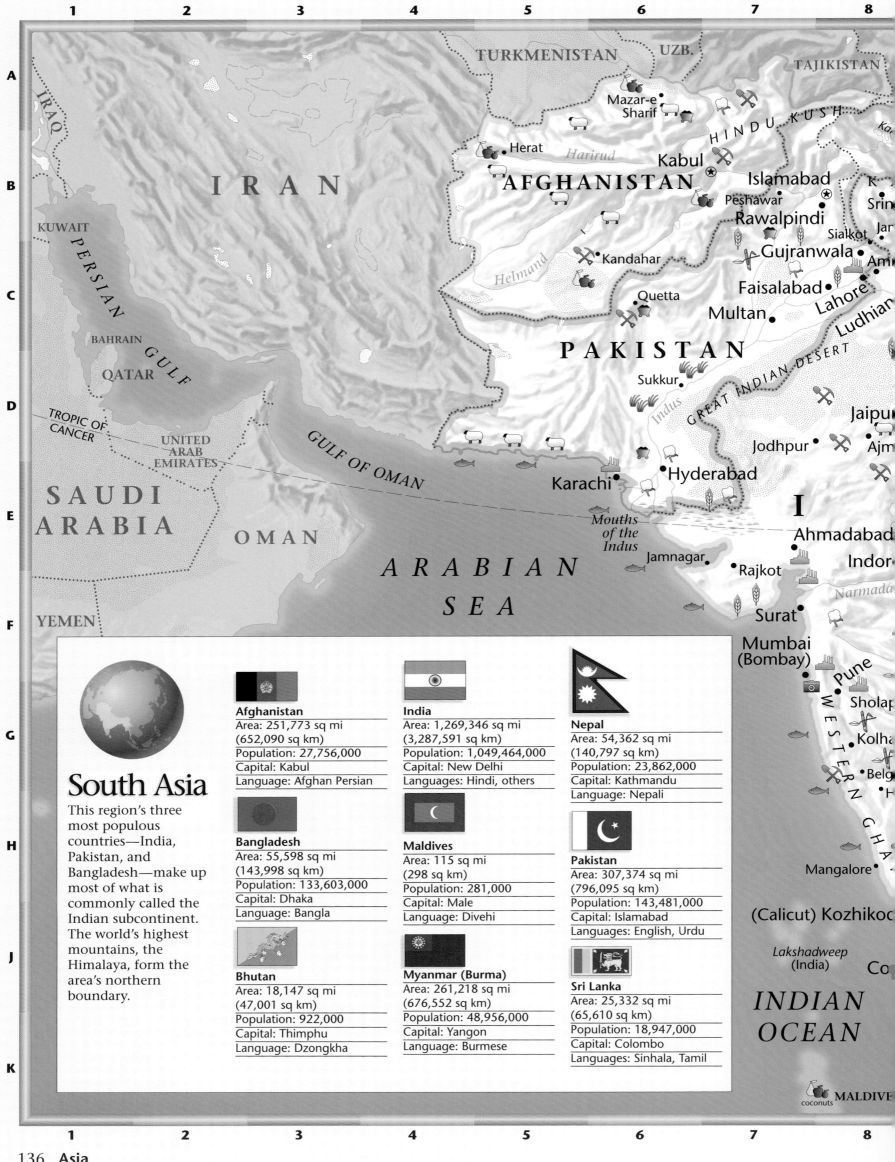

TURKMENISTAN UZB.
TAJIKISTAN

IRAQ

IRAN

Mazar-e
Sharif

HINDU KUSH

Herat · Harirud · Kabul
AFGHANISTAN
Islamabad
Peshawar
Rawalpindi
Sialkot
Gujranwala
Kandahar
Quetta
Faisalabad
Lahore
PAKISTAN
Multan
Ludhian

KUWAIT

PERSIAN

BAHRAIN
QATAR
GULF

GREAT INDIAN DESERT
Sukkur
Indus
Jaipu

TROPIC OF
CANCER
UNITED
ARAB
EMIRATES

Jodhpur
Ajm

Karachi
Hyderabad

SAUDI
ARABIA

GULF OF OMAN

Mouths
of the
Indus
Ahmadabad
Indor

YEMEN
OMAN
Jamnagar
Rajkot
Narmada

ARABIAN
SEA
Surat
Mumbai
(Bombay)
Pune
Sholap

South Asia

This region's three
most populous
countries—India,
Pakistan, and
Bangladesh—make up
most of what is
commonly called the
Indian subcontinent.
The world's highest
mountains, the
Himalaya, form the
area's northern
boundary.

Afghanistan
Area: 251,773 sq mi
(652,090 sq km)
Population: 27,756,000
Capital: Kabul
Language: Afghan Persian

India
Area: 1,269,346 sq mi
(3,287,591 sq km)
Population: 1,049,464,000
Capital: New Delhi
Languages: Hindi, others

Nepal
Area: 54,362 sq mi
(140,797 sq km)
Population: 23,862,000
Capital: Kathmandu
Language: Nepali

Bangladesh
Area: 55,598 sq mi
(143,998 sq km)
Population: 133,603,000
Capital: Dhaka
Language: Bangla

Maldives
Area: 115 sq mi
(298 sq km)
Population: 281,000
Capital: Male
Language: Divehi

Pakistan
Area: 307,374 sq mi
(796,095 sq km)
Population: 143,481,000
Capital: Islamabad
Languages: English, Urdu

Bhutan
Area: 18,147 sq mi
(47,001 sq km)
Population: 922,000
Capital: Thimphu
Language: Dzongkha

Myanmar (Burma)
Area: 261,218 sq mi
(676,552 sq km)
Population: 48,956,000
Capital: Yangon
Language: Burmese

Sri Lanka
Area: 25,332 sq mi
(65,610 sq km)
Population: 18,947,000
Capital: Colombo
Languages: Sinhala, Tamil

Kolha
WESTERN GHA
Belg
Mangalore

(Calicut) Kozhiko

Lakshadweep
(India)

INDIAN
OCEAN

Co

coconuts MALDIVE

9   10   11   12   13   14   15   16

A

B

C

D

E

F

G

H

J

K

C H I N A

K U N L U N   S H A N

Yellow

(Godwin Austen)
...50 ft
...1 m

Boundary claimed
by India

Boundary claimed
by China

M I R

Indus

Simla

T I B E T

Brahmaputra

Mekong

Salween

Yangtze

Dehra Dun

Boundary
claimed
by China

Mt. Everest
29,035 ft
8,850 m

Dibrugarh

Delhi

Meerut

Bareilly

N E P A L

Kathmandu

Thimphu
BHUTAN

A

New Delhi

gra

Lucknow

Ganges

Gorakhpur

Brahmaputra

TROPIC OF
CANCER

Kanpur

Patna

Ganges

Imphal

Gwalior

Varanasi
(Banaras)

Asansol

Dhaka
BANGLADESH

Monywa

Mandalay

Allahabad

I N D I A

Khulna

Bhopal

Jabalpur

Jamshedpur

Kolkata
(Calcutta)

Chittagong

Bagan

Taunggyi

LAOS

Akola

Nagpur

Raipur

Mouths
of the
Ganges

Sittwe

MYANMAR
(BURMA)

THAILAND

Godavari

D E C C A N

E A S T E R N   G H A T S

Hyderabad

Vishakhapatnam

(Rangoon) Yangon

rubber

Mawlamyine

P L A T E A U

Vijayawada

Pathein

Krishna

Guntur

rubber

Dawei

B A Y

ANDAMAN
ISLANDS
(India)

A N D A M A N

Myeik

Bangalore

Chennai (Madras)

O F

rubber

Mysore

Pondicherry

S E A

Isthmus
of Kra

Salem

B E N G A L

MALAY
PENINSULA

Coimbatore

Kodaikanal

Madurai

Jaffna

NICOBAR
ISLANDS
(India)

Strait of Malacca

Trivandrum

Kandy

SRI
LANKA
(CEYLON)

Colombo

0   300 miles

0   300 kilometers

INDONESIA

coconuts

Two-Point Equidistant Projection

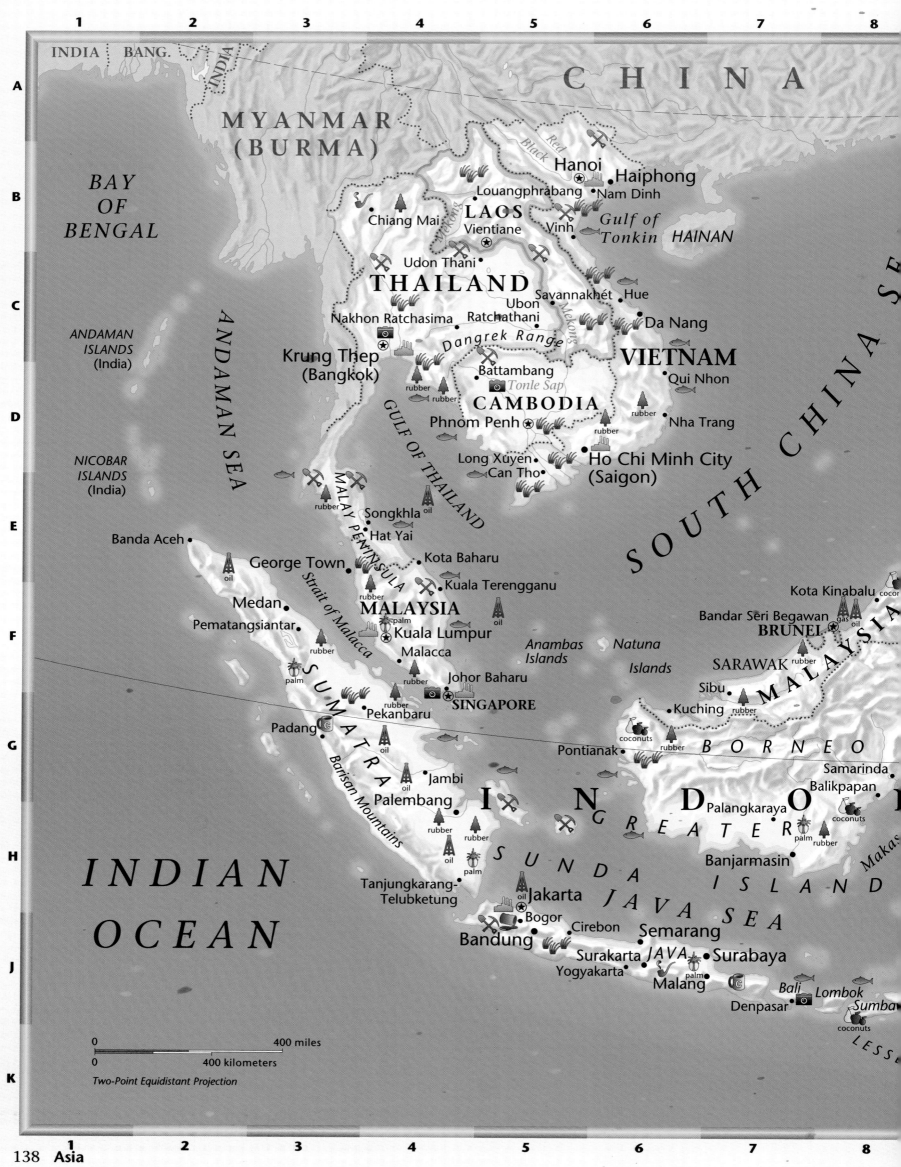

1   **2**   **3**   **4**   **5**   **6**   **7**   **8**

INDIA   BANG.   INDIA

CHINA

MYANMAR
(BURMA)

BAY
OF
BENGAL

Black   *Red*

Hanoi   ● Haiphong
Louangphrabang   ● Nam Dinh

Chiang Mai   **LAOS**   *Gulf of*
Vientiane   Vinh   *Tonkin*   HAINAN

Mekong

Udon Thani

THAILAND   Savannakhét   Hue

ANDAMAN
ISLANDS
(India)

Ubon
Nakhon Ratchasima   Ratchathani   *Mekong*   ● Da Nang

Krung Thep   **VIETNAM**
(Bangkok)   *Dangrek Range*

ANDAMAN SEA

Battambang   ● Qui Nhon

rubber   *Tonle Sap*

rubber   **CAMBODIA**   rubber

NICOBAR
ISLANDS
(India)

Phnom Penh   ● Nha Trang

rubber

Long Xuyen
Can Tho   Ho Chi Minh City
(Saigon)

GULF OF THAILAND

rubber   oil

Banda Aceh   Songkhla
Hat Yai   Kota Baharu

George Town   Kuala Terengganu

oil

Medan   *MALAY PENINSULA*

Pematangsiantar   rubber   **MALAYSIA**   *Anambas*   *Natuna*
palm   *Islands*   *Islands*

Kota Kinabalu   coconuts

Bandar Seri Begawan   gas oil
BRUNEI

Strait of Malacca   Kuala Lumpur   oil

Malacca   **SARAWAK**   rubber

rubber   Sibu

SUMATRA   Johor Baharu   Kuching   rubber

palm   rubber   **SINGAPORE**   coconuts   **MALAYSIA**

rubber   Pekanbaru   *BORNEO*

Padang   Pontianak   rubber

oil

Jambi   **I**   **N**   **D**   **O**   Samarinda

Palembang   *GREATER*   Palangkaraya   Balikpapan

rubber   rubber   palm   coconuts

INDIAN

Tanjungkarang-
Telukbetung   palm

oil   Banjarmasin

Makas...

oil   Jakarta   *SUNDA*   *ISLAND...*

Bogor   *JAVA SEA*

Cirebon   Semarang

OCEAN

Bandung   Surakarta   *JAVA*   Surabaya

Yogyakarta   palm

Malang   *Bali*   *Lombok*   *Sumba...*

Denpasar   coconuts   *LESS...*

0   400 miles
0   400 kilometers

Two-Point Equidistant Projection

SOUTH CHINA SEA

A
B
C
D
E
F
G
H
J
K

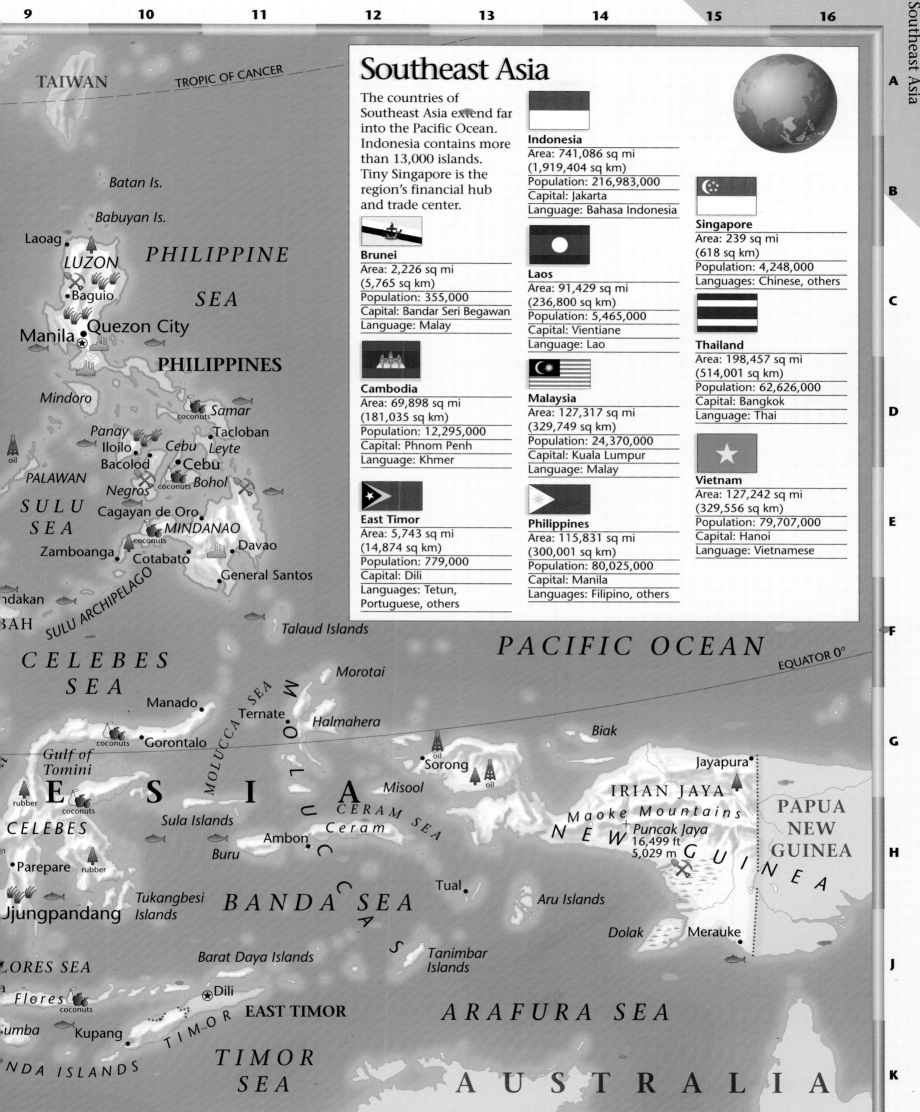

TAIWAN — TROPIC OF CANCER

Batan Is.

Babuyan Is.

Laoag

LUZON

Baguio

PHILIPPINE

Manila

Quezon City

SEA

PHILIPPINES

Mindoro

Samar

coconuts

Panay *Tacloban*
Iloilo *Cebu* *Leyte*
Bacolod *Cebu*

oil

PALAWAN

Negros *Bohol*
coconuts

SULU

Cagayan de Oro

SEA

MINDANAO

Zamboanga

coconuts

Cotabato

Davao

General Santos

ndakan

BAH

SULU ARCHIPELAGO

Talaud Islands

Southeast Asia

The countries of
Southeast Asia extend far
into the Pacific Ocean.
Indonesia contains more
than 13,000 islands.
Tiny Singapore is the
region's financial hub
and trade center.

Indonesia
Area: 741,086 sq mi
(1,919,404 sq km)
Population: 216,983,000
Capital: Jakarta
Language: Bahasa Indonesia

Brunei
Area: 2,226 sq mi
(5,765 sq km)
Population: 355,000
Capital: Bandar Seri Begawan
Language: Malay

Laos
Area: 91,429 sq mi
(236,800 sq km)
Population: 5,465,000
Capital: Vientiane
Language: Lao

Singapore
Area: 239 sq mi
(618 sq km)
Population: 4,248,000
Languages: Chinese, others

Cambodia
Area: 69,898 sq mi
(181,035 sq km)
Population: 12,295,000
Capital: Phnom Penh
Language: Khmer

Malaysia
Area: 127,317 sq mi
(329,749 sq km)
Population: 24,370,000
Capital: Kuala Lumpur
Language: Malay

Thailand
Area: 198,457 sq mi
(514,001 sq km)
Population: 62,626,000
Capital: Bangkok
Language: Thai

East Timor
Area: 5,743 sq mi
(14,874 sq km)
Population: 779,000
Capital: Dili
Languages: Tetun,
Portuguese, others

Philippines
Area: 115,831 sq mi
(300,001 sq km)
Population: 80,025,000
Capital: Manila
Languages: Filipino, others

Vietnam
Area: 127,242 sq mi
(329,556 sq km)
Population: 79,707,000
Capital: Hanoi
Language: Vietnamese

PACIFIC OCEAN

EQUATOR 0°

*CELEBES
SEA*

Manado

MOLUCCA SEA

Morotai

Ternate

Halmahera

Biak

coconuts

Gorontalo

oil

Sorong

Jayapura

*Gulf of
Tomini*

Misool

oil

IRIAN JAYA

Maoke Mountains

+ *Puncak Jaya*
16,499 ft
5,029 m

*PAPUA
NEW
GUINEA*

rubber

E

S

I

A

CERAM SEA

N E W

G U I N E A

coconuts

CELEBES

Ceram

Sula Islands

Ambon

Buru

Parepare

rubber

Ujungpandang

*Tukangbesi
Islands*

BANDA SEA

Tual

Aru Islands

Dolak

Merauke

Barat Daya Islands

*Tanimbar
Islands*

ARAFURA SEA

LORES SEA

Flores
coconuts

Dili

EAST TIMOR

umba

Kupang

T I M O R

NDA ISLANDS

*TIMOR
SEA*

A U S T R A L I A

The low peaks of the Hamersley Range along the west coast of Australia form the starting point for arrowlike clouds (right). The Hamersley Range is typical of Australia's mountains—low and located near the coast. Deserts cover much of the continent's sparsely populated interior.

Unlike Australia, which is geologically stable, New Zealand stretches along a subduction zone. In the north its landscape is marked by hot springs and geysers. In the south rise the glacier-covered peaks of the Southern Alps.

Oceania is the name that geographers commonly use for the Pacific islands that make up the regions of Melanesia, Micronesia, and Polynesia. Australia and New Zealand are often included in Oceania.

The white sands of Cable Beach, along Australia's northwestern coast, are a popular destination for tourists, including these on camelback. Although camels are not native to Australia, they are well suited to the continent's dry climate.

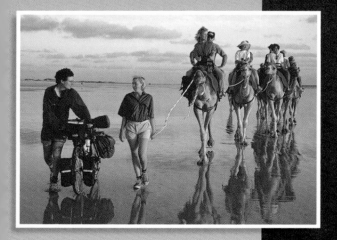

CONNECTION: *You can find Australia's west coast on the maps on pages 142–143.*

ew Zealand
ceania

Australia

Down Under and Outback

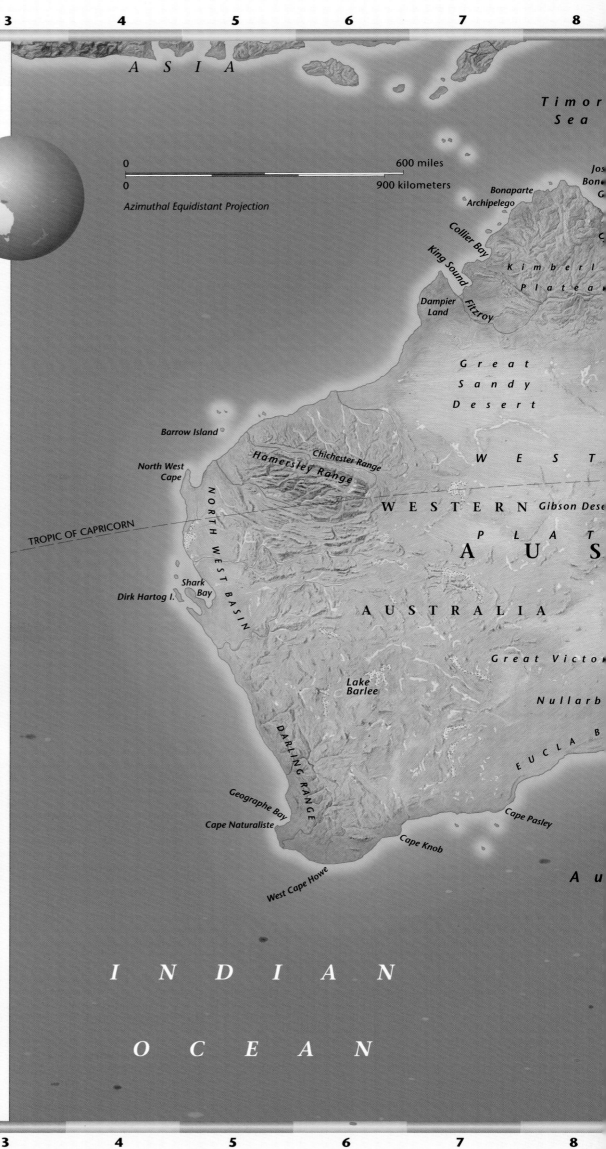

Just three times bigger than Greenland (the Earth's largest island), Australia is the smallest of the continents—and the flattest as well. It earns the nickname "land down under" because it is located entirely below the Equator. The Great Dividing Range—low mountains running north-south along the east coast—blocks rainfall from the Pacific. Inland lie the dry scrublands and vast, hot deserts of central and western Australia that locals call the outback. Australia's most famous physical feature lies offshore: the Great Barrier Reef, the largest structure ever built by living creatures.

The Land

Area
2,968,000 sq mi
(7,687,000 sq km)

Highest mountain
Kosciuszko: 7,310 ft (2,228 m)

Lowest point
Lake Eyre: 52 ft (16 m)
below sea level

Longest river
Murray-Darling: 2,310 mi
(3,718 km)

Largest body of water
Lake Eyre: 3,430 sq mi
(8,884 sq km)

Largest island
Tasmania: 26,383 sq mi
(68,332 sq km)

0   600 miles
0   900 kilometers
Azimuthal Equidistant Projection

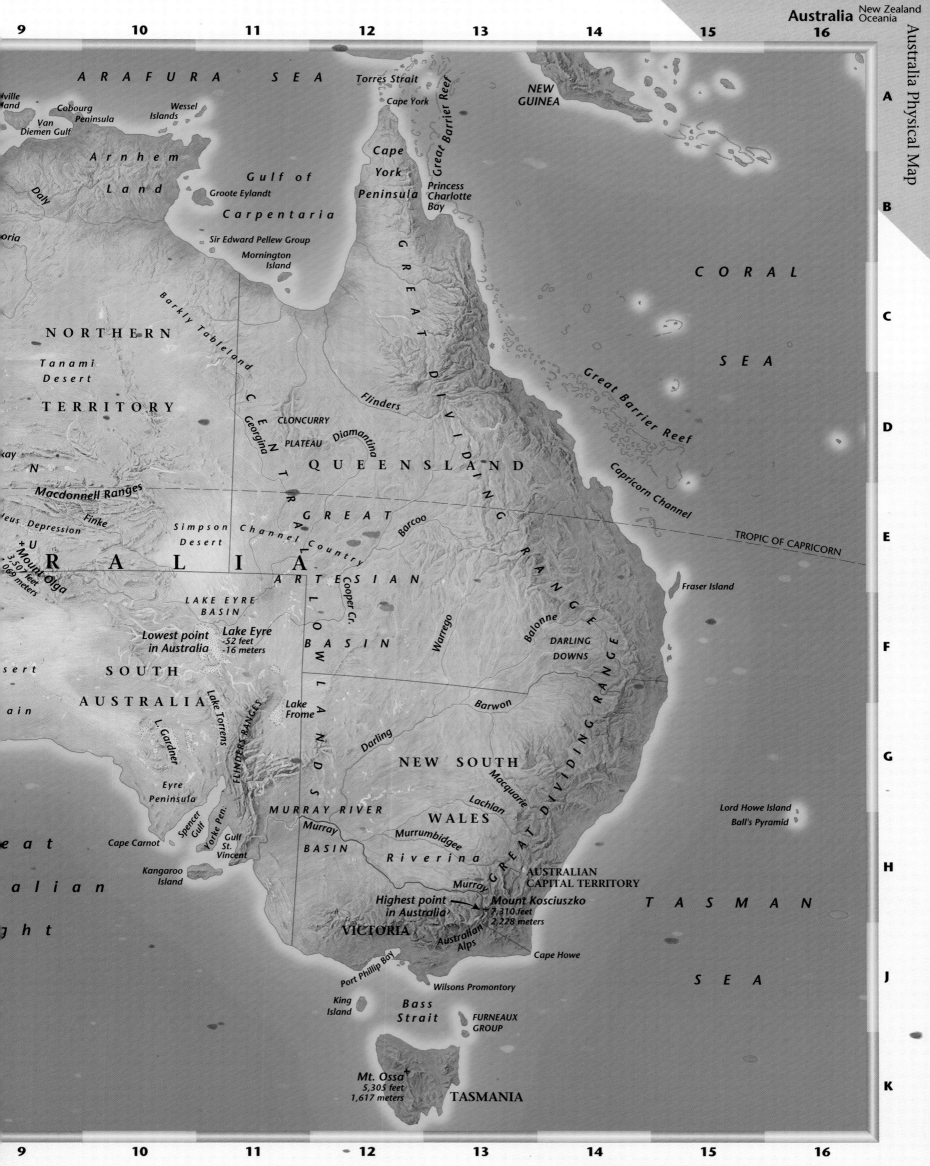

9 10 11 12 13 14 15 16

A
ARAFURA SEA
Torres Strait
Cape York
Great Barrier Reef
NEW GUINEA
ville land
Cobourg Peninsula
Wessel Islands
Van Diemen Gulf

B
Arnhem Land
Daly
Groote Eylandt
Carpentaria
Cape York Peninsula
Princess Charlotte Bay
CORAL

C
NORTHERN
Barkly Tableland
Sir Edward Pellew Group
Mornington Island
Gulf of

SEA

D
Tanami Desert
TERRITORY
CLONCURRY
PLATEAU
Flinders
QUEENSLAND
GREAT DIVIDING
Great Barrier Reef
kay
Georgina
Diamantina

E
Macdonnell Ranges
Finke
Simpson Desert
GREAT
Channel Country
Barcoo
RANGE
Capricorn Channel
TROPIC OF CAPRICORN
eus Depression
Mount Olga 3,507 feet 1,069 meters
N
RALIA
ARTESIAN
Cooper Cr.
Fraser Island

F
LAKE EYRE BASIN
Lowest point in Australia
Lake Eyre -52 feet -16 meters
BASIN
Warrego
Balonne
DARLING DOWNS
sert
SOUTH
AUSTRALIA
Lake Frome
LOWLANDS
Barwon

G
ain
L. Gardner
Lake Torrens
FLINDERS RANGES
Darling
NEW SOUTH
Macquarie
GREAT DIVIDING RANGE
Lord Howe Island
Ball's Pyramid
Eyre Peninsula
Lachlan

H
Spencer Gulf
Yorke Pen.
Gulf St. Vincent
MURRAY RIVER
Murray
WALES
Murrumbidgee
Riverina
AUSTRALIAN CAPITAL TERRITORY
TASMAN
Cape Carnot
eat
BASIN
Murray

J
alian
Kangaroo Island
Highest point in Australia
Mount Kosciuszko 7,310 feet 2,228 meters
VICTORIA
Australian Alps
Cape Howe
SEA
ght
Port Phillip Bay
Wilsons Promontory

K
King Island
Bass Strait
FURNEAUX GROUP
Mt. Ossa 5,305 feet 1,617 meters
TASMANIA

9 10 11 12 13 14 15 16

Australia
New Zealand, Oceania
Lands of Natural Wonder

When English explorers landed in Australia and caught their first glimpse of a kangaroo, words failed them. Captain James Cook wrote in 1770, "To compare it to any European animal would be impossible as it has not the least resemblance of any one I have seen."

Australia owes its odd animal life to the fact that the continent has been isolated from other land for millions of years. During that time, its animals evolved into strange and wonderful creatures. Australia is famous for its marsupials (pouched mammals)—kangaroos, koalas, wombats, and Tasmanian devils, to name a few.

Most of New Zealand's land animals have been introduced from other countries. The country has many native birds, including the flightless kiwi, whose name is a nickname for a New Zealander.

Birds—especially long-distance fliers such as albatrosses and terns—are the most common kind of wildlife native to islands that make up Oceania. Most of these islands are either coral atolls or volcanic in origin.

▲ KANGAROOS CROSSING!
A uniquely Australian road sign greets visitors to Ayers Rock. Exposed by years of wind and weather, the rock is sacred to Aborigines, Australia's native people, who call it Uluru.

▼STRANGEST IN A STRANGE LAND:
The poison-spurred, duck-billed platypus is a member of an unusual order of egg-laying mammals called monotremes.

▶BEACH MEETS CITY *along Australia's Queensland coast. More than 80 percent of Australia's population lives in coastal cities.*

▲ **PULLING FOR ALL** *they're worth as they crash through the surf, an Aussie lifeboat crew competes in a race. Australia's long beaches are popular with surfers and swimmers alike.*

▶ **SNUGGLING CHEEK** *to cheek, an Aborigine child savors a quiet moment with a pet kangaroo. In 1976 Aborigines regained title to traditional lands that make up a third of Australia's Northern Territory.*

▲ **SAFE WITHIN** *the slender fingers of an anemone, a clownfish peers out from Australia's famous Great Barrier Reef.*

▶ **SHIMMERING** *colors make opals precious stones. Most of the world's gem opals come from fields in southeastern Australia.*

▲ **A KNACK** *for looking cute and cuddly, the koala has become a symbol for Australia. Because koalas eat only leaves from eucalyptus trees, few zoos outside the continent manage to keep them.*

▲ **DRESSED TO SCARE,** *a tribesman from New Guinea's Asaro River Valley wears a clay mask in a ritual meant to ward off evil spirits. New Guinea is the largest island in Melanesia.*

◀ **RAINBOW LORIKEETS** *groom one another in a show of feathered friendship. Lorikeets and cockatoos are colorful parrots native to Australia and New Guinea.*

▲ **A SAILBOAT SCUDS** *across Sydney Harbor, its sails echoed by the arches of the city's famous Opera House. Once a giant British penal colony, Australia now boasts its own world-class music, theater, and architecture.*

◄ **SHEEPDOGS** *join their owner as he calls out across a New Zealand sheep station. Australia and New Zealand devote vast acreage to sheep and cattle ranching.*

▲ **STEAM RISING** *above the green waters of New Zealand's Emerald Lake hints at geothermal activity. North Island has many volcanoes and hot springs.*

Australia
Country and Continent

A political map of Australia highlights an unusual feature: The entire continent is one sparsely populated country. Aborigines, the first Australians, came from Asia 50,000 years ago. In 1770, England claimed Australia as a colony and British immigrants flowed in. Today, most Australians live in coastal cities such as Sydney and Melbourne, though hardy ranchers still work the country's dry interior lands. Independent and politically stable since 1901, Australia is a prosperous country. It is one of the world's largest exporters of coal and iron ore and a world leader in wool production and diamonds.

The People

Population
19,731,000

Capital: Canberra

Language: English

Largest metropolitan areas
Sydney: Pop. 3,713,500
Melbourne: Pop. 3,189,200

Population density
7 people per sq mi

Economy
Farming: livestock, wheat, fruit
Industry: mining, wool, oil

Life expectancy
79 years

Arafura Sea

Cobourg Pen.
Wessel Is.
Cape Arnhem

ville
and

⊙Darwin
ARNHEM
LAND
Gulf of

•Pine Creek
Groote Eylandt

Carpentaria

Daly Waters•
•Borroloola

•Newcastle Waters
Wellesley Is.

NORTHERN
Burketown•
•Karumba

•Normanton
Croydon•
•Forsyth

TERRITORY
Camooweal•
•Cloncurry

•Tennant Creek
Mount Isa•
Hughenden•

•Barrow Creek
QUEENSLAND
•Boulia

Macdonnell Ranges
•Winton

•Alice Springs
Aramac•

Barcaldine•
•Emerald
•Rockhampton

R
Blackall•

+Mount Olga
3,507 feet
1,069 meters
Windorah•
Mount
Morgan
•Gladstone

A
L
Charleville•

Oodnadatta•
Eromanga•
•Bundaberg
Fraser Island

SOUTH
Roma•
•Maryborough

-52 ft
-16 m
•Kingaroy

oil
Cunnamulla•
•Toowoomba

AUSTRALIA
Goondiwindi•
⊙**Brisbane**
•Gold Coast

Lake Eyre
gas oil
•Lismore

•Marree
•Moree

•Ooldea
•Grafton

I
Bourke•
•Armidale

Penong•
•Ceduna
Broken Hill•
Coonamble•
Tamworth•

Whyalla•
Port
Augusta•
NEW SOUTH
•Muswellbrook

Wallaroo•
Dubbo•

Port Lincoln•
Port Pirie•
Mildura•
Orange•
•Newcastle

Kangaroo I.
•Adelaide⊙
Murray
WALES
⊙Sydney

Wagga Wagga•
•Wollongong

stralian
ht
7,310 ft
2,228 m
•Goulburn
A.C.T.

Mount Gambier•
Bendigo•
★Canberra **AUSTRALIAN CAPITAL TERRITORY**

Ballarat•
VICTORIA
+Mt. Kosciuszko
•Cooma

Warrnambool•
Geelong•
⊙**Melbourne**

Port Phillip Bay
•Moe
oil gas

King Island
Bass Strait
Furneaux Group

Burnie•
•Devonport
•Launceston

Queenstown•
•St. Marys

TASMANIA

Geeveston•
⊙Hobart

PAPUA NEW GUINEA

Torres Str.
Cape York

•Weipa

**CORAL SEA ISLANDS
TERRITORY**
(Australia)

•Coen

•Cooktown

•Cairns
•Innisfail

•Townsville
•Ayr
Charters Towers•
•Proserpine
•Mackay

Great Barrier Reef

Coral Sea

Lord Howe I.
Ball's Pyramid
(New South Wales)

*Tasman
Sea*

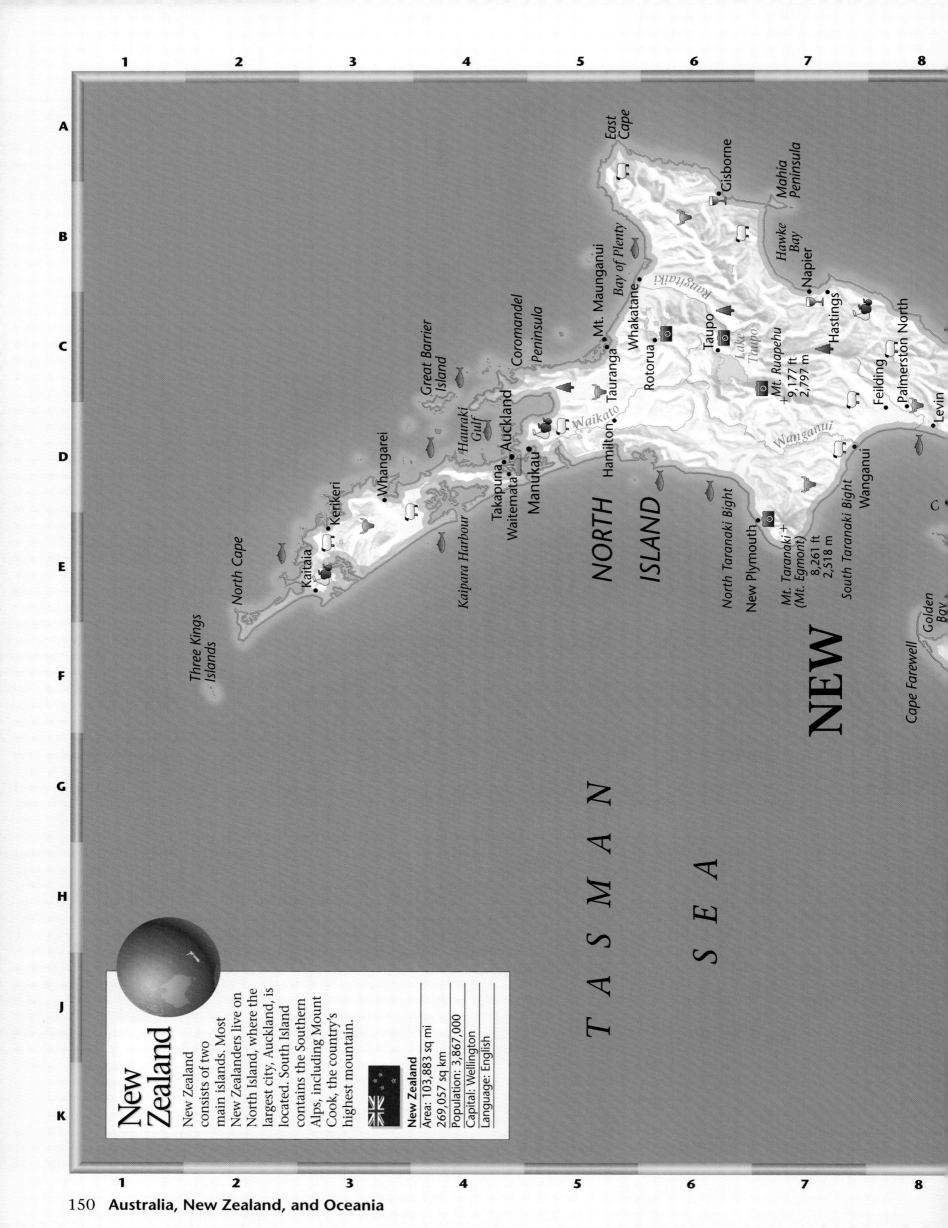

East
Cape

Gisborne

Mahia
Peninsula

Hawke
Bay

Napier

Hastings

Great Barrier
Island

Mt. Maunganui

Bay of Plenty

Whakatane

Taupo

Mt. Ruapehu
+ 9,177 ft
2,797 m

Feilding

Palmerston North

Levin

Coromandel
Peninsula

Tauranga

Rotorua

Lake
Taupo

Hauraki
Gulf

Auckland

Waikato

Hamilton

Wanganui

Whangarei

Kerikeri

Takapuna
Waitemata
Manukau

Kaipara Harbour

NORTH
ISLAND

North Taranaki Bight

New Plymouth

Mt. Taranaki +
(Mt. Egmont)
8,261 ft
2,518 m

South Taranaki Bight

Wanganui

North Cape

Kaitaia

NEW

Three Kings
Islands

Cape Farewell

Golden
Bay

T A S M A N

S E A

New Zealand

New Zealand consists of two main islands. Most New Zealanders live on North Island, where the largest city, Auckland, is located. South Island contains the Southern Alps, including Mount Cook, the country's highest mountain.

New Zealand

Area: 103,883 sq mi
269,057 sq km
Population: 3,867,000
Capital: Wellington
Language: English

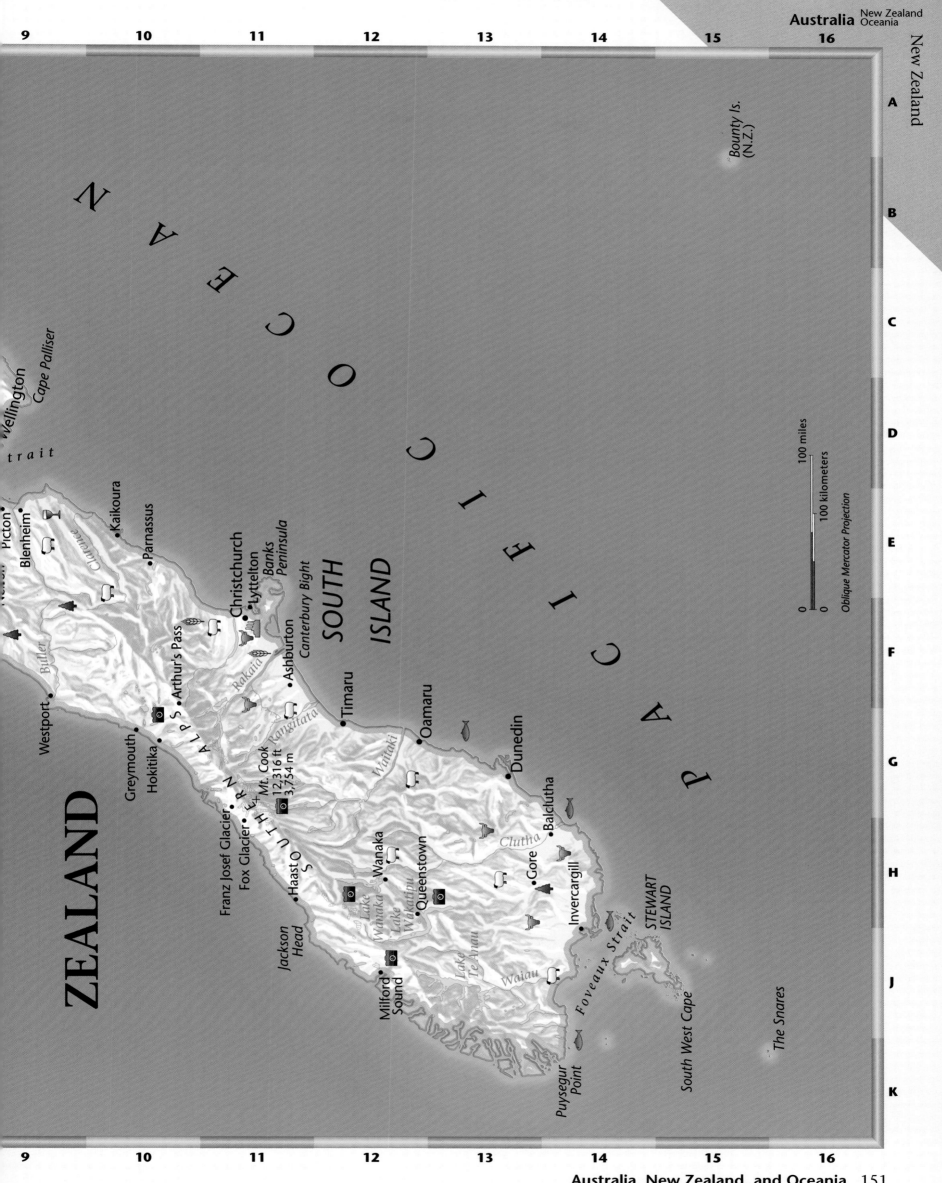

9 10 11 12 13 14 15 16

A

B

C

D

E

F

G

H

J

K

Bounty Is.
(N.Z.)

P A C I F I C   O C E A N

100 miles

100 kilometers

0

0

Oblique Mercator Projection

O C E A N

Wellington

Cape Palliser

Strait

ZEALAND

Nelson

Picton

Blenheim

Kaikoura

Parnassus

Clarence

Christchurch

Lyttelton

Banks
Peninsula

Canterbury Bight

SOUTH

ISLAND

Westport

Buller

Greymouth

Hokitika

Arthur's Pass

Rakaia

Ashburton

Rangitata

Timaru

Oamaru

SOUTHERN   ALPS

Franz Josef Glacier

Fox Glacier

Mt. Cook
12,316 ft
3,754 m

Waitaki

Dunedin

Haast

Jackson
Head

Lake
Wanaka

Wanaka

Lake
Wakatipu

Queenstown

Gore

Balclutha

Clutha

Invercargill

Milford
Sound

Lake
Te Anau

Waiau

Foveaux Strait

STEWART
ISLAND

Puysegur
Point

South West Cape

The Snares

9 10 11 12 13 14 15 16

Antarctica

Most people think ice-covered Antarctica is the end of the world, an expanse of white at the bottom of the map. This picture, made from dozens of satellite images, shows the continent as it appears from space. The curving arm reaching into the sea (lower right) is the Antarctic Peninsula, more than 800 miles (1,200 kilometers) long. To the right of the peninsula, the rough peaks of the Transantarctic Mountains snake across the continent. Above them is the flat central area of Antarctica called the Polar Plateau. Surrounding the whole continent is a vast, floating sheet of ice. In the winter, this sea ice extends for 7,300,000 square miles (18,906,000 square kilometers).

Adélie penguins appear unfazed by a researcher's presence. Antarctica provides nesting sites for seven species of these flightless birds.

CONNECTION: *You can find the continent of Antarctica on the map on pages 156–157.*

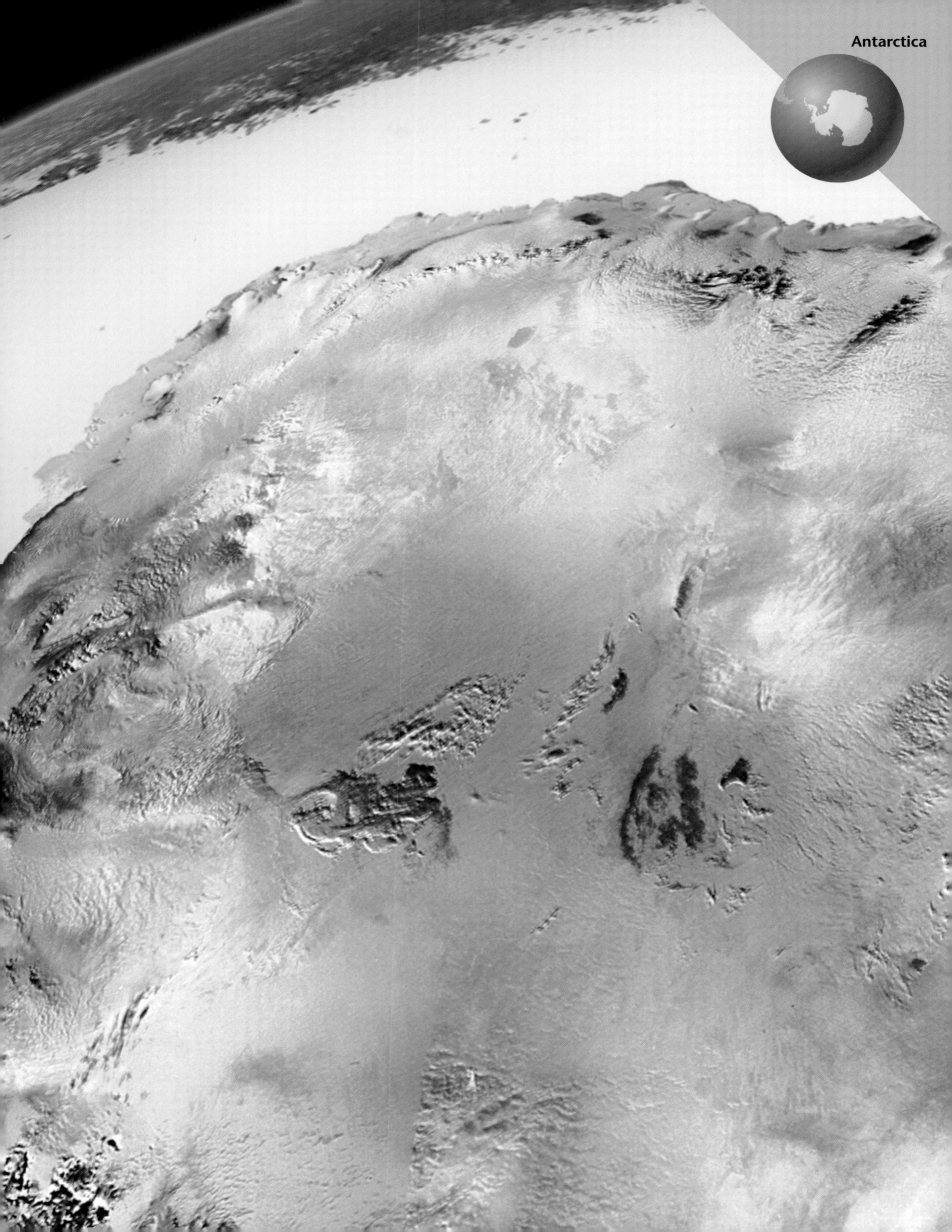

Antarctica

Antarctica

A Desert of Solid Ice

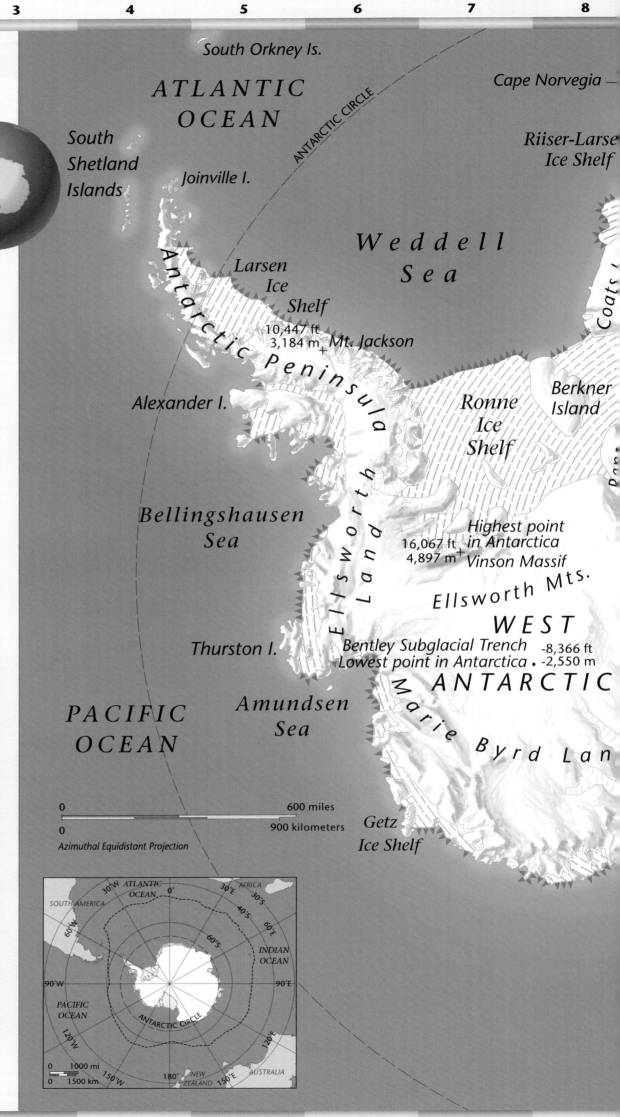

Antarctica is the coldest and windiest continent on Earth. It receives so little precipitation that it is also the world's largest cold desert. Almost all of Antarctica lies under a sheet of ice more than a mile thick. Beneath its weight, the rocky land sinks thousands of feet below sea level.

In the ocean around Antarctica is a unique zone known as the Antarctic Convergence (inset map). There, cold water meets warmer water from the north. This mix nurtures the plants and animals, such as krill, that attract whales and make these waters the most fertile on Earth.

The Land

Area
5,100,400 sq mi
(13,209,000 sq km)

Highest mountain
Vinson Massif: 16,067 ft
(4,897 m)

Lowest point
Bentley Subglacial Trench: 8,366
ft (2,550 m) below sea level

Coldest spot (record)
Vostok Station: -128.6°F (-89°C)
on July 21, 1983

Average precipitation
On the polar plateau: less than
2 inches (5 centimeters) of
precipitation a year

South Orkney Is.

ATLANTIC OCEAN

Cape Norvegia —

ANTARCTIC CIRCLE

South Shetland Islands

Joinville I.

Riiser-Larse Ice Shelf

Weddell Sea

Larsen Ice Shelf

Coats

10,447 ft
3,184 m + Mt. Jackson

Antarctic Peninsula

Alexander I.

Ronne Ice Shelf

Berkner Island

Bellingshausen Sea

Ellsworth Land

Highest point in Antarctica
16,067 ft
4,897 m + Vinson Massif

Ellsworth Mts.

WEST

Thurston I.

Bentley Subglacial Trench   -8,366 ft
Lowest point in Antarctica • -2,550 m

ANTARCTIC

PACIFIC OCEAN

Amundsen Sea

Marie Byrd Lan

0 ——— 600 miles
0 ——— 900 kilometers
Azimuthal Equidistant Projection

Getz Ice Shelf

30°W ATLANTIC OCEAN 0° AFRICA
SOUTH AMERICA   30°E
40°S   40°E
60°W   50°S
60°S   60°E
INDIAN OCEAN
90°W   90°E
PACIFIC OCEAN
120°W   120°E
150°W   ANTARCTIC CIRCLE
180°   NEW ZEALAND   AUSTRALIA
0 ——— 1000 mi
0 ——— 1500 km

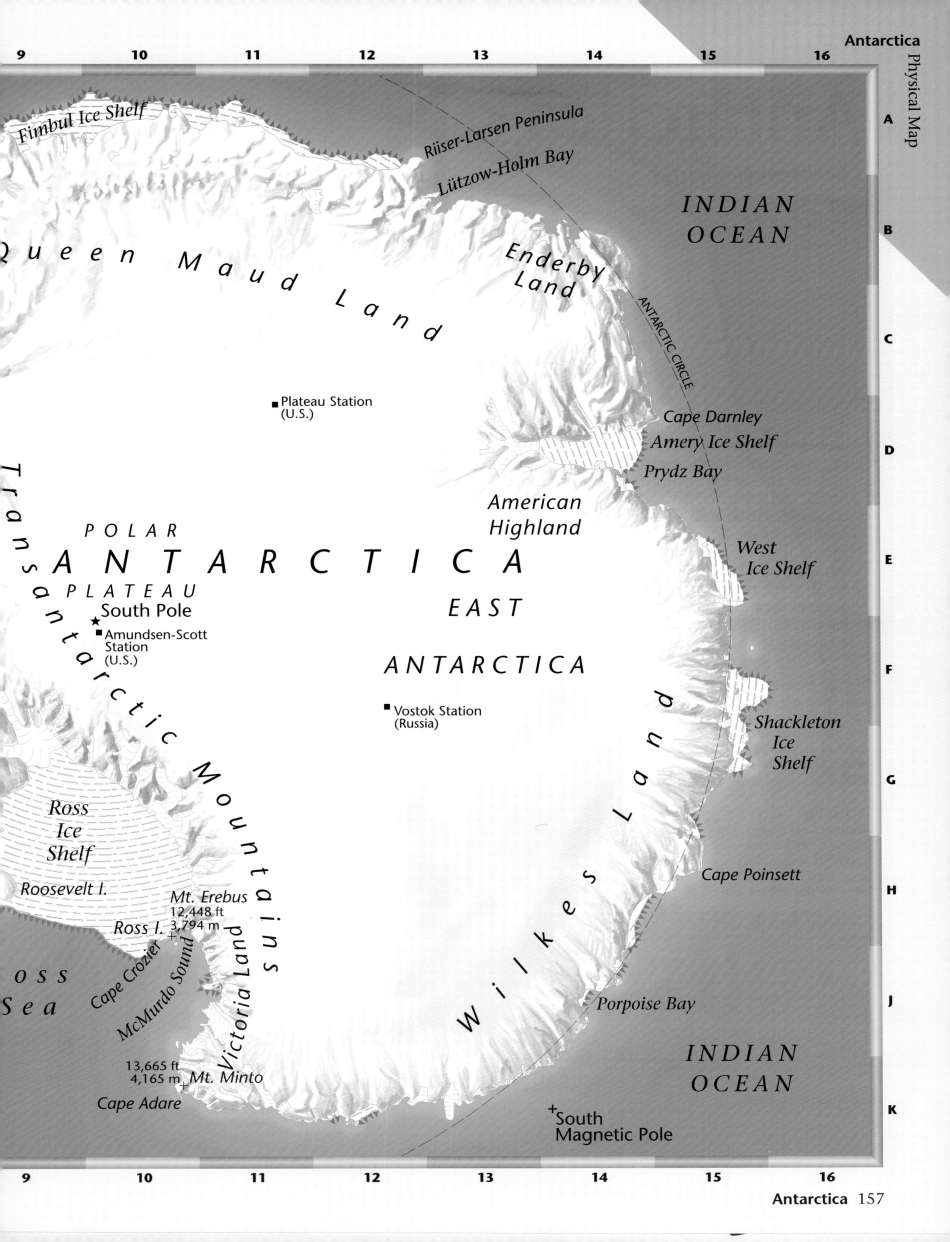

9 10 11 12 13 14 15 16

Fimbul Ice Shelf

Riiser-Larsen Peninsula

Lützow-Holm Bay

INDIAN OCEAN

Queen Maud Land

Enderby Land

ANTARCTIC CIRCLE

Cape Darnley
Amery Ice Shelf
Prydz Bay

American Highland

West Ice Shelf

POLAR
ANTARCTICA
PLATEAU
South Pole
★
■ Amundsen-Scott Station (U.S.)

■ Plateau Station (U.S.)

EAST
ANTARCTICA

■ Vostok Station (Russia)

Shackleton Ice Shelf

Transantarctic Mountains

Ross Ice Shelf

Roosevelt I.

Mt. Erebus
12,448 ft
Ross I. 3,794 m

Cape Crozier

McMurdo Sound

Victoria Land

Wilkes Land

Cape Poinsett

oss Sea

13,665 ft
4,165 m Mt. Minto

Cape Adare

Porpoise Bay

INDIAN OCEAN

+South Magnetic Pole

9 10 11 12 13 14 15 16

Oceans

We talk about the oceans as though there were many of them, but in fact there is just one big ocean with four names. The combined mass of the Atlantic, Pacific, Indian, and Arctic Oceans surrounds the rocky continents with 320 million cubic miles (1.3 billion cubic kilometers) of salty, life-filled water.

Most of this huge ocean has been a mystery to us. We know a little about the blue waters near our shores: fishing grounds and coral reefs, such as Australia's Great Barrier Reef. But the ocean's darker depths were largely unexplored until recently. Now, new technology, from satellites to deep-ocean submersibles, is helping us understand this last frontier on Earth.

A seaplane soars over the vast Great Barrier Reef (right), which stretches for 1,250 miles (2,012 kilometers) along Australia's Pacific coast. Brilliant colors of a coral reef (below) lure a diver in for closer inspection.

CONNECTION: *You can find the Great Barrier Reef on the map of the Pacific Ocean floor on pages 168–169.*

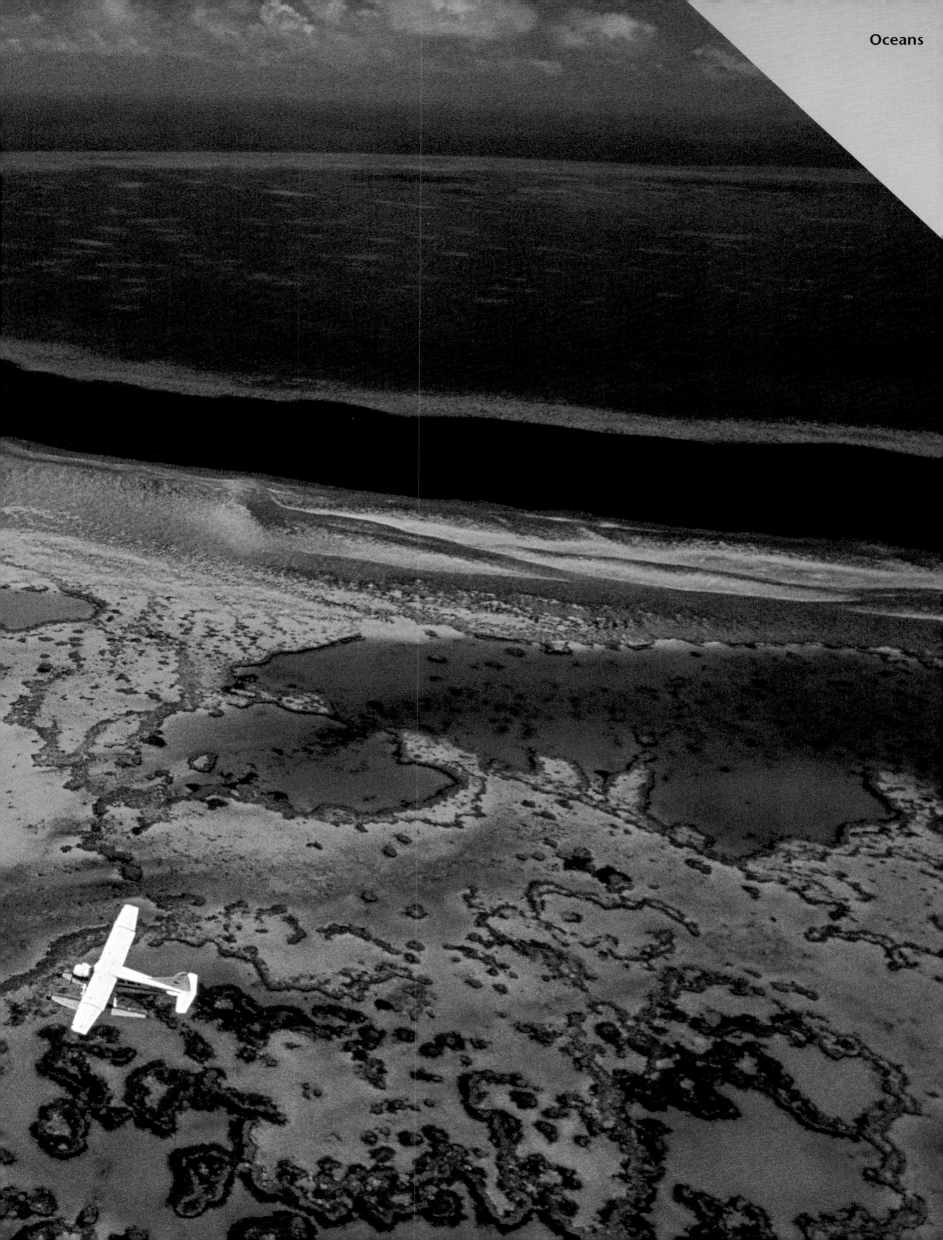

Life in the Ocean

The ocean isn't just a body of water: it's a soup, a living broth. Its water holds an amazingly rich variety of life. Every major division of animal life is found in the seas, from tiny one-celled microbes to the largest creature on the planet, the blue whale. Nowhere, not even in the rain forest, is there a greater diversity of life. (Green, yellow, and red areas in the satellite map at right show waters particularly rich in plant and animal life.)

In sunny surface waters, grazing animals such as shrimp feed on tiny plants. Deeper, in the twilight region, creatures swim to the surface each night to feed. The black depths hold the strangest animals of all: bizarre glowing predators and otherworldly life-forms on sea vents. This sea-vent life may hold the key to the origins of life on Earth.

Gentle Giant

Gulping gallons of plankton-rich seawater as it swims, the mild-mannered whale shark is the world's largest fish. Its open mouth can be 4 feet (1 meter) wide.

Chilled Krill

At home in frigid water, tiny krill (above) swim beneath Antarctic ice. Millions of these animals will be eaten by larger creatures, such as whales and seals.

The Coral Community

Coral reefs are skeletons—millions of limestone skeletons cemented together over time. The skeletons are created by the tiny coral animals that live inside them. Found in warm, shallow waters around the world, these reefs are busy neighborhoods. Their nooks and crannies provide a home for brilliantly colored fish, sponges, basket stars, and other underwater creatures.

Creatures that call the coral reef home include the parrotfish (left) and golden anthias fish (right). Parrotfish use their sharp, beaklike mouths to break off bits of coral. Then they eat the algae that live on the soft-bodied coral animals inside.

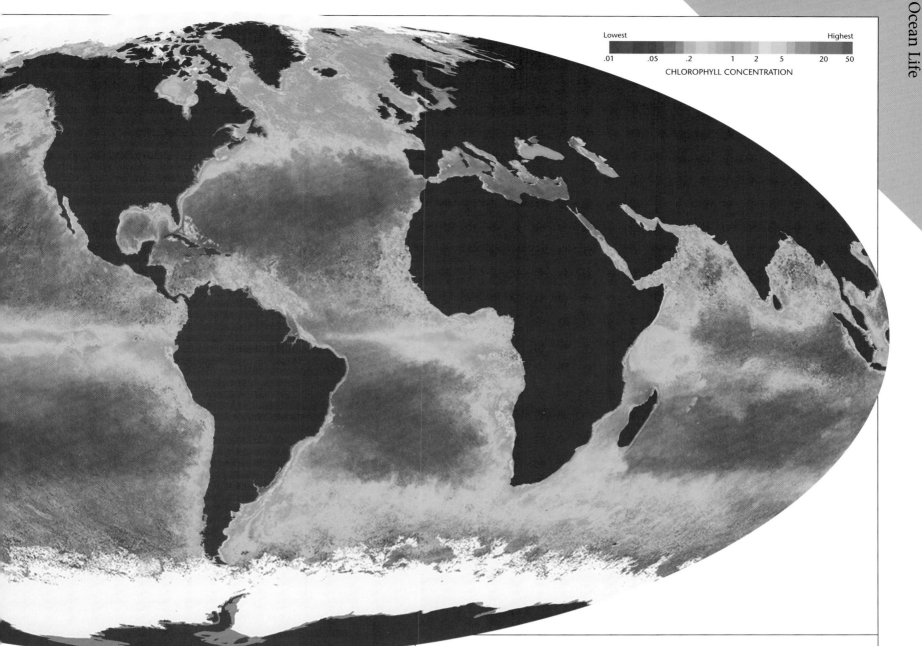

Lowest | | | | | | | Highest
.01 | .05 | .2 | 1 | 2 | 5 | 20 | 50
CHLOROPHYLL CONCENTRATION

Some Like It Hot

The ocean is cracked. An enormous seam runs through its floor, marking a place where Earth's plates are pulling apart and building a mid-ocean mountain range with cooling lava (below, right). Shooting up through the seam are jets of hot water called hydrothermal vents. They are heated to as much as 850°F (454°C) by magma below. A number of bizarre creatures live around the vents, including giant clams and tiny chemical-eating microbes.

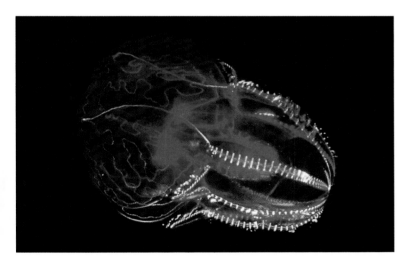

Glowing Gobblers

Many deep-sea animals make their own light through a chemical process called bioluminescence. Among them are the red, glowing Lampocteis (above) and the small but scary anglerfish (right).

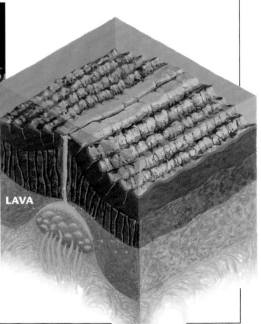

LAVA

More than 300 new species have been discovered around hydrothermal vents. They include tube worms (above), some of them six feet (2 meters) tall. Their insides are full of bacteria that provide them with food.

Mapping the Ocean

How do you map a place that moves under your feet? How do you see a land that daylight never reaches? How do you explore a world whose temperatures freeze you, whose pressures crush you, and whose inhabitants might eat you if you ventured outside?

The answer is: slowly, bit-by-bit, with high-tech equipment. Mapping the ocean is harder than mapping Mars. Yet in recent years, scientists have made great strides in picturing the sea from bottom to top. This progress is due mainly to satellites that scan the sea's surface and to clever machines that explore its depths. This new information helps us understand just how large a role the ocean plays in the world's climate and how important it is to our own existence.

How Deep Is Deep?

Not until the 1950s, when scientists used sonar to measure the ocean floor, did we first see the great mountains and valleys of the world's oceans. Now, with satellite imaging we can map everything larger than 6 miles (10 kilometers) wide, and even smaller features by using on-site sonar surveys. We can see how the ocean would look without water (right, inset) and just how deep its waters are (large map).

Undersea Geography

Around each continent is a shallow continental shelf that drops off to an abyssal plain. Running through the ocean floor is the Mid-Ocean Ridge. Underwater volcanoes form seamounts that form islands when they rise above the surface. Coral reefs may build up around these islands. Over time, the volcanoes erode and sink, leaving coral atolls. Valleys, called trenches, cut deep into the ocean floor.

0 m	0 ft.
-500 m	-1650 ft.
-1,500 m	-4,900 ft.
-3,000 m	-9,850 ft.
-5,000 m	-16,400 ft.
-7,000 m	-22,950 ft.
-9,000 m	-36,100 ft.
-11,000 m	-45,950 ft.

World Bathymetry

km

0   3,000

mi

0   3,000

Scale at the Equator, Miller Cylindrical Projection

Ups and Downs

Argo floats, like the one illustrated below, see what satellites can't. A float sinks thousands of feet below the surface, drifts for ten days, then bobs to the surface. There it sends information about the temperature and saltiness of the water to an orbiting satellite that relays the data to scientists. Then the cycle starts over as the float sinks.

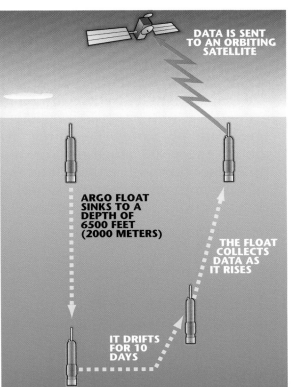

DATA IS SENT TO AN ORBITING SATELLITE

ARGO FLOAT SINKS TO A DEPTH OF 6500 FEET (2000 METERS)

THE FLOAT COLLECTS DATA AS IT RISES

IT DRIFTS FOR 10 DAYS

A New Light on the Ocean

The Sea-Viewing Wide Field-of-View Sensor (SeaWiFS) satellite (below) senses light—both visible and infrared. It can detect floating plants on the ocean surface, leading to maps of biological activity such as the one on pages 162–163.

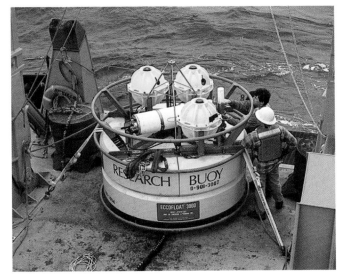

Sounding the Depths

Researchers get an acoustic buoy ready for the sea. These devices measure the seafloor by bouncing sound waves off the bottom. They can also take the temperature of seawater by measuring the time it takes for sound to pass through it.

Ocean and Climate

Air, land, and ocean work together to create the world's climate—its weather over time. Only recently did we begin to learn what a large part the ocean plays.

The ocean is Earth's radiator. It absorbs heat from the sun and releases it slowly, helping to keep the planet warm. But the sea's currents and hot and cold cycles affect the world's climate as well. As shown in the map at right, currents warmed in the tropics (red arrows) rise, move to colder regions, and sink again (green and blue arrows), evening out temperatures around the world. Huge areas of surface water heat up or cool down in regular patterns. These changes and currents affect the atmosphere and cause floods, drought, storms, and heat waves all over the world.

AFRICA

INDIAN
OCEAN

AUSTRALIA

ANTARCTICA

The Terrible Twins

It arrives around Christmas, but instead of presents it brings droughts in Africa, floods in North America, and typhoons in the Pacific. Named El Niño, after the Christ child, it is a warm Pacific current (shown in red in the top globe, below) that swings past the coast of Peru every two to seven years. Covering an area larger than the continental United States, El Niño heats the ocean by as much as 10°F (-12°C) above normal. Sometimes it is followed by a cold-water current, called La Niña (blue in the bottom globe, below). Where El Niño brings floods, La Niña brings drought.

El Niño

La Niña

Rainy Season, Before and After

Brown, dry rice fields in Goa, India (above, left), wait in May for the yearly monsoon winds to bring rain. In August, after the monsoon, the fields are green and growing (above, right). Farmers in many parts of the world rely on such predictable rains to keep their crops alive. Ocean currents such as El Niño can determine whether those rains arrive.

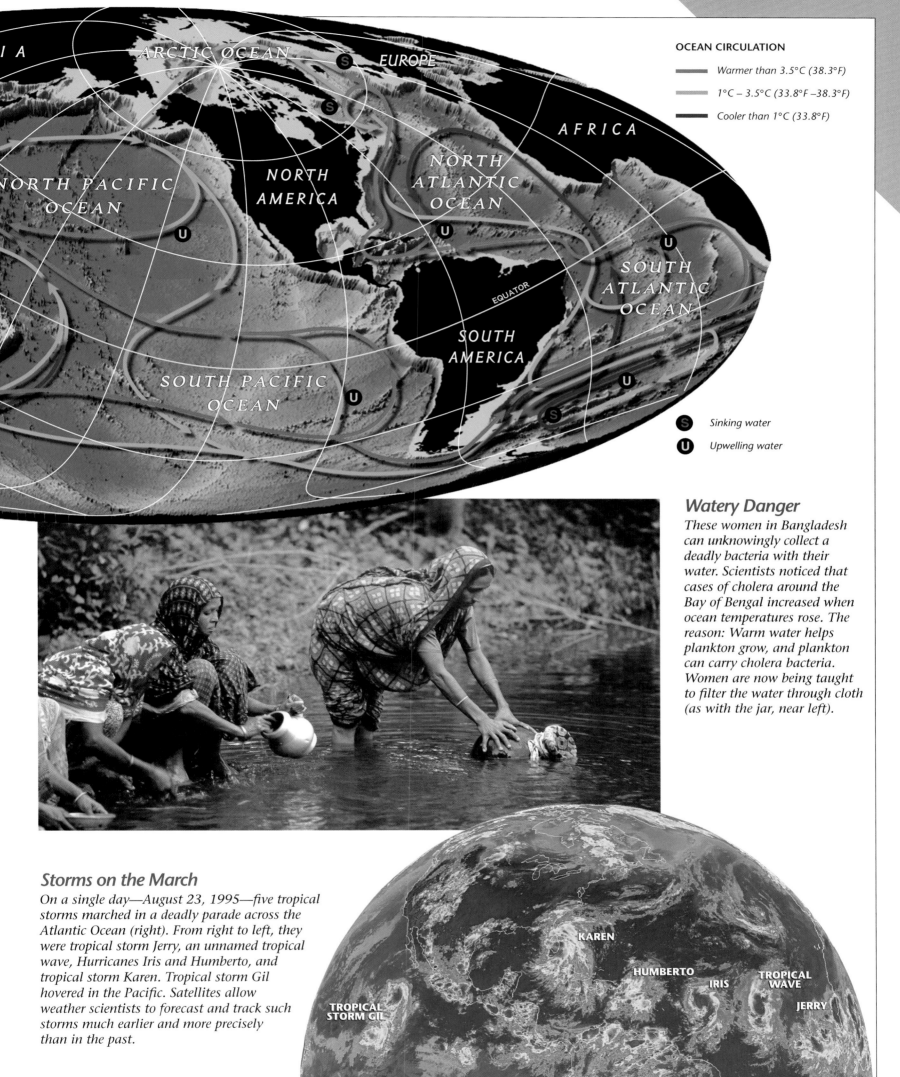

OCEAN CIRCULATION

—— *Warmer than 3.5°C (38.3°F)*

—— *1°C – 3.5°C (33.8°F –38.3°F)*

—— *Cooler than 1°C (33.8°F)*

S *Sinking water*

U *Upwelling water*

ARCTIC OCEAN

EUROPE

AFRICA

NORTH PACIFIC OCEAN

NORTH AMERICA

NORTH ATLANTIC OCEAN

SOUTH ATLANTIC OCEAN

EQUATOR

SOUTH AMERICA

SOUTH PACIFIC OCEAN

Watery Danger

These women in Bangladesh can unknowingly collect a deadly bacteria with their water. Scientists noticed that cases of cholera around the Bay of Bengal increased when ocean temperatures rose. The reason: Warm water helps plankton grow, and plankton can carry cholera bacteria. Women are now being taught to filter the water through cloth (as with the jar, near left).

Storms on the March

On a single day—August 23, 1995—five tropical storms marched in a deadly parade across the Atlantic Ocean (right). From right to left, they were tropical storm Jerry, an unnamed tropical wave, Hurricanes Iris and Humberto, and tropical storm Karen. Tropical storm Gil hovered in the Pacific. Satellites allow weather scientists to forecast and track such storms much earlier and more precisely than in the past.

KAREN

HUMBERTO

IRIS

TROPICAL WAVE

JERRY

TROPICAL STORM GIL

Pacific Ocean

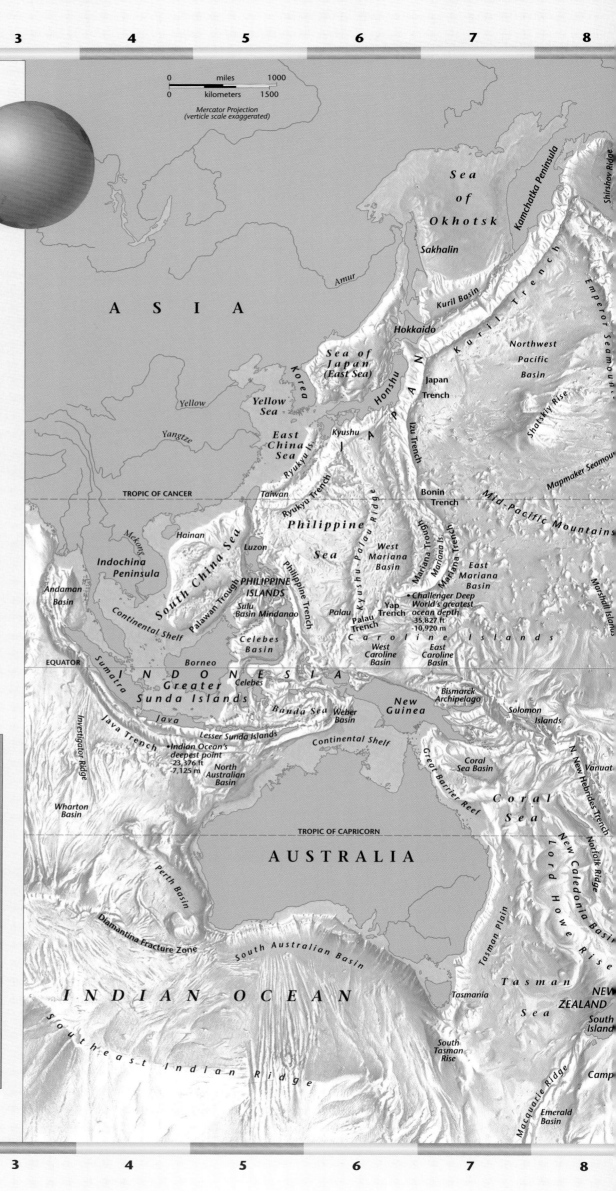

Greatest of Oceans

Biggest, oldest, deepest. The Pacific takes first place among the world's oceans in many categories. It's also the site of more volcanic activity than any other ocean. Look at the edges of the ocean floor in this map, and you'll see why. The vast plate holding most of the ocean's floor is diving down under the edges of the continents to the east and west. As the diving plate melts, molten rock rises, creating volcanoes. Where the ocean plate rubs against the continental plates earthquakes shake the land. This violent area around the rim of the Pacific is called the Ring of Fire.

Facts

Surface area
64,186,000 sq mi
(166,241,000 sq km)

Percent of Earth's water area
46%

Greatest Depth
Challenger Deep (in the Mariana Trench): -35,827 ft (-10,920 m)

Surface temperatures
Summer high: 82°F (28°C)
Winter low: 30°F (-1°C)

Tides
Highest: 30 ft (9 m) near Korean peninsula
Lowest: 1 ft (0.3 m) near Midway Islands

9   10   11   12   13   14   15   16

A

B

NORTH AMERICA

C

D

Continental Shelf

ALASKA

Yukon

Gulf of Alaska

Bering Sea

Aleutian Basin

Bowers Ridge

Aleutian Islands

Aleutian Trench

Juan De Fuca Ridge

Tufts Plain

Columbia

Hudson Bay

NORTH ATLANTIC OCEAN

Chinook Trough

Mendocino Fracture Zone

Pioneer Fracture Zone

Patton Escarpment

Colorado

Gulf of Maine

Northwest Hawaiian Ridge

Midway Islands

Musicians Seamounts

Murray Fracture Zone

Cedros Trench

Gulf of Mexico

Bahama Islands

TROPIC OF CANCER

Mexico Basin

Cuba

Greater Antilles

Atlantic Ocean's deepest point -28,232ft -8,605 m

Hawaiian Islands

Hawaiian Ridge

Necker Ridge

Hawaii

Molokai Fracture Zone

Yucatán Peninsula

Caribbean Sea

Lesser Antilles

E

Central Pacific

Magellan Rise

Basin

Clarion Fracture Zone

Mathematicians Seamounts

Middle America Trench

Line Islands

Clipperton Fracture Zone

Guatemala Basin

Cocos Ridge

Panama Basin

F

EQUATOR

Galápagos Rift

Galápagos Is.

SOUTH AMERICA

Galápagos Fracture Zone

Manihiki Plateau

Marquesas Islands

Marquesas Fracture Zone

Peru Basin

Galápagos Rise

Fiji

Fiji Islands

Plateau

Lau Basin

Cook Islands

Tuamotu Archipelago

Society Islands

Austral Islands

Easter Fracture Zone

Nazca Ridge

Peru-Chile Trench

G

Lau Ridge

Tonga Trench

Sala y Gómez Ridge

Chile Basin

H

North Island

Kermadec Trench

Louisville Ridge

Southwest Pacific Basin

Challenger Fracture Zone

Chile Rise

Chatham Rise

Bounty Trough

Pacific-Antarctic Ridge

Agassiz Fracture Zone

Valdivia Fracture Zone

J

Udintsev Fracture Zone

Eltanin Fracture Zone

Menard Fracture Zone

Southeast Pacific Basin

Humboldt Plain

K

9   10   11   12   13   14   15   16

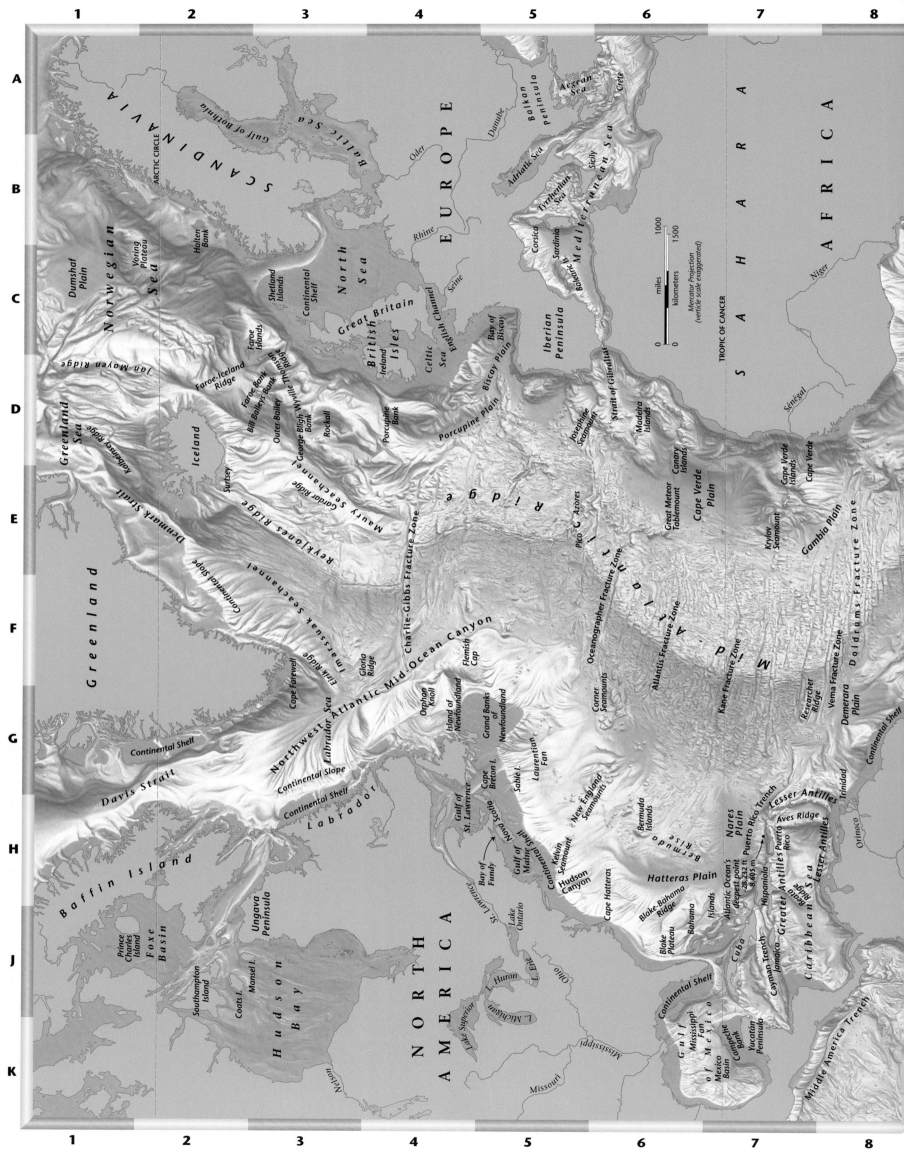

9 10 11 12 13 14 15 16

A

B

C

D

E

F

G

H

J

K

Atlantic Ocean

Realm of Hidden Mountains

Shaped like a fat "S," the Atlantic Ocean is only half as big as the Pacific, but it's getting bigger every day. That's because it's spreading apart along a seam that runs down its middle. The seam marks the place where two of Earth's plates are pulling apart, allowing magma—hot melted rock—to rise up between them. As the magma flows out and hardens, it forms new ocean floor, including an underwater chain of mountains called the Mid-Atlantic Ridge that rises as high as 2 miles (3 kilometers).

Facts

Surface area
33,420,000 sq mi
(86,557,000 sq km)

Percent of Earth's water area
24%

Greatest depth
Puerto Rico Trench: -28,232 ft
(-8,605 m)

Surface temperatures
Summer high: 86°F (30°C)
Winter low: 28°F (-2°C)

Tides
Highest: 52 ft (16 m),
Bay of Fundy, Canada
Lowest: 1.5 ft (0.5 m),
Gulf of Mexico and
Mediterranean Sea

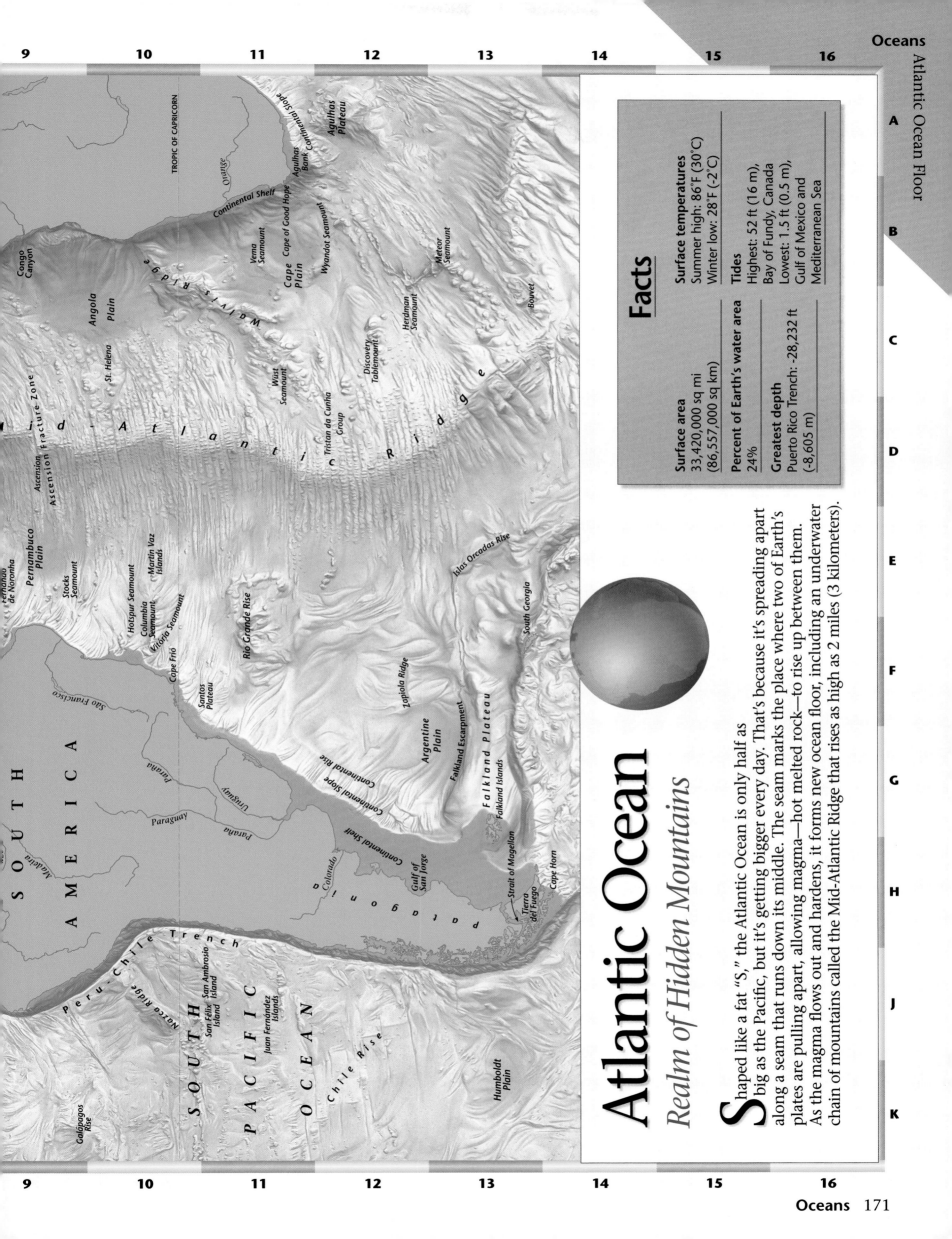

Congo Canyon

TROPIC OF CAPRICORN

Orange

Continental Shelf

Agulhas Bank Continental Slope

Agulhas Plateau

Cape of Good Hope

Vema Seamount

Wyandot Seamount

Cape Plain

Meteor Seamount

Bouvet

Herdman Seamount

Discovery Tablemount

Wüst Seamount

Tristan da Cunha Group

Angola Plain

St. Helena

Mid-Atlantic Ridge

Ascension Fracture Zone

Ascension

Fernando de Noronha

Pernambuco Plain

Stocks Seamount

Hotspur Seamount

Columbia Seamount

Martin Vaz Islands

Vitória Seamount

Cape Frio

Rio Grande Rise

Islas Orcadas Rise

South Georgia

Zapiola Ridge

Argentine Plain

Falkland Escarpment

Falkland Plateau

Falkland Islands

Santos Plateau

São Francisco

SOUTH AMERICA

Paraná

Uruguay

Paraguay

Paraná

Continental Slope

Continental Rise

Continental Shelf

Colorado

Gulf of San Jorge

Patagonia

Strait of Magellan

Tierra del Fuego

Cape Horn

Madeira

Peru-Chile Trench

Nazca Ridge

San Ambrosio Island

San Félix Island

Juan Fernández Islands

SOUTH PACIFIC OCEAN

Chile Rise

Galápagos Rise

Humboldt Plain

9 10 11 12 13 14 15 16

Indian Ocean

Passage to Asia

Warm, blue, and stormy, the Indian Ocean fills the area between Africa and Australia. In the north, India splits it into the Arabian Sea and the Bay of Bengal. Its floor reveals the slow, but violent, motions of Earth's crust. The crooked arms of the Red Sea and the Persian Gulf hug the Arabian Peninsula, which is breaking away from Africa. The longest straight-line feature on Earth, the Ninetyeast Ridge, formed over a 90-million-year period as the plate carrying India moved northward over a volcanic hot spot.

Facts

Surface area
28,350,000 sq mi
(73,427,000 sq km)

Percent of Earth's water area
20%

Greatest Depth
Java Trench: -23,376 ft
(-7,125 m)

Surface temperatures
Summer high: 90°F (32°C)
Winter low: 30°F (-1°C)

Tides
Highest: 36 ft (11 m)
Lowest: 2 ft (0.6 m)
(both along Australia's west coast)

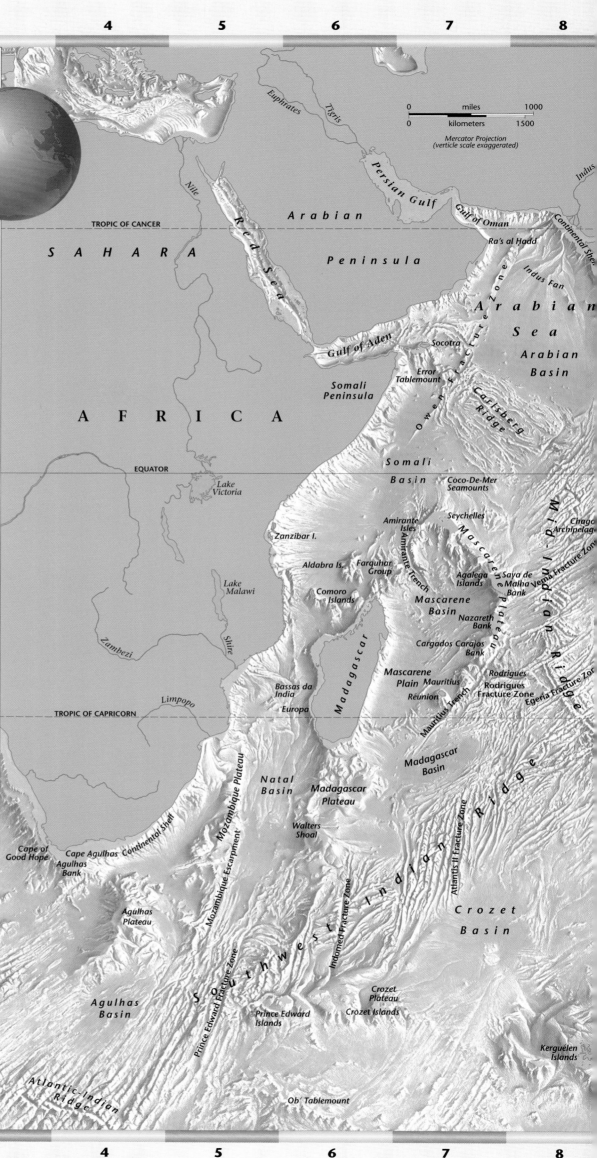

9 10 11 12 13 14 15 16
A B C D E F G H J K

ASIA

Yellow

Yangtze

Brahmaputra

Ganges

Yellow Sea

Yellow Sea

Honshu

Japan

Japan Trench

Northwest

Shikoku

Kyushu

Pacific

Isakov Seamount

Basin

Makarov Seamount

Bonin Is.

East China Sea

TROPIC OF CANCER

Mekong

Salween

Continental Shelf

Taiwan

Ryukyu Islands

Ryukyu Trench

Kyushu-Palau Ridge

INDIA

Hainan

Paracel Islands

Macclesfield Bank

South

Luzon

Philippine Sea

Philippine

West Mariana Basin

Mariana Trough

Mariana Islands

Bonin Trench

Bay

of

Ganges Fan

Bengal

Andaman Islands

Andaman Basin

Sri Lanka (Ceylon)

Nicobar Islands

Indochina

Peninsula

China

Philippine Islands

Philippine Basin

Benham Seamount

Philippine Trench

World's greatest ocean depth −35,827 ft −10,920 m

Challenger Deep

Mariana Trench

Guam

East Mariana Basin

Maldive Islands

Nikitin Seamount

Mid-Indian

Diego Garcia

Basin

Sumatra

Investigator Ridge

Ninetyeast Ridge

Palawan Trough

Sea

Continental Shelf

Sulu Basin

Mindanao

Palau Trench

Celebes Basin

Palau

Yap Trench

Equipik Rise

West Caroline Basin

Caroline Islands

East Caroline Basin

EQUATOR

Borneo

Greater

Celebes

Sunda Islands

Celebes

Bismarck Archipelago

Sea

Java

Banda Sea

Bali

Weber

Boton

New Guinea

New Britain Trench

Osborn Plateau

Java Ridge

Java Trench

Christmas I.

Indian Ocean's deepest point −23,376 ft −7,125 m

Lesser Sunda Islands

Timor

Continental Shelf

Solomon Sea

Coral Sea Basin

Coral Sea

Wharton Basin

North Australian Basin

Exmouth Plateau

Great Barrier Reef

Wallaby Plateau

Cuvier Plateau

TROPIC OF CAPRICORN

East Indiaman Ridge

Broken Ridge

Diamantina Fracture Zone

Perth Basin

AUSTRALIA

Darling

Naturaliste Plateau

Continental Shelf

Continental Slope

Murray

Continental Slope

Tasman Plain

Amsterdam

St. Paul

Continental Slope

South Australian Basin

Tasman Sea

Tasmania

Tasman Sea

Kerguelen

Plateau

Southeast   Indian   Ridge

South Tasman Rise

East Tasman Plateau

Arctic Ocean

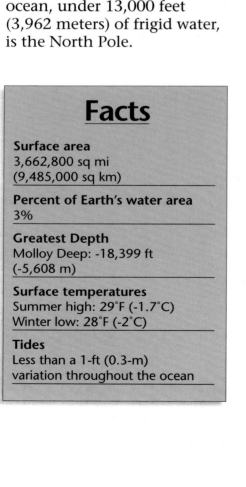

The Frozen North

The smallest, coldest, and most mysterious of the four oceans, the Arctic has been mapped in detail only recently. That's because it takes a specially built submarine to cruise under its frozen surface and collect data about the ocean floor. Maps made from this data reveal three ridges running between Greenland and Siberia as well as an unusually wide continental shelf along the Siberian coast. The shelf is so close to the surface that in some places it shows scrapes from the bottoms of icebergs. Roughly in the middle of this ocean, under 13,000 feet (3,962 meters) of frigid water, is the North Pole.

Facts

Surface area
3,662,800 sq mi
(9,485,000 sq km)

Percent of Earth's water area
3%

Greatest Depth
Molloy Deep: -18,399 ft
(-5,608 m)

Surface temperatures
Summer high: 29°F (-1.7°C)
Winter low: 28°F (-2°C)

Tides
Less than a 1-ft (0.3-m)
variation throughout the ocean

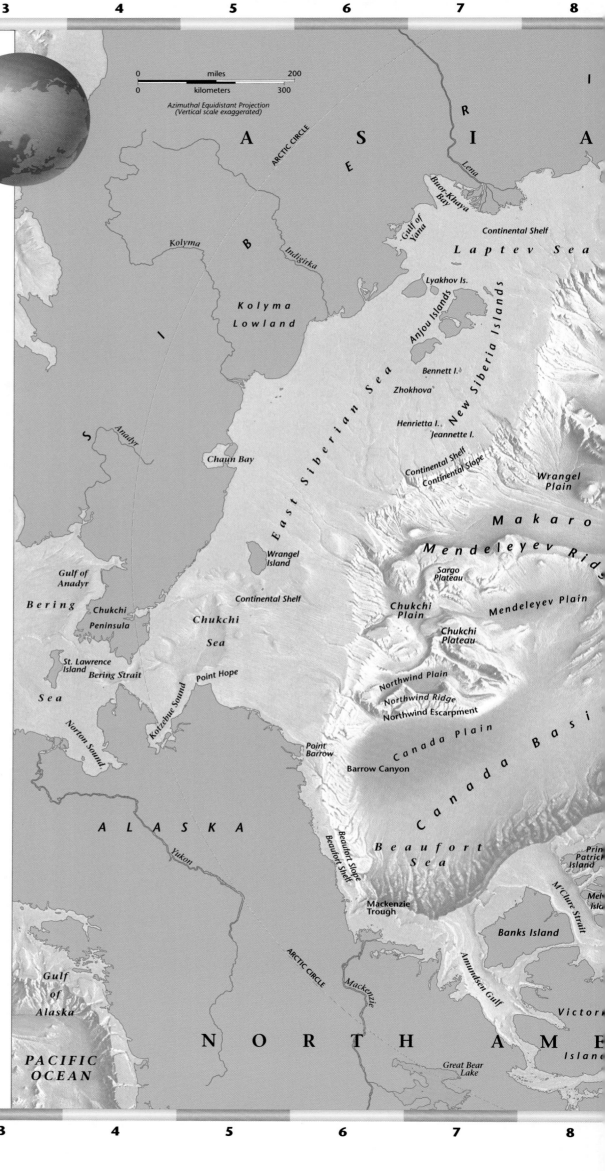

miles
0   200
kilometers
0   300
Azimuthal Equidistant Projection
(Vertical scale exaggerated)

ASIA

ARCTIC CIRCLE

Kolyma

Indigirka

Gulf of Yana

Lena

Buor-Khaya Bay

Continental Shelf

Laptev Sea

Kolyma Lowland

Lyakhov Is.

Anjou Islands

Bennett I.

Zhokhova

New Siberia Islands

Henrietta I.

Jeannette I.

Continental Shelf

Continental Slope

Wrangel Plain

Anadyr

Chaun Bay

East Siberian Sea

Makaro

Mendeleyev Rid

Sargo Plateau

Wrangel Island

Continental Shelf

Chukchi Plain

Mendeleyev Plain

Gulf of Anadyr

Chukchi Plateau

Bering

Chukchi Peninsula

Chukchi Sea

St. Lawrence Island

Bering Strait

Point Hope

Northwind Plain

Northwind Ridge

Northwind Escarpment

Sea

Kotzebue Sound

Canada Plain

Canada Basi

Norton Sound

Point Barrow

Barrow Canyon

ALASKA

Yukon

Beaufort Slope

Beaufort Shelf

Beaufort Sea

Prin Patric Island

M'Clure Strait

Mel Isla

Mackenzie Trough

Banks Island

ARCTIC CIRCLE

Mackenzie

Amundsen Gulf

Gulf of Alaska

Victori

NORTH AME

Island

PACIFIC OCEAN

Great Bear Lake

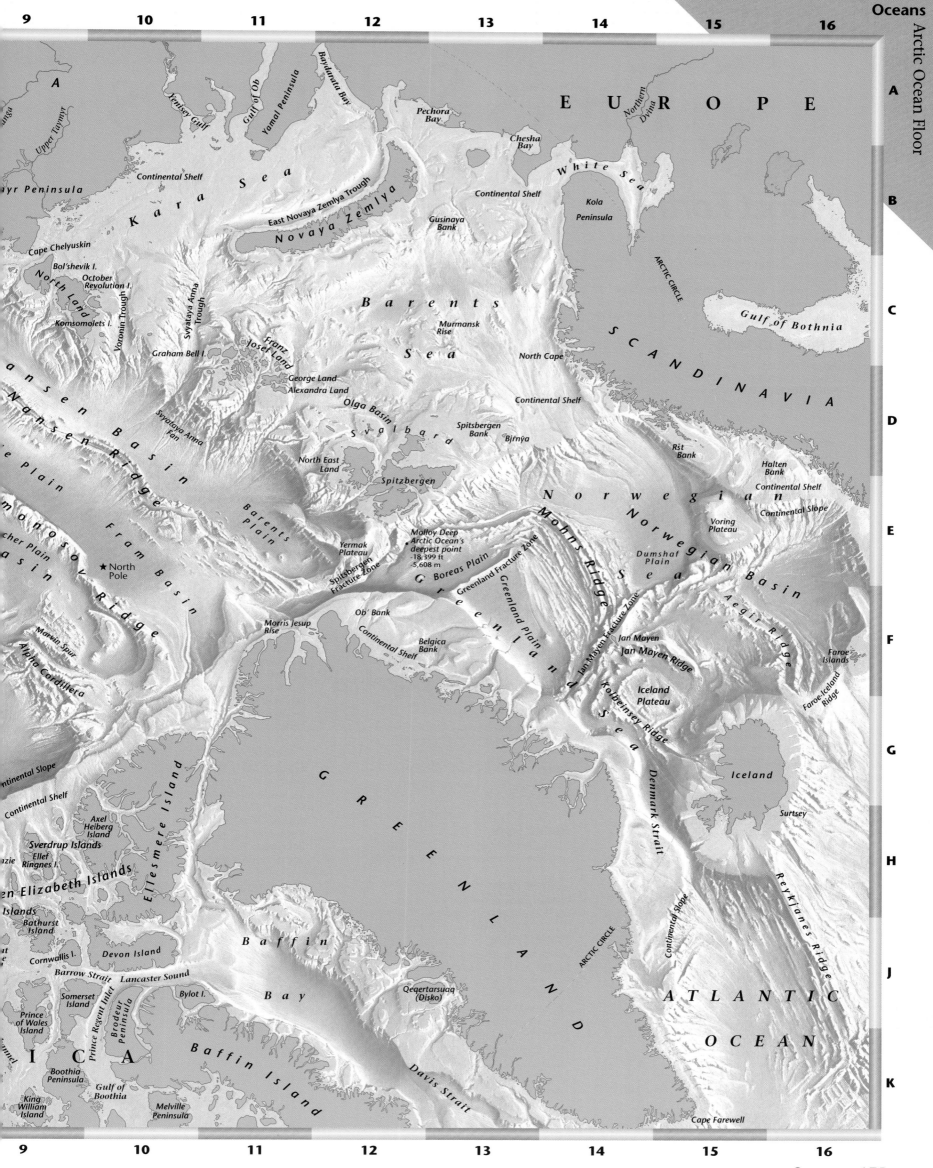

9 10 11 12 13 14 15 16

A

E U R O P E

Upper Taymyr

Yenisey Gulf

Gulf of Ob

Yamal Peninsula

Baydaratra Bay

Pechora Bay

Northern Dvina

yr Peninsula

K a r a   S e a

Continental Shelf

Chesha Bay

B

Cape Chelyuskin

East Novaya Zemlya Trough

White Sea

Continental Shelf

Kola Peninsula

ARCTIC CIRCLE

Bol'shevik I.

October Revolution I.

Novaya Zemlya

Gusinaya Bank

Gulf of Bothnia

C

North Land

Komsomolets I.

Varonin Trough

Svyataya Anna Trough

B a r e n t s

Murmansk Rise

S C A N D I N A V I A

Graham Bell I.

Franz Josef Land

S e a

North Cape

George Land

Alexandra Land

Continental Shelf

D

Hansen Ridge

Nansen Basin

Svyataya Anna Fan

Olga Basin

S v a l b a r d

Spitsbergen Bank

Bjørnya

Røst Bank

Halten Bank

N o r w e g i a n

Continental Shelf

Plain

North East Land

Spitzbergen

Voring Plateau

Continental Slope

E

Fram Basin

Barents Plain

Molloy Deep Arctic Ocean's deepest point -18,399 ft -5,608 m

N o r w e g i a n   B a s i n

Dumshaf Plain

cher Plain

monosov Ridge

★ North Pole

Yermak Plateau

Spitsbergen Fracture Zone

Boreas Plain

Mohns Ridge

Aegir Ridge

sin

Ob' Bank

Morris Jesup Rise

Continental Shelf

Belgica Bank

Greenland Plain und

Greenland Fracture Zone

Jan Mayen Fracture Zone

Jan Mayen

Jan Mayen Ridge

Faroe Islands

F

Marvin Spur

Alpha Cordillera

G r e e n l a n d   S e a

Kolbeinsey Ridge

Iceland Plateau

Faroe-Iceland Ridge

G

Continental Slope

Continental Shelf

G

Denmark Strait

Iceland

Axel Heiberg Island

R

Surtsey

Sverdrup Islands

Ellef Ringnes I.

E

H

Elizabeth Islands

Bathurst Island

Ellesmere Island

E

Continental Slope

Reykjanes Ridge

Islands

Cornwallis I.

Devon Island

N

Baffin

ARCTIC CIRCLE

J

Barrow Strait

Lancaster Sound

Bylot I.

Bay

Qeqertarsuaq (Disko)

L

A T L A N T I C

Somerset Island

Brodeur Peninsula

Prince Regent Inlet

D

Prince of Wales Island

I C A

A

Baffin Island

O C E A N

K

Boothia Peninsula

Gulf of Boothia

Davis Strait

King William Island

Melville Peninsula

Cape Farewell

9 10 11 12 13 14 15 16

Facts & Figures

Planet Earth

Mass: 6,583,348,000,000,000,000,000 tons
(5,974,000,000,000,000,000,000 metric tons)
Distance around the Equator:
24,901 mi (40,073 km)
Area: 196,951,900 sq mi (510,066,000 sq km)
Land area: 57,313,000 sq mi (148,429,000 sq km)
Water area: 139,634,000 sq mi (361,637,000 sq km)

The Continents

Asia: 17,212,000 sq mi (44,579,000 sq km)
Africa: 11,608,000 sq mi (30,065,000 sq km)
North America: 9,366,000 sq mi
(24,256,000 sq km)
South America: 6,880,500 sq mi
(17,819,000 sq km)
Antarctica: 5,100,400 sq mi (13,209,000 sq km)
Europe: 3,837,000 sq mi (9,938,000 sq km)
Australia: 2,968,000 sq mi (7,687,000 sq km)

Highest Mountain on Each Continent

Everest, Asia: 29,035 ft (8,850 m)
Aconcagua, South America: 22,834 ft (6,960 m)
McKinley (Denali), North America:
20,320 ft (6,194 m)
Kilimanjaro, Africa: 19,340 ft (5,895 m)
El'brus, Europe: 18,510 ft (5,642 m)
Vinson Massif, Antarctica: 16,067 ft (4,897 m)
Kosciuszko, Australia: 7,310 ft (2,228 m)

Lowest Point on Each Continent

Antarctica: -8,366 ft (-2,550 m)
Dead Sea, Asia: -1,365 ft (-416 m)
Lake Assal, Africa: -512 ft (-156 m)
Death Valley, North America: -282 ft (-86 m)
Valdés Peninsula, South America: -131 ft (-40 m)
Caspian Sea, Europe: -92 ft (-28 m)
Lake Eyre, Australia: -52 ft (-16 m)

Longest Rivers

Nile, Africa: 4,241 mi (6,825 km)
Amazon, South America: 4,000 mi (6,437 km)
Yangtze (Chang), Asia: 3,964 mi (6,380 km)
Mississippi-Missouri, North America:
3,710 mi (5,971 km)
Yenisey-Angara, Asia: 3,440 mi (5,536 km)
Yellow (Huang), Asia: 3,395 mi (5,464 km)
Ob-Irtysh, Asia: 3,361 mi (5,410 km)
Congo (Zaire), Africa: 2,715 mi (4,370 km)
Amur, Asia: 2,744 mi (4,416 km)
Lena, Asia: 2,734 mi (4,400 km)

Major Islands

Greenland: 840,000 sq mi (2,175,600 sq km)
New Guinea: 306,000 sq mi (792,500 sq km)
Borneo: 280,100 sq mi (725,100 sq km)
Madagascar: 226,600 sq mi (587,000 sq km)
Baffin: 196,000 sq mi (507,500 sq km)
Sumatra: 165,000 sq mi (427,300 sq km)
Honshu: 87,800 sq mi (227,400 sq km)
Great Britain: 84,200 sq mi (218,100 sq km)
Victoria: 83,900 sq mi (217,300 sq km)
Ellesmere: 75,800 sq mi (196,200 sq km)

Major Lakes

Caspian Sea, Europe-Asia: 143,200 sq mi
(371,000 sq km)
Superior, North America: 31,700 sq mi
(82,100 sq km)
Victoria, Africa: 26,800 sq mi (69,500 sq km)
Huron, North America: 23,000 sq mi
(59,600 sq km)
Michigan, North America: 22,300 sq mi
(57,800 sq km)
Tanganyika, Africa: 12,600 sq mi (32,600 sq km)
Baikal, Asia: 12,200 sq mi (31,500 sq km)
Great Bear, North America: 12,100 sq mi
(31,300 sq km)
Aral Sea, Asia: 11,900 sq mi (30,700 sq km)
Malawi, Africa: 11,200 sq mi (28,900 sq km)

Oceans

Pacific: 64,186,000 sq mi (166,241,000 sq km)
Atlantic: 33,420,000 sq mi (86,557,000 sq km)
Indian: 28,350,000 sq mi (73,427,000 sq km)
Arctic: 3,662,800 sq mi (9,485,000 sq km)

Major Seas

South China: 1,148,500 sq mi (2,974,600 sq km)
Caribbean: 971,400 sq mi (2,515,900 sq km)
Mediterranean: 969,100 sq mi (2,510,000 sq km)
Bering: 873,000 sq mi (2,261,100 sq km)
Gulf of Mexico: 582,100 sq mi (1,507,600 sq km)
Sea of Okhotsk: 537,500 sq mi (1,392,100 sq km)
Sea of Japan: 391,100 sq mi (1,012,900 sq km)
Hudson Bay: 281,900 sq mi (730,100 sq km)
East China: 256,600 sq mi (664,600 sq km)
Andaman: 218,100 sq mi (564,900 sq km)

Geographic Extremes

Highest Mountain
Everest (Chomolungma), China/Nepal:
29,035 ft (8,850 m)

Deepest Point in the Ocean
Challenger Deep, Mariana Trench, Pacific:
-35,827 ft (-10,920 m)

Hottest Place
Dalol, Denakil Depression, Ethiopia:
annual average temperature 93° F (34° C)

Coldest Place
Plateau Station, Antarctica:
annual average temperature -70°F (-56.7° C)

Wettest Place
Mawsynram, Assam, India: annual average
rainfall 467 in (11,873 mm)

Driest Place
Atacama Desert, Chile: barely measurable rainfall

Largest Hot Desert
Sahara, Africa: 3,475,000 sq mi (9,000,000 sq km)

Largest Cold Desert
Antarctica: 5,100,400 sq mi (13,209,000 sq km)

People

Most People by Continent
Asia: 3,765,711,000

Least People by Continent
Antarctica: 2,000 (transient)
Australia: 19,731,000

Most Densely Populated Country
Monaco: 34,000 people in 0.7 sq mi

Least Densely Populated Country
Mongolia: 4 people per sq mi

Biggest Metropolitan Areas
Tokyo, Japan: 26,546,000
New York, United States: 21,200,000
México, Mexico: 18,268,000
São Paulo, Brazil: 17,900,000
Bombay (Mumbai), India: 17,850,000
Osaka, Japan: 17,800,000
Los Angeles, United States: 16,374,000
Buenos Aires, Argentina: 13,250,000
Lagos, Nigeria: 13,056,000
New Delhi, India: 12,987,000
Calcutta, India: 12,900,000
Shanghai, China: 11,800,000
Beijing, China: 10,836,000
Rio de Janeiro, Brazil: 10,650,000
Seoul, South Korea: 9,862,000

Countries with the Highest Life Expectancy
Japan: 81.23 years
Switzerland: 79.78 years
Sweden: 79.72 years
Australia: 79.52 years
San Marino: 79.52 years
Iceland: 79.49 years
France: 79.34 years

Countries with the Lowest Life Expectancy
Zambia: 37.20 years
Mozambique: 37.50 years
Malawi: 37.60 years
Zimbabwe: 37.80 years
Rwanda: 39.30 years
Botswana: 39.30 years
Burundi: 40.60 years

Countries with the Highest Annual Income per Person
Luxembourg: $36,400
U.S.: $36,200
San Marino: $32,000
Switzerland: $28,600
Norway: $27,700

Countries with the Lowest Annual Income per Person
Sierra Leone: $510
Congo: $600
Ethiopia: $600
Somalia: $600
Eritrea: $710

Glossary

archipelago a group or chain of islands

bay a body of water, usually smaller than a gulf, that is partially surrounded by land

border the area on either side of a boundary

boundary most commonly, a line that has been established by people to mark the limit of one political unit, such as a country or state, and the beginning of another; geographical features such as mountains sometimes act as boundaries

breakwater a structure, such as a wall, that protects a harbor or beach from pounding waves

canal an artificial waterway that is used by ships or to carry water for irrigation

canyon a deep, narrow valley that has steep sides

cape a point of land that extends into an ocean, a lake, or a river

cliff a very steep rock face, usually along a coast but also on the side of a mountain

continent one of the seven main landmasses on Earth's surface

country a territory whose government is the highest legal authority over the land and people within its boundaries

delta lowland formed by silt, sand, and gravel deposited by a river at its mouth

desert a hot or cold region that receives 10 inches (25 centimeters) or less of rain or other kinds of precipitation a year

divide an elevated area drained by different river systems flowing in different directions

elevation distance above sea level, usually measured in feet or meters

escarpment a cliff that separates two nearly flat land areas that lie at different elevations

fault a break in Earth's crust along which movement up, down, or sideways occurs

fork in a river, the place where two streams come together

glacier a large, slow-moving mass of ice

gulf a portion of the ocean that cuts into the land; usually larger than a bay

harbor a body of water, sheltered by natural or artificial barriers, that is deep enough for ships

hemisphere literally half a sphere; Earth has four hemispheres: Northern, Southern, Eastern, and Western

highlands an elevated area or the more mountainous region of a country

inlet a narrow opening in the land that is filled with water flowing from an ocean, a lake, or a river

island a landmass, smaller than a continent, that is completely surrounded by water

isthmus a narrow strip of land that connects two larger landmasses and has water on two sides

lagoon a shallow body of water that is open to the sea but also protected from it by a reef or sandbar

lake a body of water that is surrounded by land; large lakes are sometimes called seas

landform a physical feature of the Earth that is shaped by tectonic activity and weathering and erosion; the four major kinds are plains, mountains, plateaus, and hills

landmass a large area of Earth's crust that lies above sea level, such as a continent

large-scale map a map, such as a street map, that shows a small area in great detail

latitude distance north and south of the Equator, which is 0° latitude

longitude distance east and west of the prime meridian, which is 0° longitude

mesa an eroded plateau, broader than it is high, that is found in arid or semiarid regions

metropolitan area a city and its surrounding suburbs or communities

mountain a landform, higher than a hill, that rises at least 1,000 feet (300 meters) above the surrounding land and is wider at its base than at its top, or peak; a series of mountains is called a range

nation people who share a common culture; often used as another word for "country," although people within a country may be of many cultures

ocean the large body of saltwater that surrounds the continents and covers more than two-thirds of Earth's surface

peninsula a piece of land that is almost completely surrounded by water

plain a large area of relatively flat land that is often covered with grasses

plateau a relatively flat area, larger than a mesa, that rises above the surrounding landscape

point a narrow piece of land smaller than a cape that extends into a body of water

population density in a country, the number of people living on each square mile or kilometer of land (calculated by dividing population by land area)

Prairie Provinces popular name for the Canadian provinces of Manitoba, Saskatchewan, and Alberta

prime meridian an imaginary line that runs through Greenwich, England, and is accepted as the line of 0° longitude

projection the process of representing the round Earth on a flat surface, such as a map

reef an offshore ridge made of coral, rocks, or sand

Sahel a semiarid grassland immediately south of the Sahara in western and central Africa

savanna a tropical grassland with scattered trees

scale on a map, a means of explaining the relationship between distances on the map and actual distances on the Earth's surface

sea the ocean or a partially enclosed body of saltwater that is connected to the ocean; completely enclosed bodies of saltwater, like the Dead Sea, are really lakes

small-scale map a map, such as a country map, that shows a large area without much detail

sound a long, broad inlet of the ocean that lies parallel to the coast and often separates an island and the mainland

Soviet Union shortened name for the Union of Soviet Socialist Republics (U.S.S.R.), a former communist republic in eastern Europe and northern and central Asia that was made up of 15 republics of which Russia was the largest

spit a long, narrow strip of land, often of sand or silt, extending into a body of water from the land

steppe a Slavic word referring to relatively flat, mostly treeless temperate grasslands that stretch across much of central Europe and central Asia

strait a narrow passage of water that connects two larger bodies of water

territory land that is under the jurisdiction of a country but that is not a state or a province

tributary a stream that flows into a larger river

tropics region lying within 23 1/2° north and south of the Equator that experiences warm temperatures year-round

upwelling process by which nutrient-rich water rises from ocean depths to the surface

valley a long depression, usually created by a river, that is bordered by higher land

volcano an opening in Earth's crust through which molten rock erupts

Index

Map references are in boldface (**50**) type. Letters and numbers following in lightface (D12) locate the place-names using the map grid. (Refer to page 7 for more detail.) Illustrations appear in italic (*140*) type and text references are in lightface.

National Geographic Society

John M. Fahey, Jr.
President and Chief Executive Officer

Gilbert M. Grosvenor
Chairman of the Board

Nina D. Hoffman
*Executive Vice President, President of Books
and Education Publishing Group*

Ericka Markman
*Senior Vice President, President of Children's Books
and Education Publishing Group*

Staff for this book

Nancy Laties Feresten
Barbara Lalicki
Editorial Directors

Patricia Daniels
Suzanne Patrick Fonda
Project Editors

Marianne R. Koszorus
Bea Jackson
Peggy Archambault
Art Directors

Dorrit Green
Designer

Carl Mehler
Director of Maps

Susan McGrath
Patricia Daniels
Writers

Marilyn Mofford Gibbons
Janet Dustin
Illustrations Editors

Alex Novak
Managing Editor

Jennifer Emmett
Assistant Editor

Kristin Edmonds
Sean M. Groom
Jocelyn Lindsay
Keith R. Moore
Text Research

Thomas L. Gray
Joseph F. Ochlak
Nicholas P. Rosenbach
Map Editors

Matt Chwastyk
Map Production Manager

Jehan Aziz
John S. Ballay
George Bounelis
Geosystems Global Corp.
James Huckenpahler
Mapping Specialists Ltd.
Martin S. Walz
Beth N. Weisenborn
Scott Zillmer
Map Production

Tibor G. Tóth
Map Relief

Stuart Armstrong
Map Illustration

Cindy Min
Production Design

Carrie E. Young
Editorial Assistant

Judith Klein
Copy Editor

Ellen Teguis
*Assistant Vice President
Marketing Publications*

Ruth Chamblee
Rachel Graham
Marketing Managers

Mark Caraluzzi
Heidi Vincent
*Directors of Direct Response Sales
and Marketing*

R. Gary Colbert
Production Director

Lewis R. Bassford
Production Manager

Vincent P. Ryan
Manufacturing Manager

National Geographic Maps

Allen Carroll
*Vice President and
Chief Cartographer
National Geographic Maps*

Richard W. Bullington
Project Manager

Neal J. Edwards
Senior Pre-Press Cartographer

Eric Lindstrom
Edit Cartographer

Dianne C. Hunt
Production Cartographer

Sally Summerall
Senior Design Cartographer

Alfred L. Zebarth
Senior Production Cartographer

Consultants

*Geography Education
Consultants*

Billie Kapp
*Teacher Consultant
Connecticut Geographic Alliance*

Lydia Lewis
*Geography Education
National Geographic Society*

Martha Sharma
*National Cathedral School
Washington, D.C.*

Jacki Vawter
*Educational Consultant
Alexandria, VA*

Regional Consultants

Africa
Dr. C. Gregory Knight
Pennsylvania State University

Antarctica
Dr. Deneb Karentz
University of San Francisco

Asia
Dr. Clifton Pannell
University of Georgia

Australia/Oceania
Dr. Michael Brown
University of Washington

Europe
Dr. Craig ZumBrunnen
University of Washington

South America
Dr. Stephen Frenkel
University of Washington

North America
Dr. Stephen Birdsall
University of North Carolina

Oceans
Dr. Eric Lindstrom
*Oceanography Program Scientist
NASA Headquarters*

World Economy
Daniel Cannistra
*Ernst & Young LLP
Customs and International
Trade Practice*

Illustrations Credits

Photographs are from Getty Images unless otherwise noted.

Abbreviations for terms appearing below: (t) top; (b) bottom; (l) left; (r) right; (c) center; NGIC-National Geographic Image Collection; NGS-National Geographic Staff; NGP-National Geographic Photographer.

Cover globe: WorldSat International Inc. from NOAA data; Robert Stacey. Photographs (t–b): Yao Hill tribe family, TAXI/Getty Images; Cathedral of St. Basil the Blessed, Steve Raymer/NGIC; Great Sphinx, Richard T. Nowitz/CORBIS.

All locator globes created by Theophilus Britt Griswold

2–3 WorldSat International Inc. from NOAA data; Robert Stacey.

How to Use This Atlas
6 (t) Original NASA photograph printed from digital image © 1996 CORBIS; (b) Doug Armand.

Understanding Maps
8 (art) © 1998 Sally J. Bensusen/Visual Science Studio. 10 (art) Shusei Nagaoka. 10–11 Lockheed Martin. 11 Kenji Yamaguchi/NGS. 12–13 (art) Shusei Nagaoka. 14 (art, bl and br) Shusei Nagaoka. 14–15 (art) Ron Miller; 15 (tr) Robert Hynes; (cr) John Pervet; (art, br) Shusei Nagaoka.

Planet Earth
16 (art, t) Shusei Nagaoka; (art, b) Christopher R. Scotese/PALEOMAP Project, University of Texas, Arlington. 17 (art, t) Shusei Nagaoka; (art, b) Susan Sanford. 18–19 (art) Shusei Nagaoka; 18–19 (l–r) Jason Hawkes; Tom Bean; Robert Frerck; Glen Allison; Art Wolfe; Harvey Lloyd; Ron Sanford; Gerald Brimacombe.

The World
23 (bl–r) University of Miami; Cary S. Wolinsky. 24 (t) Raymond Gehman; (art, l–r) John D. Dawson; Freddy Storheil; Tim Davis. 25 (l) Ed Pritchard; (tr) Chris Baker; (br) Michael K. Nichols/NGP; (art) Stuart Armstrong. 24–25 Desertification data UNEP. 28 (c) Macduff Everton/CORBIS. 29 (graph) Stuart Armstrong. 30 (graphs) Stuart Armstrong; 30 (br) Vernier Jean Bernard/CORBIS SYGMA. 31 (t) David Madison; (bl–r) Zane Williams; Charles O'Rear/CORBIS.

North America
32–33 Original NASA photograph printed from digital image © 1996 CORBIS. 36 (l) Robert Frerck; (r) Hiroyuki Matsumoto. 36–37 Kim Heacox. 37 (art) Tony Chen. 38 (tl) Gary John Norman; (cl) Chad Ehlers; (bl) (art) Tony Chen. 38–39 (t) A. Hyde; (b) Rosemary Calvert. 39 (tl) Glen Allison; (tr) Yves Marcoux; (c) Sarah Stone; (b) Paul Chesley

South America
64 William J. Hebert. 64–65 Original NASA photograph printed from digital image © 1996 CORBIS. 68 (l) Erik Svenson; (r) Richard T. Nowitz/NGIC. 68–69 Eduardo Garcia. 69 (art, l) Tony Chen; (r) Kevin Schafer. 70 (art, tl) Richard Schlect; (bl) Ed Simpson; (art, br) Richard Schlect. 70–71 David Levy. 71 (l) Jacques Jangoux; (r) Ken Fisher.

Europe
80 Nicholas DeVore. 80–81 Original NASA photograph printed from digital image © 1996 CORBIS. 84 (l) Phil Cole. 84–85 Steve Raymer/NGIC. 85 (t–b) Bail and Spiegel; Martine Mouchy; Stuart Franklin/NGIC. 86 (tl) Richard Elliot; (art, bl) Harry Bliss; (br) Guy Marche. 86–87 Bob Handelman. 87 (tl) Anthony Cassidy; (tr) Will & Deni McIntyre; (cl) Vince Streano; (cr) James L. Stanfield/NGIC; (b) Rob Talbot.

Africa
100 Marc Chamberlain. 100–101 Original NASA photograph printed from digital image © 1996 CORBIS. 104 (l) (art) John D. Dawson; (r) Michael Lewis/NGIC. 104–105 Bob Krist/CORBIS; Bruno De Hogues. 105 Art Wolfe. 106 (art, tl) John D. Dawson (cl) Penny Tweedie. 106–107 (t) John Beatty; (b) Bruno De Hogues. 107 (tl) Bruce Dale; (tr) Nicholas DeVore; (art, br) Christopher A. Klein.

Asia
118 Doug Armand. 118–119 Original NASA photograph printed from digital image © 1996 CORBIS. 122 (art, l) Robert Cremins; (r) Terry Vine. 122–123 (t) Paul Chesley; (b) Steve Raymer. 123 Peter Turnley/CORBIS. 124 (t–b) Erica Lansner; Orion Press; Keren Su. 124–125 (t) Chris Shinn; (b) Robert Frerck. 125 (art, t) Kinuko Y. Craft; (c) Paul Harris.

Australia, New Zealand, and Oceania
140 R. Ian Lloyd/Productions Pte. Ltd. 140–141 Original NASA photograph printed from digital image © 1996 CORBIS. 144 (art, bl) Tony Chen; (br) Hideo Kurihara. 144–145 Doug Armand. 145 (bl) Robin Smith; (br) Penny Tweedie. 146 (tl) Paul McKelvey; (cl) Christopher Arneson; (bl) Fritz Prenzel; (tr) Stuart Westmoreland; (cr) J. Scherschel/NGIC. 146–147 John Eastcott/Yva Momatiuk. 147 (t) Suzanne & Nick Geary; (b) William J. Hebert.

Antarctica
154–155 National Remote Sensing Centre, Farnsborough, England, and NOAA, Suitland, Maryland; digital composition created by Theophilus Britt Griswold. 154 Art Wolfe. 158 Art Wolfe. 158–9 (t) Maria Stenzel/NGIC; (b) Galen Rowell/CORBIS. 159 (t) Joel Bennett; (bl) Gordon Wiltsie; (art, br) Richard Ellis.

Oceans
160 Joan H. Membery. 160–161 David Doubilet/NGIC. 162 (tl) Flip Nicklin/Minden Pictures; (tr) Ron & Valerie Taylor/Innerspace Visions; (bl) Sylvia A. Earle; (br) Jeff Jaskolski/Innerspace Visions. 163 (tl) Bruce Robison; (tr) Stephen Low/Woods Hole Oceanographic Institute; (bl) Peter Herring/Imagequest3d.com; (art, br) Christopher A. Klein. 165 (art) Stuart Armstrong adapted from Jack Cook/Woods Hole Oceanographic Institute; (bl) L. Green & Kevin Hardy/Scripps Institute of Oceanography; (br) Provided by the Sea-WiFS Project, NASA Goddard Space Flight Center and ORBIMAGE. 166 (art, l) NASA/Goddard Space Flight Center; (cl–r) Steve McCurry/Magnum; 167 (c) Cary S. Wolinsky.

Library of Congress Cataloging-in-Publication Data

National Geographic Society (U.S.)
National Geographic world atlas for young explorers—Rev. and expanded ed.
   p.   cm.
   Includes index.
   Summary: Presents world, regional, and thematic maps as well as photographic essays on each continent and the oceans.
   ISBN 0-7922-2879-0
   1. Children's atlases.   [1. Atlases.]   I. Title: World atlas for young explorers. II. Title.
G1021 .N43   2003
912—dc21

                                         2003055004

Published by the National Geographic Society
1145 17th St. N.W.
Washington, D.C. 20036-4688